Those DASHING McDONAGH SISTERS

MANDY SAYER is an award-winning novelist and narrative non-fiction writer. Her work has been published in the UK, the United States, Brazil, Germany, Japan and China. Sayer's honours include the Vogel Award, the National Biography Award, the South Australian Premier's Award for Non-Fiction, *The Age* Book of the Year for Non-fiction and the Davitt Award for Young Adult Fiction. She was the recipient of the 2021 Hazel Rowley Literary Fellowship, which supported her research and writing of *Those Dashing McDonagh Sisters*. She lives in Sydney with her husband, writer Louis Nowra, and their rescue dog, Basil. For more information, visit mandysayer.com.au.

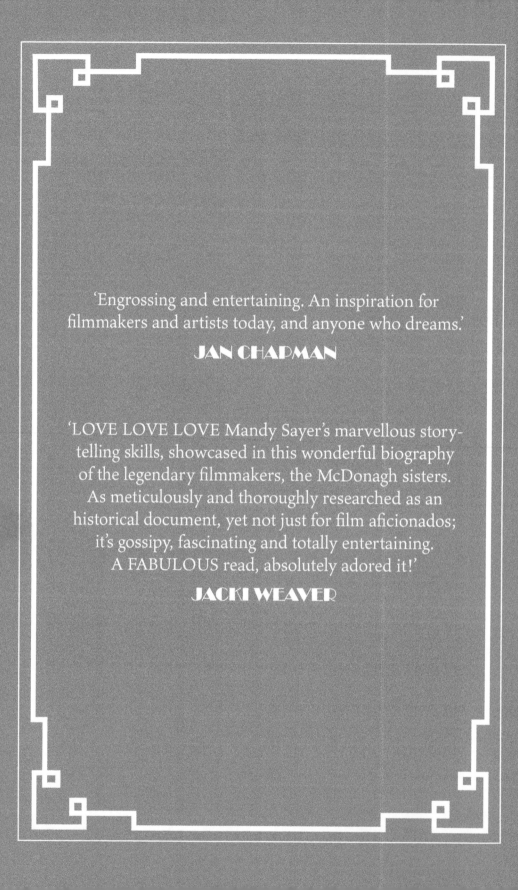

'Engrossing and entertaining. An inspiration for filmmakers and artists today, and anyone who dreams.'

JAN CHAPMAN

'LOVE LOVE LOVE Mandy Sayer's marvellous story-telling skills, showcased in this wonderful biography of the legendary filmmakers, the McDonagh sisters. As meticulously and thoroughly researched as an historical document, yet not just for film aficionados; it's gossipy, fascinating and totally entertaining. A FABULOUS read, absolutely adored it!'

JACKI WEAVER

To Louis, with love

A NewSouth book

Published by
NewSouth Publishing
University of New South Wales Press Ltd
University of New South Wales
Sydney NSW 2052
AUSTRALIA
http://unsw.press

© Mandy Sayer 2022
First published 2022

10 9 8 7 6 5 4 3 2 1

A catalogue record for this book is available from the National Library of Australia

ISBN   9781742237435 (paperback)
        9781742238517 (ebook)
        9781742239415 (ePDF)

Internal design Josephine Pajor-Markus
Cover design Debra Billson
Cover images Portraits of Paulette McDonagh, Isabel McDonagh, and Phyllis McDonagh courtesy of National Film and Sound Archive of Australia

Those DASHING McDONAGH SISTERS

Australia's first female filmmaking team

MANDY SAYER

NEWSOUTH

CONTENTS

EXTRAS

⹁RAILER

In October 2020, the London Film Festival honoured the achievements of Australian pioneer filmmakers, sisters Paulette, Isabel, and Phyllis McDonagh, with a screening of their most famous silent feature, *The Cheaters* (1929), which attracted rapturous reviews.

Between 1926 and 1933, these three remarkable siblings, born within thirty months of one another, made four independent feature films in Sydney, and a series of documentaries. Paulette wrote and directed most of the scenarios; Phyllis undertook producing, art directing, and publicity; and Isabel, under the name of Marie Lorraine, acted as the female leads. They were in their twenties at the time and mostly self-taught. Together, they helped to transform Australian cinema's preoccupations with the outback and the bush, with what the sisters mocked as 'haystack movies', into a thrilling, urban modernity. Under Paulette's careful direction, and through the judicious use of close-ups, melodramatic overacting was jettisoned for subtle naturalism, a style that Isabel perfected. The sisters did not make deliberately 'Australian' films with recognisable local settings, preferring the cinematic techniques and themes of Hollywood melodrama and German Expressionism. Expressionist films such as Fritz Lang's *Metropolis* and *Dr Mabuse, the Gambler* were screened in Sydney when the three were young adults.

During the 1920s and early '30s, Paulette was one of only five female directors in the world. And in the history of cinema, there has never been a trio of sisters that has formed an independent film company, producing full-length features.

Their father was a prominent doctor with an abiding love of recreational activities such as rollerskating, boxing, and theatre. He was honorary surgeon for the Sydney Stadium during boxing matches, and for the JC Williamson Theatrical Company, the latter of which presented the best international actors to Australian audiences, including French diva Sarah Bernhardt and American actor Lionel Belmore.

Growing up, the sisters shared a bedroom and would stay up most nights discussing the details of the latest play or silent film they had seen and, if they didn't like it, mock the bad acting and directing. The sisters were so close that one would not even consider buying a comb without discussing it with the other two. Friends and relatives tried to discourage them from investing their time, money, and energy in such a risky, male-dominated enterprise. And when they approached industry professionals to help with distribution, they were told, 'Go home, little girls'. Still, they were convinced that with their combined intelligence, talent, and discernment, they could produce feature films that would transcend the national masculinist tropes of bushrangers and squatters, and the female stereotypes of farmers' wives and downtrodden servants. They would go on to create female characters who could crack safes, brandish pistols, perform the Charleston on the beach, and give birth to a child whose conception was the result of a sexual assault.

The resilience of their female characters reflected their own form of self-reliance. Orphaned in their early twenties, the sisters dedicated themselves to raising their four younger siblings and caring for a disabled aunt, while simultaneously writing, directing, and producing feature films. Together, they adapted from the silent era to the demanding technology of the talkies with an almost ferocious determination.

Their first feature, *Those Who Love* (1926), was an instant hit with audiences around the country, taking more at the box office at the time than Charlie Chaplin's *The Gold Rush*. It also caused the governor of New South Wales to weep at the premiere. Reviews of the film were ecstatic. 'The result is a dazzling triumph and which is said to be the best Australian film that has yet graced the screen', claimed arts and entertainment magazine *Everyone's*. '... a splendid performance [that] ranks with some of the best characterisations ever given to the screen by the world's greatest stars'. This debut, considered a fluke by some critics of the time, was followed by the even more acclaimed *The Far Paradise*, *The Cheaters*, and the first Australian anti-war film, *Two Minutes Silence*, which poet and critic Kenneth Slessor claimed was, 'A powerful and convincing story, intelligently directed and capable of challenging comparison with world standards ... The whole effect ... is one of beauty and strength'. Most of their films were screened in the UK, where today they are better known than they are in their own country.

In the 1920s and '30s, Australian cinema was struggling to compete with powerful Hollywood studios that controlled the means of production and distribution in this country. Always coping with self-raised low budgets, the sisters were just as creative off the set as they were on it. Through their charm and determination, they often borrowed costumes, props, equipment, and properties to make up the budget shortfalls. Their younger siblings often played small parts or stood in as extras. Phyllis even managed to secure for free the use of the personal train of the premier of New South Wales for the shooting of a key scene in *The Far Paradise*. They also used their own home, a mansion called Drummoyne House, as a set. It was richly furnished with antiques, paintings, and gilded mirrors, collected by their father, lending an authenticity to the interior scenes. The plots usually revolved around class differences between two ill-fated lovers, a rich young man and lower-class lass, challenged by societal and parental expectations. Although the sisters did not set out deliberately to blaze a trail of feminism, their collective confidence and independence were striking at a time when the only career option open for women was marriage.

Despite the extraordinary achievements of the McDonagh sisters, duly celebrated in London in 2020, there has never been a book published on their lives and works anywhere in the world. The main reason for this oversight is that although their surviving films have been preserved and digitalised by the National Film and Sound Archive of Australia (NFSA), their features, unlike those of Raymond Longford and Lottie Lyell, have never been made available to the public on video, DVD, or streaming services. Drawing from recorded oral histories, newspaper articles, essays, and my interviews with McDonagh descendants and friends, this biography sets out to rescue these dashing sisters from their omission from our national and cinematic history, and to facilitate access to their astonishing body of work.

Ten Myths About the McDonagh Sisters

1. Their father left them 1000 pounds in his will to finance their first film.
2. Their father left a will.
3. They were rich society girls.
4. Their mother died within a year of their father.
5. Their first film, *Those Who Love*, was inspired by historical documents found in the cellar of their convict-built home, Drummoyne House.
6. After they made their final film, Phyllis met her future husband in New Zealand.
7. They wrote the first draft of their first film while they were still in high school.
8. Their maternal grandfather was a Spanish diplomat.
9. They broke up as a filmmaking team after the arrival of talkies.
10. During a reconnaissance trip for their second film, they got lost in the Burragorang Valley for three days.

MAIN
FEATURE

1

UPSTAIRS, DOWNSTAIRS

(1816–1897)

The existence of the McDonagh sisters was the result of a calamitous accident that would unite two totally different families, one from 'upstairs' and the other from 'downstairs'.

At around midnight on 15 February 1896, Dr John McDonagh was summoned to the Royal Hotel, on George Street, to attend to an ill guest. He promptly arrived with his medical bag, hurried through the foyer, and pressed the bell for the lift. After it descended and stopped, he pulled back the gate, entered the elevator and pressed the button for the third floor. The lift rose and halted at the appointed level. The doctor once again pulled back the gate and exited as a woman he knew entered. She made a comment that he did not hear clearly, and so he stepped back into the lift to catch what she was saying. But as he did this, the lift began to descend and the doctor, half in and half out, suddenly felt the ceiling of the lift slam against his head and twist his neck. The lift jerked and groaned as the woman screamed and the doctor struggled. Panicked guests strove to pull him free, but as they did so, the doctor's leg became sandwiched between the lift ceiling and the floor of the third level, completely crushing it.

Once freed, he was rushed to Sydney Hospital, where his severely broken leg was set in a cast and the intense pain was treated with morphine. Unable to practise medicine or take care of himself, he would be bedridden at home for the next six months. His two sisters and mother could help a little, but they were not prepared or trained to care for a full-time patient, so a live-in nurse was hired. The nurse who arrived, Anita Amora, was slim and pretty, with luminous, wide blue eyes and lustrous black hair that she pinned up in a bun beneath her starched white cap. She was twenty-nine years old and had never been married.

The relationship between a nurse and a patient is an intensely intimate one. The patient is dependent upon the nurse for hygiene, food, drink, mobility, and pain relief. The nurse is dependent on the patient for cooperation, communication, and an even temper. They are confined to the patient's bedroom, with few distractions. There is a lot of spare time during which to converse.

Anita would eventually learn that the Irish-Catholic McDonagh clan originally hailed from Maguiresbridge, County Fermanagh, in the country's north. John's father, Patrick, studied medicine in Dublin, graduating as a doctor and surgeon. He went on to marry Isabella Grant, who was the daughter of a comfortably middle-class Kilkenny solicitor, and through her mother, she was related to the Catholic branch of the aristocratic Ormond family of Ireland. Their first child, Mary, was born in Dublin in 1857, followed by John in 1859.

By the time of John's birth, his mother's brother, John Grant, had been living in the colony of New South Wales for twenty-six years. John Grant was also born in Kilkenny, in 1816, and had immigrated alone to Australia as a nineteen-year-old Catholic missionary. Catholicism was vitally important to both the Grant and McDonagh sides of the family.

Four years after his arrival in Sydney, Grant received his subdeaconship and his deaconship on the same day and subsequently worked in the parishes of Picton, Appin, Berrima, and Windsor. During a later trip to Rome, he received the title of Doctor of Divinity from Pope Pius IX. He was appointed Dean of Bathurst upon his return, and spent the rest of his life there, attending to his parishioners, and raising funds for the building of the first Catholic Cathedral outside of Sydney.

Grant was a highly respected beacon of faith and forbearance in a wild and reckless colony. On 3 December 1863, as part of his duties as Dean, he accompanied notorious bushranger John Vane to Bathurst Gaol after Vane's mother had finally convinced her son to surrender himself to the authorities. Earlier that year, Vane had joined John Gilbert's gang and ridden with the legendary bushrangers Ben Hall and John O'Meally.

After Patrick McDonagh completed his medical training in Dublin, and when son John was about two years old, the family left Ireland and settled for a time in Cape Town, South Africa. But no doubt lured by letters from his brother-in-law in New South Wales, detailing the fortunes to be made by industrious young men there, Patrick and the family then emigrated to Australia, also settling in Bathurst, at the time the most remote township in the colony. Ten years before, in 1851, Bathurst's economy had been boosted by the discovery of gold, and at the time of the McDonaghs' immigration, the town was booming with both opportunities and wealth. Patrick established a medical practice there and treated all kinds of patients, from convicts to clergy, bushrangers to barristers.

In 1857, the foundation stone of Bathurst's St Michael and St John's Cathedral was blessed by the first Catholic Archbishop of Sydney, Dr John Polding, and it finally opened for services in April 1861. The red brick, English Gothic–style cathedral was designed by English architect Charles Hansom. Dean Grant was held in such high esteem by the Catholic community in and around Bathurst that, following his death from diphtheria in

1864, at the age of forty-eight, he was buried in a vault beneath the southern side of the archway separating the nave from the chancel/sanctuary, with a block of marble placed on top of the vault.

Three years after the death of Dean John Grant, Patrick McDonagh had amassed enough savings in the goldrush town to move to Sydney, to the elite medical address of Burdekin Terrace on College Street. There, he immersed himself in charitable work, contributing to a fund for the relief of the wives and children of Irish State prisoners. He also sat on a committee with Archbishop Polding to raise money for the rebuilding of St Mary's Cathedral, which had been destroyed by fire in 1865, a fund to which he also regularly contributed. On 12 May 1867, his wife, Isabella, gave birth to a daughter, whom they named after the child's mother and paternal grandmother. The following year, Isabella gave birth to yet another daughter, who was christened Annie. When John McDonagh was nine years old, his baby sister, Isabella, died at the age of two. In the 19th century, it was not uncommon to lose an infant to illness, even one of an eminent doctor. Later, the family moved to 173 Macquarie Street. Patrick established a surgery on the first floor and living quarters on the two upper levels.

Young John McDonagh had a beautiful singing voice, so much so that he could have performed professionally. But John's surgeon-father expected him to study hard and enter a more stable profession. He first attended Lyndhurst College in Glebe, which had been established to train young men for the clergy. The premises had been designed by visionary colonial architect John Verge.

After his tenure at Lyndhurst, John completed his secondary education at St Patrick's College, Melbourne. He then gained admission to the University of Sydney and was issued his licence to practise midwifery in 1883. He then travelled overseas and studied at the University of Brussels, earning his medical degree in 1884. The following year he acquired even more surgical skills from the Royal College of Surgeons in Ireland and the Royal College of Physicians in London, before returning to Sydney after a three-year absence.

In 1889, his adored father died prematurely of cirrhosis of the liver, coupled with cancer of the liver, suggesting that McDonagh Senior regularly enjoyed the favoured Irish ritual of getting bladdered. He was afforded a full military funeral, one that included his beloved horse, in honour of his previous charitable and civic activities, which included helping to establish Sydney Hospital and the nearby St Mary's Cathedral. As his cortège wound through the streets of Sydney, many shops and businesses closed in respect.

At the time of his father's death, John was thirty, and his unmarried sisters Mary and Annie were thirty-two and twenty-one respectively. Following Irish-Catholic tradition, as the eldest child, John immediately became the new head of the family, assuming care and responsibility for his mother and sisters. By this time, he had developed a love of popular entertainments, and adored theatre, rollerskating, and boxing. He also developed a taste for the finer things in life and would only drink expensive Moët champagne.

During the late 19th century and beyond, John was honorary surgeon to JC Williamson Theatrical Company, formed in 1882, which specialised in importing some of the finest actors and productions from England and America. Williamson, an American and a former actor, was also of Irish descent, and the son of a doctor, and so he and John McDonagh shared a similar family background and a love of drama, opera, and music.

In 1890, Williamson seized control of the company from his other two business partners and began to run it on his own. This was at a time when theatre was still considered a somewhat bohemian enterprise and not quite respectable; those in the upper echelons of society would still consider playhouses as 'Synagogues of Sin'. During the first year of his monopoly, however, Williamson challenged this prejudice by bringing to Australia one of the most acclaimed women in the world at the time, the French actress Sarah Bernhardt.

Bernhardt arrived in Sydney in a tornado of publicity, officially opening the Hotel Australia on Castlereagh Street and becoming its first guest. Williamson and the hotel staff also generously accommodated her menagerie of koalas, possums, parrots, St Bernard, and pug dogs, her 100 pieces of luggage, and her spectacular temper tantrums. Wide-eyed John McDonagh was not only in the audience at Her Majesty's Theatre during her final performance of *Fedora* and *Camille*, but he also treated her ailments and became a valued acquaintance. He even treated and befriended actors Lionel Belmore, Albert Chevalier, Henry Irving, and French American operatic soprano Clementine de Vere Sapio when they toured the colonies. The Theatre Royal on Castlereagh Street, where Williamson staged his lavish productions, was only a five-minute walk from Dr McDonagh's surgery.

McDonagh was also honorary surgeon for the Sydney Stadium, where he enjoyed free tickets to boxing matches. When he wasn't patching up post-fight boxers in locker rooms, he served on several arts committees.

In 1893, the doctor himself appeared on stage at the Lyceum Theatre, after a performance of *Lucretia Borgia*. He sat on a throne swathed in luxurious drapes, as part of a committee in tribute to manager George Goodman, who was about to be married. The doctor appeared in the place of JC Williamson, who was otherwise engaged, and read out a letter from the theatre entrepreneur, detailing Williamson's regret at not being able to attend the celebration and expressing his 'earnest and deepest wishes for the future happiness of Mr Goodman and his future lady'. As a leading doctor and surgeon, John made a handsome living and enjoyed his place in high society, but a big part of him would always yearn to be close to the stage and the performers who enlivened it.

By the mid-1890s, social butterfly Dr McDonagh was in his late thirties and still a bachelor, with a gregarious Irish charm that mesmerised his female patients. At around this time, he became engaged – we don't know to whom – but at the last minute panicked and called off the wedding. Still, the doctor unwittingly expressed his relief at the broken engagement by proceeding with the honeymoon solo.

With his sisters, John threw sumptuous soirées at his home and invited famous actors and singers to celebrate with him. One such soirée was reported in the social pages of May 1894, which had been thrown specifically for his older sister, Mary, who was by then thirty-seven years old and still unmarried. Mary was plain-looking but a gifted pianist and singer. Twenty-six-year-old Annie was attractive and enjoyed wearing expensive clothes and, for the late 19th century, scandalous amounts of make-up. The guest list included ship captains, marine officers, singers, doctors, musicians, and Lady Windeyer, the wife of Lord Windeyer.

For the occasion, the rooms of the Macquarie Street home were filled with chrysanthemums, and from the balcony, guests enjoyed the spectacular views of the Royal Botanic Gardens and glimpses of the harbour. Mary wore a fashionable velvet blouse and a peach-coloured double skirt. Around the piano, vocal performances were given by Madame Emily Soldene, her brother John, and famous French pianist and composer Henri Kowalski, who 'charmed his hearers with a fantasia of his own on the "Austrian National Hymn", "Valse in C Minor", and "Mazurka" by Chopin'.

John was also regularly on the guest lists of society balls, dinners, and charity functions, and would usually take one of his sisters as his plus-one. Even so, the doctor's social connections varied widely, from raffish boxers to the judge Sir Edmund Barton, who a few years later would go on to become Australia's first prime minister.

Just a ten-minute walk away from John's gilded world lived Jane Annie (Anita) Amora. She was born in 1869 in a squat worker's cottage with an outdoor kitchen in the wharf-side slum of Woolloomooloo. There were no parks or trees in the neighbourhood and the most popular game for children was catching rats down at the wharves. At night, toxic miasmic air hung in clouds over the narrow streets and lanes. The area was populated with poverty-stricken families of fishermen, tradesmen, and shopkeepers.

Anita's mother was Irish immigrant Annie Gaffney, born in Lurgan, Armagh, in 1846. Her father, Joseph Horatio Amora, had been born in Valparaíso, Chile in 1843. He was the son of Jane Berger and Ernesto de Silva Amora and had been trained as a junior ship's officer. Amora was dark and handsome, with olive skin, black hair, and brown eyes, though at five-foot three-and-a-half inches, he was hardly tall. He immigrated to Australia in 1864 on the ship *Gravina*, not as a crew member, but as an unassisted passenger. Annie and Joseph married in Paddington in 1868, and Anita was born the following year. Annie would go on to bear another three children, one of whom, a boy, would die when Anita was four.

We do not know why Amora fled Valparaíso at the age of twenty-one, never to return. It's certainly possible that he was running away from scandal, or the law, or that he was simply in search of youthful adventure. But once settled in Sydney, Amora morphed into an inveterate social climber and opportunist. How he managed to become a founding member of the Sydney

Amateur Sailing Club and commodore of the institution between 1872 and 1875 is a mystery, but he seems to have had charm and uncontrollable ambition. Ten years after his arrival in Sydney, he became a naturalised citizen of the colony. At the height of his popularity, in 1882, Amora was appointed Honorary Chilean Consul in Sydney, and later as Honorary Vice-Consul for the Netherlands, Hawaii, and Nicaragua. By the mid-1880s, however, he was working as a lowly ferry master for Charles Jeanneret's Parramatta River and Hunters Hill Steam Ferry Company.

In late November 1882, when Anita was only thirteen, her mother, Annie, died. Curiously, the funeral procession did not assemble and leave from the Amora family home, but from the home of Annie's father, Patrick Gaffney, at 238 George Street, Sydney, on 1 December. This suggests that the father arranged and financed the funeral, or that there was bad blood between the father and son-in-law, or both. Following the funeral, responsibility for the care of the younger children, eleven and four, naturally fell on Anita's slight shoulders.

A few years later, Anita and her younger sister, Nell, began training as nurses. By the time they were eighteen and sixteen respectively, Anita's father had become romantically involved with thirty-two-year-old Elizabeth Longstaff, marrying her in 1886. The following year, Elizabeth gave birth to a daughter, Inez Carmen Amora, in Paddington.

After graduating, Anita and Nell joined the staff of the Thomas Walker Hospital, in Concord, on the banks of the Parramatta River. It was a public hospital that treated non-infectious convalescents, and initially, Anita was appointed head nurse. By July 1893, however, there was a reshuffle in the hierarchy, with younger sister, Nell, being appointed to the position.

-*≈○◐≈*-

Over sponge baths and sheet changes, bedpans and Bovril, the patient and nurse inevitably grew closer. Six months later, by the time the doctor's leg had healed completely, John McDonagh and Anita Amora had fallen deeply in love. For the rest of his life, the doctor would walk with a pronounced limp, but he no doubt believed that the accident and the prolonged convalescence had been a blessing in disguise, because without it he would never have met his wife, nor have gone on to father the children whom he would cherish.

Photographs of Anita as an adult reveal a raven-haired beauty with an insouciant air, and it is obvious that she had taken after her Chilean father physically. She would go on to pass these genetic traits to her first three daughters, who were often admired in the press during the 1920s and early '30s for their glossy black hair and startling hazel eyes. The girls' father, however, could not have been more different; he was well over six feet tall, with pale skin and fair hair.

During the same year that John and Anita fell in love – 1896 – the first public season of moving pictures in Sydney was screened by American magician Carl Hertz at the Tivoli Theatre, as part of a variety program. Less than two weeks later, cinematographer and projectionist Marius Sestier, a travelling representative of Frères Lumière company in France, opened the first auditorium devoted entirely to the screening of films. The Cinématographe had been invented and patented by the Lumière brothers in Paris the year before, and they had sent Sestier and other representatives overseas to open new markets for this novel form of entertainment. The machine was surprisingly versatile, as its design incorporated a camera, a printer, and a projector. Sestier's mission was to not only screen films, but also to produce them in whichever country he found himself in. Before his arrival in Australia, he'd screened and shot films in India.

As a lover of contemporary and cutting-edge entertainments,

it's more than likely that the now-recovered Dr McDonagh squired his fiancée to the theatre to view the new-fangled amusement flickering across a screen. After all, the event was facilitated by McDonagh's old friend, JC Williamson, who donated the use of his theatre, the Lyceum, for a single afternoon preview.

The press reports of the screening were so enthusiastic that soon a more permanent venue, dubbed 'Salon Lumière', was established a few doors down from the Lyceum at 237 Pitt Street, a former branch of Lewis Phillips Auctioneers. The open-plan room was spacious enough to hold rows of seating that faced a back wall holding a ten by twelve–foot screen with a highly ornamental frame. The programming consisted of twelve short films on rotation, with new ones frequently added. In fact, the very first film shot in Australia was screened on 27 October 1896, the final night of Salon Lumière, when enthralled audiences watched their fellow Sydneysiders disembarking from SS *Brighton* at Manly, which had been filmed by Sestier and his Australian concessionaire, renowned photographer Henry Walter Barnett. Because the Salon was not associated with the bawdier vaudeville and variety programs at the Tivoli, it began attracting a more high-class clientele, a circle within which Dr McDonagh moved with ease, such as the governor, Lord Hampton; the Anglican Primate of Australia; the Roman Catholic Bishop of Goulburn; and priests and students from Riverview College. After Sestier and Barnett left Sydney to travel south and shoot footage of the Melbourne Cup, Australia's first cinema closed, but for only a brief time. It was reopened by James McMahon as Salon Cinématographe to capitalise on Sestier's extraordinary precedent and success.

Later that year, in Sydney, Sestier again came within Dr McDonagh's orbit when he shot what is now Australia's oldest surviving first film, *Patineur Grotesque*, or *The Humorous Rollerskater*, in Prince Alfred Park. The action of the sixty-second-long film takes place in the centre of an unmoving frame. A slim man in a loose costume and wearing rollerskates performs for a growing crowd. As part of his vaudeville-type routine, the skater trips and falls, then drops his hat. As he tries to retrieve the hat he continues to fall about, and as he bends over and flips his coat tails, he reveals a white handprint on the seat of his pants. When the hat is finally restored to his head, the film fades to black. Fifteen years later, Dr McDonagh would open a rollerskating rink in the very same park where *Patineur Grotesque* was filmed.

In 1897, the same year that his daughter Anita would marry one of the most eligible bachelors in the colony, Joseph Horatio Amora was charged by the Water Police Court in Sydney for stealing 290 pounds. (In those days, the average price of a home was just under 100 pounds.) Amora's boss had given him the cash as a deposit for him to purchase the schooner *Oscar Robinson* on behalf of a New Hebrides client. Instead of obeying orders, however, Amora absconded with the money. The theft was so brazen, and so easily traced, that one can only assume that it had been born out of desperation to pay off mounting debts. His bail was set at 300 pounds, more than the amount that he was alleged to have stolen.

Far from being shocked or repelled by the actions of his father-in-law-to-be, not only did Dr McDonagh offer moral support to Amora, but he also appeared as a character witness for him on 26 February 1897. It's likely that his experiences as a doctor and with theatre people and boxers from all walks of life had allowed him to empathise with the greyer areas of human behaviour. He had that rare quality of tolerance and a non-judgmental attitude towards the fallibility of humans.

During Amora's trial, the respected surgeon stood up in court and gave evidence under oath that the accused had been under his continual medical care since April the year before, and that 'Amora's mental condition had caused much anxiety'. Despite McDonagh's valiant attempts to protect the father of his bride-to-be, the judge and jury of four did not believe either testimony: Amora was sentenced to two years' hard labour in Darlinghurst Prison. An appeal lodged after the sentencing was dismissed three months later. By then, Amora was fifty-two years old.

Although Amora's defence team had argued that their client was a first offender, this was not the first time that he had clashed with authorities. In 1872, he'd been fined five shillings, plus two shillings sixpence costs, for 'failing to keep his (Glenn St) premises clean'. In August 1882, the Marine Board ruled that the shipwreck of the steam collier, *Llewellyn*, near Wollongong in May of that year had been caused by negligent actions of the master, Amora, in 'navigating the vessel too close to the shore, and in not taking sufficient precautions for her safety in the thick, hazy weather'. In a later hearing, his mariner's licence was suspended for three months. Due to the severity of the accident, he was lucky not to have had it cancelled permanently. Further humiliation came in 1892 when landlord William Lloyd seized all the furniture and belongings of the Amora family home on Moore Park Road, Paddington, for failure to pay the rent. Unsurprisingly, three years later Amora was forced to claim bankruptcy: in June 1895, the Insolvency Court recorded his assets as twenty-two pounds and ten shillings, while his liabilities added up to a staggering 540 pounds and twelve shillings. This was a man who seemed to crave power and prestige, but who took far too many risks in his struggle to achieve them.

By the time his daughter Anita married Dr John McDonagh at St Joseph's Catholic Church, Woollahra on 4 December 1897, Amora had already been imprisoned for ten months. Not only did he miss his eldest daughter's society wedding, but he also missed the birth of his first grandchild.

After he was released from gaol, Amora struggled to find work and sunk into ignominy. While his daughter enjoyed living with her husband in a grand Victorian building in the city – one of the best and most respected addresses in Sydney – Amora failed to pay his rent on a house in Paddington and was subsequently evicted. Five years later he died in Leichhardt Hospital at the age of fifty-six.

The plots of the first three silent films the McDonagh sisters produced all revolve around a girl from the wrong side of the tracks falling in love with a rich gentleman, and the subsequent reactions of both sets of parents. The first, *Those Who Love*, tells the story of an upper-class misfit besotted with a lowly showgirl. *The Far Paradise* is a classic romance centred around the lovers Cherry Carson and Peter Lawton, who are driven apart by family loyalties and meddling by Cherry's father, who has a shady criminal past and who accidentally murders his business partner. In *The Cheaters*, the female lead's father figure is a lifelong criminal intent on drawing his social-climbing albeit kidnapped daughter, in love with a rich man, back into his nefarious underworld.

We don't know how much the sisters were aware of their grandfather's criminal past. But they certainly knew of steep class differences and possibly one shameful skeleton in the family closet. As younger sister Paula commented, 'Mother was sensitive about her family because, you know, she felt that they mightn't have quite made the grade that she enjoyed as Daddy's wife ... Mother kept quiet about a few of her relatives. They never came to light ...' In fact, the McDonagh siblings would grow up believing that their maternal grandfather had been a highly respected Spanish diplomat.

The narrative about a poor young woman from the wrong side of town finding love and protection in the arms of a wealthy man belonged to the sisters' own mother as much as to the female protagonists of their first three feature films. Through their filmmaking in the 1920s and early '30s, this trio of sisters managed to transform real and imagined family scandals into compelling and sophisticated cinematic stories.

2

THE URBAN PLAYGROUND
(1898–1909)

In 1900, among Australia's earliest film sequences were those shot and incorporated into a mixed medium performance created by the Salvation Army, which included hymns, lectures, coloured lantern slides and moving pictures entitled *Soldiers of the Cross*. It attracted enormous interest and praise from both critics and audiences. Within a few years, individual show-men, mostly magicians and conjurers keen to augment their performances, were investing in rudimentary projectors and short cinematograph films and travelling around the country. They set up improvised screens in church halls, sheds, tents, amusement parks, rollerskating rinks, pubs, and on the backs of flatbed trucks, attracting patrons from remote areas desperate to experience this novel form of entertainment.

The three McDonagh sisters were born within thirty months of one another: Isabel on 3 January 1899; Phyllis on 7 January 1900; and Paulette on 11 June 1901. With the girls being born in such quick succession at the turn of the century, they also entered the world at the same time as motion pictures were entering the Australian experience.

The property in which the sisters were born still stands, a three-storey Georgian building with floor-to-ceiling windows and wrought-iron Juliet balconies directly across the road from the State Library of New South Wales, and a three-minute walk to Sydney Hospital where their father was a consultant. The green plaque near the front door of the house proclaims, HORBURY TERRACE, which was originally part of a series of eight identical homes, built in 1847, whose distinguished tenants have included Isaac Nathan, Australia's first classical composer, and colonial politicians Robert Lowe and Edward Broadhurst.

Mother Anita was extremely fond of dogs, and the family would own many over the next few decades. At the time of her wedding, she was the adoring owner of a little black pug, who two years later she had to rehome because it repeatedly tried to attack baby Isabel.

A manned hansom cab was parked outside the terrace twenty-four hours a day, seven days a week, to transport the doctor on emergency house calls. Being Irish and Catholic, John had a keen sense of social justice and was aware of the severe disparities that existed in Sydney between the rich and the poor, and the simmering tensions between Protestants and Catholics. This often showed in his practice as a doctor. He would regularly and deliberately overcharge his wealthier patients while refusing payment from those who were working class or unemployed. He often travelled into the countryside to deliver the babies of rich graziers and landholders and would charge them 300 guineas for a single confinement, more than twice the amount of his regular fee.

The doctor's generosity was no more in evidence than when he was treating a single mother, Laura Chegwidden, née Meyer, who was dying of tuberculosis. The patient's biggest fear, however, was not her imminent death, but the fact that she'd be leaving behind a teenage daughter, Stella, with no one to care for her. Laura's husband was Welsh-born Constantine Chegwidden, a house painter. When Stella was eight years old, her father deserted them, and warrants for his arrest were issued in New South Wales and Victoria, which describe him as '5 foot 9, medium build, fair complexion, fair moustache, with a scar or a stab on the left side of his arm. Dresses respectably'. Stella was a small, slight girl and an accomplished seamstress who designed and made her own clothes. After meeting the girl, Dr McDonagh promised Laura that after she died, he and his wife would adopt Stella unofficially and welcome her into the family.

In 1902, the same year that Mrs McDonagh gave birth to her fourth child, a boy, Laura Chegwidden passed away. True to his word, the doctor and his wife moved Stella into their home, where she became a much-loved family member and nanny to the four children.

Across the road from their home lay the Royal Botanic Gardens, with smooth lawns patterned with winding paths that undulated down to the harbour, and which became the play-ground of the McDonagh children. In some ways, they mirrored the tight-knit Bronte siblings, with three inseparable girls finding emotional sanctuary in imaginary worlds, and a brother who could never quite rise to the hothouse intensity of their play-acting and storytelling. This creative closeness would gain momentum and saturate their lives for the next thirty years.

The sisters began upstaging young John before they could even read. In 1903, their father's older sister, Mary, aged fifty-three, accepted a marriage proposal and held her wedding to Patrick O'Connell, fifty-two, at St Patrick's Catholic Church, Sydney, in January 1904. Isabel, Phyllis, and Paulette – aged five, four, and three respectively – were invited to be a part of the service, serving as three of the five bridesmaids. The girls appeared at the church hand in hand, wearing white silk dresses with blue sashes, and bonnets decorated with chiffon, fancy straw, and feathers, all designed and sewn by Stella. Around their necks were gold chains and crosses, gifts from the nervous bridegroom. The three also carried floral crooks tied with eau de Nil and white silk ribbons. With their adorable chubby cheeks and ringleted black hair, the sisters almost stole the show from the blushing bride.

A reception was later held at Petty's Hotel, and descriptions of their mother Anita's outfit convey a vision of feminine loveliness: 'an ivory embossed silk dress prettily insetted with fancy stitching and fans of accordion-pleated chiffon, edged with black velvet ribbon, the bodies made en-suite with Brussels lace'. The newlyweds spent their honeymoon at a popular romantic destination in the Blue Mountains.

Aunt Mary's groom, Patrick O'Connell, was a wealthy Catholic grazier. In 1877, with his older brother Eugene, he'd purchased 12 000 acres of prime land west of Gulgong, New South Wales. The area was called Goodiman, said to be the Wiradjuri name for 'happy playground'.

Pat, Eugene, and their mother, Margaret, had been the publicans of the Goodiman Hotel, Gulgong, which they changed to O'Connell's Wine Saloon, and together they ran it for six years until 1889. The saloon was a popular resting place for drovers, and Pat and Eugene earned a reputation for playing cards and enjoying a dram or two of rum.

After the honeymoon, Mary moved with Pat to Goodiman, and Pat at once set to work building a large and elegant homestead for his bride, which he would name 'Tarawong'.

Due to their advanced years, Aunt Mary and Uncle Pat did not have children, and so her three nieces became their beloved surrogate offspring. Isabel, Phyllis, and Paulette adored travelling to Gulgong during the holidays and spending weeks at a time in the company of their aunt and uncle on the farm. The girls would always remember the time they spent at Tarawong as the happiest of their lives.

In his later years, after the sun went down, Uncle Pat would get fantastically drunk. One night he grabbed a gun and began staggering through the paddocks on his property, crying out, 'Caesar's Ghost!' During his drunken rambling, he accidentally shot one of his cows.

By the time of John's birth and the adoption of teenage Stella, the family had outgrown the house on Macquarie Street, so Dr McDonagh decided to rent a fashionable and large terrace at 14 College Street. It was part of a row that housed other professional men such as lawyers and other doctors, and where his own family had first lived after their departure from Bathurst. Hyde Park was just across the street and became the new playground for the McDonagh children.

In the basement of the house was the kitchen; on the ground floor was the doctor's surgery and a large reception room with a grand piano. Both the foyer and the office were decorated with theatrical memorabilia and framed signed photographs from stage stars such as Sarah Bernhardt and Lionel Belmore. The first floor was devoted to the family's living areas, furnished with expensive antiques and artworks that the doctor had collected during his trips overseas, prior to his marriage. The doctor couldn't resist beauty in any form. During a trip to Vienna, he arranged to have portraits of his relatives stencilled onto china vases and painted in gold leaf. A treasured part of his collection was a small portrait of himself painted by Tom Roberts. The third floor housed the various bedrooms. The three young sisters shared a single bedroom and would continue to do so well into adulthood.

In the early 20th century, it was still common for babies to be born at home and for relatives to die at home. But the McDonagh siblings would have had even more exposure than the average child to the confronting cycles of life and death. The top floor of the terrace was converted into the McDonagh Private Hospital, where longer-term patients were treated. People could and did expire directly above the sisters' bedroom.

As a child, Phyllis developed a phobia about operations and hospitals after her father determined that she needed her tonsils out. The sight of him in his white coat, standing in the doorway of the operating theatre, triggered a panic attack, and she fled screaming from the house and down College Street. After her mother and Stella ran after her and hauled her back, her father performed the tonsillectomy without further incident, but from that day on, and for the rest of her life, Phyllis would always avoid seeking medical attention, even for the late-life illness that would eventually kill her.

It is not clear who taught the girls reading, writing, and arithmetic, but the parents most likely followed the upper-class Victorian model of hiring a governess. Some of Phyllis's most vivid memories are of when she first learned to read and became enchanted by the power of words. 'Nothing that has happened to me since through my adult years has equalled the thrill of that discovery', she wrote. She would avidly read anything lying about the house, and even raided her father's surgery to devour his bulging medical books.

At the age of ten, she had her first short story published. 'The success went to my head. I thought I had it all made as an authoress – and commenced to write furiously.' Throughout her teens, she learned her craft by writing and submitting stories and mostly suffering rejection. 'I was born with a stubborn streak that refused to allow me to give up. In my young mind I blamed the editors for not knowing a good thing when they saw it.' At the age of seventeen, her stubbornness paid off when one of her stories would secure second place in the *Bulletin* short story competition, netting her a prize of eighteen pounds. 'That was a turning point in my literary career.'

In the early part of the century, almost everybody in Australia could read and write, but roughly 90 per cent of Australians received no secondary education. The McDonagh sisters would soon become part of the elite and fortunate 10 per cent to receive a thorough schooling beyond the sixth grade.

On Sunday nights, their father and mother entertained visiting international actors and opera singers. John, still a delightful singer, would often join the impromptu performances. The girls were not permitted to join the soirées but were allowed to observe from the fringes. 'We three would sit there', said Phyllis, 'quiet as mice, looking and listening to all these fabulous theatricals. We cut our teeth on theatre'.

The doctor's growing family and his busy surgery and hospital did not interfere with his abundant social life outside of the home. In fact, if anything, his attendance at rollerskating rinks, boxing matches, the theatre, and society functions seems to have increased. In September 1902, for example, he was instrumental in organising a farewell party for English actor and theatre manager Mr George Rignold, nicknamed 'Handsome George', at the Tattersalls Hotel. Her Majesty's Theatre had been built for Rignold in 1886, which he'd managed for nine years; and he was known internationally as a grand Shakespearean actor. John presented Rignold with a handsome travelling bag, and made a rousing speech, in which he 'dilated at length on the many excellent qualities of the recipient, both as an actor and a man'.

John was also present at the famous 1908 boxing match between Canadian Tommy Burns, nicknamed 'the great white hope' and African-American sensation Jack Johnson, at the open-air Sydney Stadium, which made headlines around the world. McDonagh, wearing a top hat, attended to the immediate medical needs of Tommy Burns as Johnson toyed with and teased the underprepared rival, and after the record-breaking knockout that flattened him. Also in attendance was the Irish-Catholic boxer, Larry Foley, who'd introduced the Queensberry code of boxing into Australia, and who was also part of 'The Fancy', a local fraternity that patronised pugilism. A gentleman in Sydney of any sporting quality, including Dr McDonagh, was socially obliged to join The Fancy, as its members included lawyers, rich businessmen, fellow doctors, and politicians, all of whom gambled regularly on their favourite boxers. Dr McDonagh soon acquired the nickname 'Sporting Mac'.

Foley was keenly aware that those in The Fancy could help him make money, not only in the ring but also later in business. With the acquisition of the White Horse Hotel, on George Street, he was able to combine his role as a publican with that of a boxing instructor and entrepreneur, building a stadium out of scrap tin and wood in the back block of the White Horse, with bleachers that could hold 2000 spectators. Those in The Fancy called it 'Foley's tin pot', which would become a forerunner of the Sydney Stadium in Rushcutters Bay, similarly nicknamed 'the old tin shed'. The tin pot was only a ten-minute stroll from Dr McDonagh's home on College Street, which made an easy escape from the demands of both domesticity and surgery.

There was a gap of five years between the birth of John Junior and the McDonaghs' next child. On 11 January 1908, a birth notice appeared in the *Sydney Morning Herald* stating that a daughter had been born to the couple on 28 December 1907. Her birth, however, was never registered. Searches through ancestry websites reveal the registrations of the births of all the other children, but not that of the McDonaghs' fourth daughter, Anita. This oversight would later cause problems for her, as she was never quite sure of her true age. Growing up, she was led to believe that she'd been born on Boxing Day 1908, which also happens to be the same date as the famous boxing match between Tommy Burns and Jack Johnson and where Dr McDonagh had been in attendance as the stadium's official medic.

A second son was born on 13 August 1909. The parents named him Grant, after Dr McDonagh's famous Uncle Dean John Grant, the Bishop of Bathurst. Grant would inherit his ancestor's spiritual calling but would be prevented from entering the priesthood due to unforeseen circumstances.

In 1911, a cartoon of Dr McDonagh appeared in Sydney's *Truth*, accompanied by a satirical poem about his obsession with, and acquisition of, rollerskating rinks. Rollerskating had been introduced in Australia in the late 1860s by entrepreneur George Selth Coppin, and it soon became a wildly popular recreational activity. By the 1890s, almost every suburb in Sydney and Melbourne, as well as many country towns, could boast about having their own rink. Burlesque rollerskating had been included on the theatre stage since the 1880s and, from the late 19th century, the doctor would have been highly familiar with this slapstick form of popular entertainment. In Sydney, a burlesque rollerskater would often be booked to perform outside venues such as circuses, aquariums, and other places of amusement. By the time of the cartoon's publication, the doctor had already become one of the principal controllers of the Coliseum Rink in North Sydney, the Exhibition Rink near Central Station, and with Larry Foley was building another on William Street, adjacent to Hyde Park. The sketch reveals a moustachioed, potbellied, determined man in profile, wearing a hat and carrying a cane. That the doctor could be the subject of a cartoon and poem reveals the extent of his fame and influence in Australia's biggest city:

Feast your eyes, do, on McDonagh
At his classic visage blink
In this world, you see, he had a mighty mission
In Yurong Street's pious regions

Soon he'll have a skating rink
This nob of the Prince Alfred Exhibition.

The poem was correct in its rhyming prediction. On 1 May 1912, Dr McDonagh and Larry Foley opened the Imperial Skating Rink, near William Street in the city. In front of a crowd of curious onlookers, the paunchy fifty-three-year-old doctor, ever the show-off, elegantly executed a delicate *pas seul* on rollerskates, demonstrating how easily the skill could be acquired. Press reports on the Imperial Skating Rink emphasised that it catered only to a 'high-class clientele'. The doctor wanted to lift the reputation of skating into an elite recreation, to be enjoyed by the upper echelons of Sydney society.

His interest in rollerskating had been piqued a few years earlier. In 1909, a man named Mr W Eckard committed to a marathon at the Sydney Skating Rink. The doctor was on site to monitor Eckard and to attend to any emergencies. A band accompanied the skater while he was cheered on by an enthusiastic public. After Eckard skated for fifty-one consecutive hours, the doctor examined him and found that 'his general physical condition was marvellously good'. Eckard's marathon had set an endurance record in Australia, and possibly a record for public interest in this popular recreational activity.

Before opening the Imperial Skating Rink, the doctor appointed as manager a twenty-one-year-old champion roller-skater named James (Jimmy) Bendrodt. Two years earlier, Bendrodt had arrived in Sydney with only five pounds, after working for his passage from Canada to Sydney as a stoker on a ship. When the doctor met Jimmy, he was concerned to find a teenager who was sick and penniless, and far from home, and so, in a typical gesture of generosity, invited him to come and live with him and his family on College Street. The Canadian settled well into the McDonagh household and grew particularly close to

Anita Senior, who warmly mothered the skinny youth. In return, Jimmy taught the entire family how to refine their skating skills. In Canada, he'd held national rollerskating titles and was eager to exploit his talent in this new, foreign land as a trick skater.

Rollerskating was not the only business in which the doctor had invested. Six years before, he had secured the lease of the Palace Theatre, on Pitt Street, a theatrical house that boasted baroque arches and cornices, a French-style roof pavilion, topped by an Indian cupola. However, his adventures in theatrical production were stalled when the actor Henry Lee asked the doctor if he could borrow the staggering amount of 150 pounds. Only a month earlier the actor had broken his contract with Anderson Management after starring in only seven performances of what was planned to have been a month-long season of *Cyrano de Bergerac* at the Palace Theatre. Moreover, on opening night, during the final act of the play, the actor was disturbed by the murmurings of audience members in the gallery. He suddenly broke from character, abused the offending party for their 'outrageous conduct', and vowed that he would never appear on stage in Sydney again.

It says something about the doctor's empathic but sometimes naive and forgiving nature that he determined to help an erratic actor, who was also suffering from arthritis. He referred Lee to a business associate, Kitching, who, on 6 December 1902, arranged for the cash to be forwarded to the actor and for a promissory note to be drawn up. The agreement was that if Lee defaulted on the bank loan, the doctor and Kitching would each be liable for half the amount. A month later, Henry Lee skipped the country and went back to America via South Africa.

When the case went to court four years later, the doctor's lawyer argued that McDonagh had not received a notice of dishonour and therefore was not guilty of any offence, but witnesses stated the opposite.

Since no other press reports about the case were published, we can safely assume that McDonagh reluctantly delivered on the promissory note. The doctor was an optimist who always dreamed big, but whose dreams were often devilled by the necessary financial details, and by less scrupulous friends and business partners. As adults, his daughters would display the very same competing strengths and weaknesses.

At one point the doctor owned the town of Wyong, where a McDonagh Road still hugs the curves of the Wyong River. He'd also invested in gold mines, silver mines, and racehorses. However, he also contributed to charity, including Lewisham Hospital, which he'd helped to establish. In the foyer of the hospital, a bust of him was prominently displayed to commemorate his generosity.

Even as young children, the girls mirrored their father's love of show business by dressing up and stealing the limelight from their less flamboyant peers. In 1911, a charity event was staged at the Sydney Skating Rink, near Central Station, where their father was the managing director, and where the extroverted trio, along with two friends, entered the Juvenile Skating Carnival's 'Best Fancy-Dress Competition' in the 'Team' category. The group appeared hand in hand in identical Dresden shepherdess costumes and proudly glided around the rink to rounds of applause. According to a report in the *Bulletin*, 'Dr McDonagh's three little girls ... snatched the prize from all competitors'.

The following year, second daughter, Phyllis, stole the show yet again in another fancy dress skating competition held at the Exhibition Rink, which that night had been transformed into a fairyland decorated in pale pink chrysanthemums, roses, and Chinese lanterns. An orchestra played light dance music to accompany the competition, including the gently mocking, 'You Can't Judge a Woman by her Clothes'. Among the participants dressed variously as Nell Gwynne, Mother Goose, and Joan of Arc, twelve-year-old Phyllis, by now an accomplished skater, stood out as 'A Doll in a Box', with a journalist describing her as 'being a splendid representation of a waxen doll with long golden hair'. She won first prize in the category of 'Best Sustained Character'. What wasn't reported in the *Sunday Times* article was that the judges were Dr McCarthy, Dr John McDonagh, and the doctor's close friend and business partner, Larry Foley.

Phyllis seems to have taken a special liking to fancy dress, because only the month before she appeared with her mother, older sister, Isabel, and her best friend, Gertie Purcell, in the 'Team' category of the Cinderella Fancy Dress Carnival at the Imperial Skating Rink, which attracted 800 participants. The quartet came dressed as the 'Kismet Eastern Princesses'. Not only did Mrs McDonagh help to design the fancy dress costumes, but she also threw herself into the fun as well. By the age of forty-three, she had become a lithe and flexible skater.

Two years later, no doubt helped by the doctor's connections, the sisters graduated from entering fancy dress skating comp-etitions to judging them. At the ages of fifteen, fourteen, and thirteen, and assisted by 'a woman from Sydney', the girls sat in judgment of hundreds of participants at the Parramatta Skating Rink, handing first prize to the 'silvered brilliance of the ancient Eastern costumes' worn by skaters Miss Dorothy Thomas and Mr Frank Cruikshanks. Growing up with such an unusual mixture of freedom and responsibility, the girls were also learning the virtues of discernment and critical scrutiny. These virtues would strengthen as they grew older and began experiencing plays, opera, and that thrilling new art form, cinema.

3

THOSE GIRLS ARE GOING TO DO SOMETHING OUTSTANDING ONE DAY

(1909–1920)

The city that the sisters grew up in was defined by grand sandstone buildings in the city, gracious Edwardian mansions in Potts Point, and crumbling Victorian terraces around The Rocks and Millers Point. The backyard of the McDonagh home overlooked the slums of east Sydney and Woolloomooloo. From 1904, new electric street lighting magically transformed dark, sepia-toned nights into dazzling brightness. By 1910, public transportation had graduated from horse-drawn trams to electric 'toast rack' ones. There was no bridge connecting Millers Point to Milsons Point, and ferries foamed across the harbour, taking passengers to the northern and eastern suburbs.

Moving pictures were being exhibited in existing buildings such as halls and former theatres: some eighteen in the city and ninety-six in the suburbs. The first designated cinema, the Bijou Picture Palace, opened in 1909 and was a simple Edwardian design with three half-circle windows. In the same year, early film entrepreneur JD Williams opened Australia's first continuous cinema at the Colonial Theatre in George Street, Sydney, only three blocks from the McDonagh family home. The shows ran

31

from 11 am to 11 pm. Admission prices were cheap: threepence for adults and a penny for children.

But money never seemed to be a problem in the McDonagh household. Before John's marriage, he had set up credit accounts for his younger sister, Annie, at the city's leading department stores: Mark Foy's, David Jones, and Anthony Hordern and Sons. The accounts were to fund her extravagant tastes for expensive clothes and jewellery, which she regularly displayed with ostentation at high-society events. A regular guest at the governor's many functions, Annie defied Victorian standards of femininity by having the audacity to wear make-up at balls and formal dinners. Unlike the doctor's introverted other sister, Mary, Annie was flirtatious, exuberant, and had such a sense of entitlement that she refused to wear any dress twice.

Prior to his marriage, the expense of funding Annie's abundant wardrobe had not been difficult for John, but that was about to change. When his new wife first sighted the department store bills, she was horrified by Annie's profligacy, and the doctor's enabling of it, and forced him to go to all the stores personally and cancel every one of Annie's accounts. The arrangement was typical of the doctor's lifelong generosity and his carelessness about money. He had an almost obsessive need to make those around him – from strangers to his beloved relatives – as happy and content as possible.

But soon, responsibility for his youngest sister would be jettisoned through the powerful medium of scandal: skittish Annie ran off with a married man and disappeared with him overseas. She wrote regularly to the doctor for the rest of his life, though he did not share her news with his children. Improprieties such as these were hidden and never discussed. Family legend maintains that Annie bore a son to her lover, who turned out to be a child prodigy, and who as an adult became a famous violinist. This legend fascinated the sisters so much that when they reached adulthood, they would try to track him down.

As the McDonagh sisters approached puberty, whenever they were tempted to wear or do something garish, they were invariably told by their Aunt Mary, 'You be careful, or you might turn out like Aunt Annie'.

Despite Aunt Mary's conservatism, the children grew up in a permissive environment and were given free rein in the house. They would often playfully transform the back garden into an outdoor theatre. Isabel, Phyllis, and Paulette would dress up and perform pantomimes for the extended family and the doctor's patients, who could watch from wheelchairs positioned on the veranda.

Throughout her married life, their mother kept in close contact with her father's brother, Ernesto, who still lived in Valparaíso, Chile. They corresponded regularly, and when she fell pregnant for the seventh time, in early 1911, she wrote to her uncle to tell him that if the baby were a boy, she was going to name the child Ernest, in honour of him. Later that year, however, when a girl was born, mother Anita wrote to Uncle Ernesto and led him to believe that the child had been christened Paula Ernestina Leonora, not to be confused with the now eleven-year-old Paulette. As with older daughter Anita, parents Anita and John, in a strange bout of forgetfulness, lost track of her correct date of birth, and she was raised believing that she was four years younger than her actual age. This discrepancy wouldn't be discovered until Paula was in her fifties and applied for a copy of her birth certificate to obtain her first passport. Due to this misunderstanding, she would start school late, and wouldn't graduate from high school until she was twenty-two.

On College Street, the bedroom of the three older sisters had French doors leading onto an iron lace balcony overlooking Hyde Park. On Sunday mornings, pedestrians clothed in their best finery would stroll past the terrace, on their way to the Domain, to listen to various soapbox speakers and military bands. A regular amusement for the girls was to stand on the balcony and throw pitchers of water over the people parading below, and then duck out of sight in fits of giggles. When any victims of the girls knocked on the front door to complain, the doctor would placate their anger by slipping them some cash.

With such unbridled energy and mischievousness, their mother decided that the girls needed a firmer hand. At the age of thirteen, second daughter, Phyllis, was enrolled in the exclusive Kincoppal Sacred Heart School in Elizabeth Bay as a weekly boarder, only returning home on weekends and holidays. The property, originally owned by the Hughes family, had stunning views across the bay and a private beach for bathing. The following year, both eldest daughter, Isabel, and third daughter, Paulette, also enrolled, and the three sisters were back together again, sharing the one room, or in this case, the one dormitory, with seventeen other girls.

Kincoppal Sacred Heart School seems to have been a curious mixture of austerity and levity. It was run by French nuns who each wore a black habit with a white frill circling the face. Every time a student passed a nun, she would have to curtsy for four seconds going down and four seconds coming up. The girls had to attend mass every day in the chapel at 7.30 am, followed by breakfast in the refectory, where conversation was forbidden. The infraction of 'talking in the refectory' resulted in immediate expulsion, with no questions asked. Conversely, on Reverend Mother's intermittent 'feast days', which included the girls all donning fancy dress, playing musical instruments, and picnicking on the rocks by the sea, socialising and enjoyment were warmly encouraged. In summer, the students were permitted to go swimming in the harbour before morning mass. In the evenings, they could sneak out onto the long balcony that ran the length of their dormitory and hear the lions roaring across the water from enclosures at Taronga Zoo.

The teenage sisters blossomed under such a structured regime. The three joined Catholic societies formed within the school, and Paulette took advantage of the superlative sporting facilities, excelling at basketball. Phyllis steeped herself in literature and wrote a lot of heartfelt poetry. Her best friend at school, Estelle McDermott, remembers Phyllis as 'a very nice girl, a very kind girl. Dreamy – as her eyes showed'. Her eyes often drifted into dreaminess whenever she was contemplating an idea for a short story or poem. Estelle remembers Isabel as being 'very lovely' and always smiling, while Paulette used to become 'very excited' and loud, and at the time spoke with a slight speech impediment.

On the weekends, the girls would make the short trip back to their home on College Street, but they spent little time with their family, preferring to enjoy their Saturdays and Sundays going to the pictures, later excitedly discussing the acting, directing, and scenario-writing late into the night.

In years to come, when the sisters began publicising their films, they promoted the myth that they'd written the first draft of their first film, *Those Who Love*, in the recreation room of Kincoppal school. This claim is highly unlikely, however, as at that stage Paulette had no idea of how to structure and format a film scenario and wouldn't learn how to do so until 1924. Moreover, their friend Estelle maintains that when the sisters were at school, there was no sign at all that they would graduate into the world of producing motion pictures. Dramatics of any kind were not only discouraged at Kincoppal but entirely forbidden – no Christmas pageants were staged or amateur theatricals mounted. In fact, the nuns took such a dim view of the theatre that when Estelle confessed to a nurse that she wanted to become an actress, her mother was immediately summoned and ordered to explain to the naive girl why the stage was a disreputable profession for a woman. Moreover, the social milieu within which the McDonagh sisters lived actively discouraged any sort of professional aspiration.

'It wasn't the thing for a young lady to work', said Estelle. 'She went in for accomplishments. Music and so forth ...'

In 1914, the First World War was declared, and the doctor's expertise would soon be in demand in Sydney for wounded and traumatised returning soldiers. That year, film stock in Australia suddenly became difficult to access because the ingredients used to manufacture it were needed to make explosives. It was during this time that Hollywood, with its mix of glamorous studio stars and powerful marketing strategies, not only filled that gap in the global industry, but completely redefined it. While America's European competitors were overwhelmed by the war, Hollywood films flooded the Australian market, and were absorbed by the porous imaginations of three impressionable schoolgirls.

A year later, the JC Williamson company grew concerned about the pattern of Americans producing film adaptations of the plays it was presenting on stage. However, due to the lack of a copyright agreement between Australia and the United States, the Williamson company was able to turn the predicament to its advantage. It formed its own film company and started shooting moving picture versions of its theatrical productions, allowing them to cut out the Americans and reap more profits for the firm. Therefore, from their early teens, the sisters were cognisant not only of the wonder of the cinema experience, but also alert to the possibilities of producing films in Australia.

Locally, many independent companies would pop up and fold after one or two films, and the quality, of course, would vary. This phenomenon created the perception among exhibitors and distributors that Australian features were vastly inferior to their Hollywood counterparts.

This perception was underscored by the stubbornly local settings of films made in Australia. The prime example of this crude form of nationalism was the series of films made by Beaumont Smith, six comedies about a family of farmers, the 'Hayseeds', who hailed from the back of beyond. Produced from 1917 onwards, the series played on national stereotypes and relied on crass, slapstick humour to entertain audiences.

In the early 20th century, the Australian industry also concentrated on films set in colonial times: *Eureka Stockade* (1907), *Robbery Under Arms* (1907), and *For the Term of his Natural Life* (1908). Bushranging stories were also wildly popular with the public: *The Story of the Kelly Gang* (1906); *The Life and Adventures of John Vane, the Notorious Australian Bushranger* (1910); *Captain Starlight*; *Captain Moonlite*; *Captain Midnight: The Bush King*; *Ben Hall and his Gang*; *Frank Gardiner, King of the Road*; and *Keane of Kalgoorlie* (all in 1911). Between 1911 and 1926, there were approximately 220 features produced in Australia, and 170 of them contained bush settings. In fact, so popular did the bushranging film become, that in 1912 the NSW police force, wary that the subject matter might corrupt innocent audience members, banned the subject in films completely. Clearly, there was an opening in the market for more sophisticated, urbane subject matter and fresher talent.

By the time the sisters began attending the cinema regularly on weekends, they had sixteen movie theatres within walking distance from their home on College Street. And while Hollywood was coming to Australia, the reverse was also true: the McDonaghs were still in high school when actresses Enid Bennett and Sylvia Breamer joined the exodus of Australian talent to Hollywood. Bennett left in 1915 and launched a successful acting career with Triangle Film Corporation. Breamer joined her the following year, also signing up with Triangle. By December 1917, she'd already starred in five films, and Australian newspapers were publicising Bennett as the second Australian actress to make a splash in Hollywood. No doubt these press reports about local talent conquering American film studios fuelled the sisters' dreams and imaginations, especially Paulette's.

At school, Isabel developed a close friendship with fellow student, Kathleen Coen. During the school holidays, she frequently stayed with Kathleen at the Coen home. Originally named Kenmare, it was on Yass's main thoroughfare, Comur Street. As a joke, someone had scratched out the 'a' and changed it to an 'o', so that the sign read 'Kenmore', which was also the name of the local 'lunatic asylum', the term used at this time. The house had once been the old Braidwood Store, with ten rooms, two storeys, soaring ceilings, and an upstairs balcony that stretched twenty feet over the footpath. In summer the Coen girls slept on the balcony; in winter they used it as a rollerskating rink. But by the time Isabel began staying with Kathleen in Yass, Kathleen's four older sisters had either entered a convent or were preparing to become nuns. Kathleen herself longed to become a nun, too, but, being the youngest daughter, was persuaded to stay at home and care for their widowed mother.

The mother owned a cockatoo that demanded tea and toast for breakfast every morning, and invariably the pet received it. Also living there were her two ageing sisters, Linda, a retired schoolteacher, and Lizzie. Each of the three women wore a red wig well into their eighties and nineties. With its amusing combination of eccentricity and religiosity, teenage Isabel would have felt right at home. Kathleen's niece, Margaret Coen, remembers Isabel as beautiful and charming, with a great sense of humour, who loved fun and games. Red-haired Kathleen also had a warm personality and her hobbies included playing cards, gambling and, later, driving cars with the roof collapsed while wearing kid gloves and a hat secured by a large pin.

The family owned the shop, Australian Stores, next door to the house, which was managed by Kathleen's uncle, Luke Trainor. The store serviced the local Irish landowners with produce and supplies, as well as women's and men's clothing, shoes, drapery, and bespoke hats fashioned by an in-house, full-time milliner.

Like the home of the McDonaghs, the Coen house was always open to visitors, and the front door was never locked, allowing for friends to come and go as they pleased. The dining room table had so many leaves that it could accommodate sixteen guests, and there were never fewer than twelve during meals.

Afternoon teas were served in the courtyard at the back of the property, threaded with wisteria and grapevines. Snapdragons and columbines nodded in the breeze; a single orange tree grew on the site of a former well, next to a mulberry and a persimmon. After making their purchases in the Australian Stores, the landed gentry would gather in this flowering yard, trading gossip and nibbling scones. And during these shopping expeditions, many a young man visiting the Coens would take one glimpse of attractive Isabel poised on an iron lace chair and fall hopelessly in love. One such suitor was so smitten with Isabel that he followed her to Sydney, knocked on the door of the home on College Street, and asked her father for permission to escort her that night to the theatre.

Wily Dr McDonagh smiled, and at once put the nervous suitor at ease. 'Isabel and I would be delighted to attend', he warmly replied, disabusing the man of the hope that he would ever have a chance to spend time with his precious daughter unchaperoned.

But her protective father was not always around to fend off unwanted attention from love-struck men. During one holiday in Yass, a young air force hero was passing through town. He fell for Isabel immediately, and one of Kathleen's relatives invited the airman to tea, and to afterwards play cards with Kathleen and Isabel. In the meantime, fun-loving Isabel was playing with Kathleen's niece, Margaret, who at the time was nine or ten years old. She led Margaret down to the laundry at the back of the house and showed her how to cut up cakes of Sunlight soap into small squares. Isabel then demonstrated how to roll the little cubes in flour, so that they looked as if they had been dusted in icing sugar.

While playing cards that night, Isabel, in the company of an excited Margaret, offered the air force hero what he assumed to be a dish of marshmallows. He accepted immediately and little Margaret watched on with glee as the airman bit into the cube, jumped from his seat, and began frothing at the mouth. Apparently, he did not appreciate the innocent practical joke, and the romance was over before it had even begun.

Isabel was not the only sister who enjoyed kidding around and playing practical jokes. Back at Kincoppal, Paulette was honing her talents as a satirist. There were two nuns at the convent to whom she'd taken a dislike, so much so that she began writing disparaging poems about them, highlighting their flat noses, leaden faces, and overbearing bulk. Amused by her own descriptive flourishes, she began sharing the poems with another girl, Gladys Oxman, who was in her year. The naive Gladys stored the poems in her desk drawer while she and Paulette, and the rest of the boarders, went home for the weekend. On Monday morning, having returned to Kincoppal, a startled Paulette was summoned to the office of the Mother Superior, where she was met by Gladys, also summoned. Mother Superior appeared, ashen-faced, the collection of unflattering poems in her hand. She sat down at her desk and verbally abused them. 'She took us to pieces', admitted Paulette.

Until they apologised, the girls were forced to sit at a small table in the middle of the dayroom while the rest of the student body was forbidden to speak to them. A terrified Gladys folded almost immediately, trailing the offended nuns, apologising profusely, and grovelling on her knees for forgiveness. An unwavering and slightly disgusted Paulette continued to sit on her own, refusing to utter a word, let alone an apology. Again, Mother Superior summoned her to the office and this time threatened her with expulsion, reminding Paulette that she came from a respectable family, and that her rejection from the school would cause a scandal.

Paulette, characteristically, remained unmoved.

Eventually, one of the targets of Paulette's poison pen gently intervened. The nun took her to her private room and admitted that she knew why Paulette had written the poems. 'She knew she was obese. She knew (she had a) lead face and big nose ... And she knew I hadn't given in. And I think she liked me for not giving in ... And do you know from then on she said, "You and I from now on are going to be the best (of) friends".'

At last, the threats of expulsion were dropped, and Paulette learned her first lesson about never blindly yielding to authority – or, even worse, intimidation.

During the Christmas break of 1916, Phyllis developed a yearning to appear on the stage. Like her father, she had a perfect pitch and loved to perform. One day she noticed an advertisement in the paper for extras to appear in a play by well-known English actors at the old Opera House. She begged her father to be allowed to audition for the play, but her mother, when she found out, was scandalised by the idea of her teenage daughter performing in public. The doctor, however, was more sanguine in his response, advising his wife that Phyllis's naiveté and innocence would protect her from any unsavoury elements associated with the underworld of backstage theatre. Anita Senior finally relented and young Phyllis auditioned for and was offered one of four small parts in a Christmas show, which ran for four weeks. 'It was not that I had any particular talent for the stage', she reflected, 'but I wanted to experience the actual background if I ever decided to write a stage novel'. After the four weeks were up, the company moved on to Melbourne, 'and I was back at school, feeling immeasurably superior and grown-up'.

Phyllis and Paulette passed their Intermediary Exams easily, but Isabel seems to not have taken hers as she left abruptly in June 1916, in the middle of the academic year, possibly due to her mother needing help in both the home and the hospital. Isabel also regularly assisted her father in his surgery – even during operations. Her calm and unruffled demeanour made her perfect for the exacting work.

In December 1917, Phyllis also left Kincoppal, while Paulette remained until 1919. Her final-year subjects for the Intermediary Exam were English, History, Geography, Art, and Needlework. She received a mark of 'B' for every subject, as did virtually every other student. It is unfortunate that she didn't have the foresight to also take the subject of Business Principles that was offered that year, for in her future role as a film director and producer, she certainly would have benefited from an understanding of the fundamentals of running a profitable enterprise. Still, the nuns did recognise the sisters' natural intelligence, drive, and confidence, with one remarking in the last months of Paulette's tenure there, 'those girls are going to do something outstanding one day'.

As one by one the sisters left school, thirty-three-year-old nanny, Stella, expressed a long-held desire to her surrogate father, John: to marry and have a family of her own. She'd lived with the McDonaghs for sixteen years and the youngest child, Paula, was now seven. The protective doctor immediately took charge of the situation, promising that he would find a suitable match for her. He soon introduced Stella to one of his colleagues, William Waddock, an analytical chemist, who was a year her junior. After courting for a suitable period, Stella and Willy married and moved to a home called 'Carmel' at 35 Spencer Street, Rose Bay.

In the year that Paulette left Kincoppal, the sisters were gifted with an Australian role model in the form of Lottie Lyell. By

42

1919, she was being celebrated as the country's first film star, playing the lead in Raymond Longford's acclaimed feature, *The Sentimental Bloke*. Critics overwhelmingly praised Lyell's natural presence onscreen and her wide, expressive eyes, which in a brief, single close-up could convey a multitude of feelings. But Lyell was not just a bit of frivolous eye candy to brighten up the screen; she was also Longford's creative partner, assisting him as a scriptwriter, designer, editor, and associate director. She was also an accomplished horse rider, and her roles were often written to exploit this skill. Through press reports, her multiple contributions to Longford's features were well known to the movie-going public, and the McDonaghs, particularly Paulette, would have been inspired by this precedent.

Other female filmmaking pioneers who contributed to the films of their male partners include Kate Howard. In 1921, she co-directed the film adaptation of her stage play, *Possum Paddock*. After arriving in Australia, English-born actor, writer, and producer Yvonne Pavis formed a company with husband Lawson Harris that produced three films in 1922: *Circumstance, A Daughter of Australia* and *Sunshine Sally*. American-born screenwriter Bess Meredyth travelled to Australia with husband Wilfred Lucas in 1918 to work on three films with the legendary sportsman Snowy Baker. With Lucas, Meredyth co-directed *The Man From Kangaroo* (1920) and *The Jackeroo of Coolabong* (1920). And then there was the trailblazing Louise Lovely, who, after enjoying an acting career in Hollywood, returned to her home in Sydney to form a production company with husband Wilton Welch. After securing the backing of several businessmen, the company accrued a budget of 30 000 pounds, which allowed the husband-and-wife team to construct a sophisticated studio in Sydney containing several large sets to produce the feature *Jewelled Nights* (1925). During the silent era, a minority of women were able to find a firm foothold in the motion picture industry.

On 11 November 1918, the First World War ended. Diggers began returning in early 1919 and continued to do so throughout the year. Accompanying them were infections of Spanish influenza and the early months of peace were disturbed by this new and unforeseen crisis. Between 27 January and 30 September, the pandemic swept through the country in three waves of increasing severity, causing approximately 12 000 deaths, mostly in New South Wales. By the autumn of 1919, hundreds of people were dying every day. Schools were closed and pedestrians were forced to wear white gauze masks; anyone who refused to do so risked immediate arrest. A family friend of the McDonaghs, Bud Macken, nephew of Francis Foy of the Foy retail empire, wrote of the crisis: 'First, a few cases – diagnosed as influenza. But they all died. Panic set in as the death toll grew to 12 daily, then 20, then started to soar to over 100 daily, then to over 400'. At the time, Macken was attending Riverview College with John McDonagh Junior, and when schools were closed indefinitely, all the students were sent home. Macken remembers that the boys who delivered groceries would merely throw meat and bread over the back fence.

At the same time, free medical treatment was offered to returning soldiers for injuries and illnesses suffered during the war. And so, between caring for the injured and infected, those attending at the McDonagh Private Hospital would have been working overtime.

Many soldiers returned from the war only to suffer the ignominy of unemployment, their jobs filled by men who had not enlisted or – to their shock – by single women. The rise of feminism was an unintended consequence of the war and Australian women gaining the vote in 1902. Now that women had become accustomed to working in factories, offices, and department stores, they were unwilling to return to non-paid domestic work, even though they earned only about fifty per cent of the wages of men. Those women who did earn their own money could spend it on modest luxuries such as clothes, cosmetics, and, of course, the cinema.

The sisters came of age precisely at a time when single women were redefining their gender roles and seeking more independence as individuals. For the first time in history, young women such as Isabel, Phyllis, and Paulette could walk in pairs or groups throughout most parts of the city in the daytime and well-lit areas at night without endangering either their safety or their reputations.

Some of the older traditions, however, still overlapped with the new, especially in upper-middle-class society. Girls were expected to wait until they were eighteen before accepting an invitation to go out with a boy. Chaperones were still common. It was not polite for a girl to dance all night with only one boy. Three dances with the same boy was almost scandalous, and indicated to all the other guests, and the lucky boy, that she was serious about becoming engaged to him. At balls and formal dinner dances, girls clutched programs and excitedly reserved dances for certain boys who had expressed an interest in them. If the McDonagh parents were worried about preserving the innocence of their daughters, they shouldn't have. According to Paula, until they turned eighteen, all the McDonagh daughters were taught that, after being kissed by a man, a girl would automatically fall pregnant.

At the same time, due to technological advances, America was developing the most dramatically expanding economy in the world, and Sydney-based department stores enthusiastically imported mass-produced items from the United States: machines, gadgets, magazines, fashions, and homewares. All were marketed as 'modern' and 'new' and exuded an air of potential and excitement. America was the epicentre of cosmopolitan modernity, but its ripple effects were felt keenly across the Pacific Ocean in moving pictures, radio serials, jazz music, dances, and the loosening of social mores. Living in the middle of Australia's biggest city, with a father enchanted by popular amusements and entertainment, the sisters were well placed to absorb the advantages of modernism and reimagine them into the most glamorous and contemporary form of storytelling: the 'Hollywood' type of motion picture.

On Thursday 5 June 1919, the girls made their debut, along with seventy other young socialites, at a Peace Ball held at the Sydney Town Hall, which was a benefit for the Church of England Homes for Children. The ball was the first grand social event since the outbreak of the war, and anticipation was at such a fever pitch that every one of the 1800 tickets was sold. Seven years later, Paulette would register for copyright an early film scenario that she'd written, 'A Greater Love'. It featured a young woman anticipating her first ball, no doubt inspired by her own and her sisters' experience: 'Her dress was chosen and rechosen, the excitement was delicious, Jaycenth existed in a whirl of expectancy. Eliza [was] impressed [by] the solemnity of the occasion, it was to be the crowning day of her young life'.

In preparation for the event, volunteers spent months crafting tinted paper flowers to decorate the hall in the colours of gold and green. The pillars were wreathed with sunflowers and ivy; galleries festooned with tulips and poppies. Floral arches had been placed in each corner of the venue, while the vice-regal dais was erected below the southern gallery, with a scenic backdrop of hanging baskets and palms. Electric lights and chandeliers were veiled in yellow muslin, casting a pale golden light over the paradisiacal setting. And the stage was magically transformed into a fragrant orange grove, with actual orange trees, foregrounded by mirrors framed by blossoms. Between the hanging fruit, twenty musicians from Torville's Orchestra played foxtrots and waltzes, with a splash of syncopated jazz. Some of the new dance crazes from America percolated onto the dance floor, including the 'scissor step' and 'the tickle toe', while jazz dancing in general was described as 'a sort of mad tango'. It was a celebration to announce that the deprivations and suffering of the war, and the fear and isolation engendered by the Spanish flu, were now over. There were many naval and military attendees, as well as women from the Red Cross, whose bright scarlet capes stood out in the crowd. Some young female attendees had already had their hair cut and styled into the modern, fashionable bob that would go on to define the style of the 1920s jazz age, but not the McDonagh sisters, who were still under the watchful eye of their Victorian mother.

The debutantes were trained for presentation by Mrs Albert Littlejohn, who endeavoured to teach the coltish Australian girls how to perform a royal curtsy. The vice-regal party, headed by Governor and Lady Davidson, arrived at 9.30 pm to the strains of the national anthem as they passed through a guard of honour. The sisters were twenty, nineteen, and eighteen respectively and, in a studio portrait taken specifically for the event, later published in the *Sydney Mail*, the three pretty debutantes are still round-faced and childlike. But with their upswept black hair, wide-set hazel eyes, and matching ankle-length white tulle gowns, they would have turned more than a few heads as they threaded through crowds and graced the polished dance floor.

The war may have ended, but their lives as women were just beginning.

4

THE MANSION BY THE RIVER

(1920–1924)

On 29 January 1920, shortly following her twenty-first birthday, Isabel was enjoying one of her many stays with Kathleen Coen in Yass when a telegram arrived stating that her beloved father was ill and that she should return home immediately. At once, Isabel packed her bags, caught a steam tram from Yass Junction to the railway station, and boarded a train to Sydney. With no way of contacting her family directly, and knowing no details of her father's ailment, it would have been a long, lonely, and agonising three-hour trip north-east through the countryside, while paddocks and parched creeks flashed past her window in the stultifying heat.

John McDonagh's best friend was also his doctor, a fellow Irishman and surgeon, Dr Nash, who was Head of Sydney Hospital. On the morning of 29 January, John had an appointment with Dr Nash at his surgery on Macquarie Street. During the consultation, Nash prescribed cocaine, which was legal at that time, though it is unclear if McDonagh was suffering from a genuine physical complaint or, at the age of sixty-one, he merely needed a stimulant to maintain his vibrant energy and demanding schedule. In the early 20th century, cocaine use was popular among older people and prostitutes requiring a pick-me-up.

'His energies never stopped', said Paula of her father.

Unfortunately, either Nash miscalculated the required amount, or the substance was much purer than at previous times, because after leaving the surgery and taking a five-minute hansom cab ride home, McDonagh collapsed on his doorstep.

His horrified wife had the servants lift him into the house, and later, the children were asked by their mother to file into the room where he lay. Phyllis and Paulette were now twenty and nineteen respectively. As Paulette once remarked, 'at twenty we were still children. Young children'.

Once Isabel arrived at Central Station, she grabbed her luggage and took a cab ride back to College Street. She rushed up the stairs of her home but, when the front door opened and she saw the servants dressed in black, she knew she'd arrived too late.

A funeral was hastily arranged to take place in two days' time. It's unclear why it was staged so soon after his death; also unclear is why it wasn't held at St Mary's Cathedral, where his father's funeral was held. Perhaps Mrs McDonagh wanted to avoid an official autopsy and the possibly scandalous reason for his sudden and unexpected death. On the following Saturday at 9.45 am, a cortège left 14 College Street and wound through the city and down New South Head Road towards Waverley Cemetery for the ceremony and burial, which was highly attended. Youngest daughter, Paula, aged nine, was deemed too young to attend the funeral, and so she stayed the weekend with former nanny, Stella, and her husband, Willy, in Rose Bay. On the night following the funeral, the Sydney boxing community paid tribute to the doctor at Sydney Stadium, where he'd attended so many matches as a surgeon-in-general and fan. The referee and participants in the main event wore black crepe armbands.

A few days after the funeral, Dr McDonagh's safe was opened and the contents were examined by the family solicitor. Mrs McDonagh was expecting to find cash, property deeds, and details of the doctor's many other investments. But after sifting through the paperwork, the solicitor informed the devastated widow that her husband had left no will. She later learned that all the deeds to the various properties and businesses he owned amounted to very little, and that there were many debts to settle. Their social fall was spectacular: in a single week, the family was suddenly toppled from their privileged position in Sydney society to an existence dependent on the kindness of friends and relatives.

At the time, the Australian government did not provide unemployment benefits to the jobless, or widow's pensions to the bereft. A popular saying was that 'the slate is the working man's bank', and families without a steady income, such as the McDonaghs, would come to rely on credit from the grocer, the butcher, the milkman, and the baker.

In the 1920s, buying household items on time payment became a popular form of credit, with customers enjoying the benefits of such modern technologies as wirelesses, vacuum cleaners, refrigerators, and stoves for the price of a five or ten per cent deposit. Within the next fifteen years, this reliance on time payment would cause innumerable problems for the family.

Mrs McDonagh could have solved their immediate financial difficulties by selling the doctor's vast collection of art, antiques, and furniture. However, in her paralysing grief, she and the children clung to the relics of the doctor's life. Now that they could no longer afford to rent the College Street property, they put most of the collection into storage and moved to a leased house on the northern beaches, at Narrabeen Lakes, where Anita could figure out how to support herself and seven children without a regular income. At this hellish time, Aunt Mary and Uncle Pat provided succour and financial assistance to soften the shock of their multiple losses. By this time, Uncle Pat had retired and they had sold their country property, Tarawong. The couple had gone on to purchase a large house in leafy Wahroonga.

Paula believes that, at the time of the doctor's death, her mother was several months pregnant and, due to severe stress, miscarried the baby. However, in early 1920, Mrs McDonagh would have been forty-nine and, despite her prolific fertility, it's highly unlikely that she could have conceived a child. More likely, she was suffering from the onset of menopause and the symptoms of a phantom pregnancy which, in the squall of deep bereavement, she mistook for an actual one.

One of the few investments made by the doctor that still held any value was land he'd purchased around and on the Wyong River, about 100 kilometres north of Sydney. 'Wyong' is an Indigenous word meaning either 'edible yam' or 'place of running water', and at the time both were plentiful in the area, as well as pristine bushland studded with eucalyptus trees, home to koalas, bandicoots, quolls, and the sonorous yellow-bellied glider. Miniature seahorses thrived in lakes, and platypuses bred in the many waterways. The town had been established by colonisers in 1888 and, by 1920, Chapman's Store had been built, as well as the Alison Homestead, St Cecilia's Church, Wyong Public School, the Wyong Milk Factory, and the railway station. The McDonagh holdings were only a fifteen-minute walk from the train, which led directly to Sydney. Today, the family is still commemorated in the area by the winding 'McDonagh Road', a 1.6-kilometre thoroughfare that hugs the curves of the Wyong River.

On 19 March 1921, a desperate Mrs McDonagh tried to auction off as much land as possible to keep the family out of debt, advertising that it was 'an extension of the town of Wyong, embracing fine river frontage blocks and interior lots in a go-ahead town on the Northern line, within easy distance of Tuggerah Lakes, the great boating and fishing resort'. She was unable to auction off all the lots that day and three months later advertised another two lots on the Wyong River for 110 pounds each.

A local doctor and friends of the family suggested that Mrs McDonagh should rely on her training as a nurse and open a convalescent home to support herself and her children. She recognised the opportunity and found a mansion big enough to house herself, her seven children, her potential patients, and her husband's collection of antiques, furniture, and art. It was called Drummoyne House and stood on a bank of the Parramatta River. Unfortunately, she did not have the funds to purchase the property, so Aunt Mary's retired husband, Pat O'Connell, stepped up and bought the mansion himself so that the family could live and work there independently. We don't know the exact terms of the agreement between Anita McDonagh and O'Connell, but the property was purchased and the deed was drawn in his name only.

The three older sisters were entranced by the mansion's history. The forty-room stone property had been built by convicts in the mid-1850s from plans submitted by the owner of the land, Captain Wright, a successful merchant and island trader, formerly of Essex, who'd recently retired. Wright had been so meticulous in his vision of the mansion that he'd inspected every stone before it was laid. Those that were considered defective he smashed with a sledgehammer. The walls of the main rooms were sixteen feet high and thirty feet long, and the mantles were fashioned from rare and expensive Sienna marble, the shutters of polished mahogany, and the floors of inlaid New Zealand kauri timber.

Wright had also employed around seventy European artisans in the construction of steps and balustrades. Wood carvings inside the house were crafted by Italian masons, one of whom had fashioned the eagle in the British House of Commons. Wright retained one mason for three years, whose brief was to collect the flowers and fruits from the lush gardens, such as trumpet lilies and night cactus, and reproduce the plants in delicate carvings around the many window frames. He also had built within the mansion a secret room, discovered years later, in which to store valuables.

After the death of Captain Wright in 1889, the house changed hands and, in March 1894, the extensive gardens were subdivided and sold, along with the mansion. In the mid-1900s, it was purchased by Elizabeth Hordern, the wealthy widow of Australian department store owner and entrepreneur, Anthony Hordern. Elizabeth moved in and lived there happily until her death on 21 November 1919, at the age of seventy-three. It was from the Hordern estate that Pat O'Connell bought the property in late 1921.

The old mansion creaked and groaned at night, and the younger children were convinced that it was haunted. The main body of the property had six upstairs bedrooms, which housed the patients, and a large bathroom at either end of the floor. Downstairs was the reception area, an enormous drawing-room, a cavernous ballroom, and a dining room. Along a passageway was a bedroom with an attached bathroom and pantry. Two wings extended from the main body of the house, and the family resided upstairs in one of them. The other side was reserved for the staff, which was comprised of a cook, a nurse, and a gardener. Each wing contained six bedrooms, so there were eighteen in all. The kitchens were located beneath the living area.

By this time, John had enrolled in medical school at Sydney University and would invite his fellow students home, where they would stay indefinitely. 'It was open house, our family, always, to people', said Paula. 'And they'd come and not just to visit, but they'd stay, you know, for days on end ...' John also brought home specimens to complete his anatomy classes. One day he found one of the family dogs playing with a human brain in the backyard, using it as a ball.

During their years at Drummoyne House, the family had a total of four dogs, including a St Bernard. A collie they owned would later make an appearance in their second film, *The Far Paradise*, as would their black Pekingese, 'Nip', who used to bite the ankles of arriving guests.

Between the two wings of the house was a stone-flagged courtyard. One of the stones had a metal ring attached to it, and one day, when John and a university friend lifted it, they discovered an underground stream. The youngest child, Paula, believed that a trip down a primitive ladder revealed tunnels that led to the Parramatta River.

Lucy, the housekeeper and cook, was a 'dear old thing', who drank on Fridays, her day off. Paula remembers that she'd disappear for hours and return home drunk and singing to herself.

Dr Menzies, a local doctor and friend who also ran a private hospital, knew of Anita's dire financial circumstances and referred rich patients to her. Anita had no assistant except a maid to help with cleaning and bedding, and daughter Isabel, who was second-in-command. Anita was meticulous about her work and took nursing very seriously, to the extent that she wouldn't allow a tray to be carried into a room without inspecting it herself. And if one aspect of the tray was not up to scratch, she'd immediately send it back to the kitchen.

Soon after the move to Drummoyne House, Anita's younger sister, Nellie, with whom she had trained as a nurse, also moved into the home. However, her arrival wasn't to assist with the nursing but to become yet another patient. Even though she was only in her late forties Nellie suffered from crippling rheumatoid arthritis and required round-the-clock care from her extended family.

During the 1920s, Drummoyne's large old estates were being subdivided and sold, to be replaced by smaller, red-roofed villas. Drummoyne House was one of the few colonial mansions in the area to survive the redevelopment of the post-war period. The suburb was serviced by electric trams, ferries, and a primitive bus service that was comprised of oversized motor cars with the chassis extended and filled with extra seats. But if the McDonaghs wanted to see a film, they did not have to travel to the city as regular motion picture programs had been screening in the area for several years, firstly in the Chelmsford Hall on Great North Road, which in 1921 was refurbished and renamed 'The Regal Theatre'. In January 1925, an open-air movie show began screening films on First Avenue, and later that year, a splendid venue was added to the suburb with the opening of the 'Victory Theatre' on Great North Road, which seated 1150 people.

Even though Drummoyne House contained eighteen bedrooms, Isabel, Phyllis, and Paulette still opted to share the one bedroom. The unexpected death of their father had drawn them even closer together, and their shared grief began to merge into a form of emotional dependence. As articulate and educated young women, they would sit up in their bedroom, discussing books, art, plays, poetry, and silent film into the early hours of the morning. 'They were like different components of the one character', observed Paula. 'One wouldn't even consider buying a comb without discussing it with the other two.'

The younger children amused themselves by entering competitions. At the age of nine, Paula was thrilled to see her name in the Sunday papers as the first-prize winner of a Beauty and the Beast drawing competition. Fourth daughter Anita won a writing competition with a sophisticated Christmas story that was printed in the *Sun* newspaper, though Isabel's sons, Alan and Charles Stewart, later claimed that they could hear Phyllis's narrative voice in the prose and suspected that the older sister had had a hand in drafting it.

In the meantime, Grant, who was being taught by Jesuits, was becoming more and more religious. He looked up to the priests as he had his own father. Grant craved direction, authority, and spiritual succour, and decided that, after graduating high school, he would study for the priesthood. Unfortunately, like Paulette earlier, Grant suffered from a speech impediment and, due to the disability, the Jesuits at Riverview rejected his plans. So, when a disconsolate Grant completed his Intermediate Certificate, majoring in English and History, he refused to return to complete his secondary education and left school at age fourteen. The grieving and disappointed boy insisted upon remaining at home indefinitely, just moping about, and at a loss.

Soon, yet another relative moved into Drummoyne House – this time a grief-stricken Aunt Mary. Only eight months after her husband, Pat O'Connell, had purchased the property for the McDonagh family's use, he'd suddenly died at the age of sixty-eight. Mary took up residence on the ground floor, in the large bedroom with the attached bathroom and pantry.

After so much sickness and grief, Anita Senior tried to resume some of the social activities that had defined the family's former glamorous life. She and the three older girls volunteered to join committees that organised dances and balls in aid of raising funds for various charities. In April 1922, the McDonagh matriarch opened Drummoyne House to the social elite of Sydney for a dance to raise money for nearby Riverview College. Guests were encouraged to bring gifts that could be later sold at a stall when a school fete was held.

The sisters and younger children decorated the ballroom and hung colourful Japanese lanterns that gently swayed in the autumn breeze from the balcony roofs. Anita and her three eldest daughters received the guests as they entered the great hall of the home. All were dressed fashionably, with Isabel wearing a gown of 'white satin and tulle with flowers', Phyllis in pink 'mousseline de soie', and Paulette in 'unrelieved white'. Even grieving Aunt Mary, a widow of two months, made an appearance to support the cause, wearing 'black georgette with garlands of pink roses'.

In 1923, when construction of the Sydney Harbour Bridge commenced, the city officially entered the age of modernism. Over the following decade, the steel arches would rise from the north and south banks of the harbour, eventually joining at the summit nine years later in a momentous crowning of ambition and architecture. Its opening in 1932 would be a beacon of hope for Sydney's residents suffering through the Depression, a reminder that their city was fresh, cosmopolitan, and international. The building of the bridge would later feature in the McDonaghs' third film, *The Cheaters*, as a metaphor for the rapid pace of change.

At the end of Mrs McDonagh's gruelling work week, the only entertainment she enjoyed was going to the pictures on Saturday nights. She and the seven children would file into the local cinema together and take up an entire row. By this time, Isabel had appeared as an extra in *A Daughter of Australia* (1921), most likely as a result of answering a newspaper advertisement. During a screening of that film, Anita experienced the pleasure and pride of seeing a close-up of her beautiful eldest daughter projected onto the screen. It would be the only time that she would see Isabel in a movie.

During another night at the pictures in March 1924, only four years after the death of her husband, Anita complained of a severe headache. Knowing that she wouldn't be able to endure the five-minute walk home, she instructed her eldest son, John, to quickly leave the theatre and arrange for a taxi to collect them. The children helped her into the car and piled in after her. When they arrived home, Mrs McDonagh made it up the stone stairs of Drummoyne House, but collapsed on the doorstep from the effects of a stroke. She never regained full consciousness.

Their mother lingered in bed for a few days, paralysed. But whenever one of her children approached the bed, her eyes would turn to look at them with pleading intensity. A second stroke soon snatched away this final ability to communicate. Isabel, panicking, rang her best friend, Kathleen Coen, for support. Kathleen immediately took a train from Yass to Sydney and arrived in time to help Isabel nurse her mother through the last hours of her life.

Five of the McDonagh children and their aunt:
(clockwise from top left) Isabel, Aunt Mary, Phyllis,
Paulette, Anita (on Mary's knee), and John.
Courtesy of Graham Shirley

Phyllis, Isabel, the children's nanny Stella, Paulette, and Anita
in the garden of Drummoyne House.
Courtesy of the NFSA

Siblings (clockwise from left) Paulette, John, Phyllis, and Isabel
wearing fancy dress in the 1920s, displaying their theatrical flair.
Courtesy of the NFSA

Drummoyne House, where the family lived from 1921.
University of Sydney Archives

Clockwise from left: Isabel, Anita Jnr, Anita Snr, a friend of Anita Jnr's, Paulette, and Paula.
Courtesy Graham Shirley

Above Bruno Valletty, Rahman Bey, and John McDonagh.

Courtesy of the NFSA

Left Phyllis, Paulette, Paula, and Isabel play-acting their worship of Rahman Bey.

Courtesy of the NFSA

Portrait shot of Paulette.
Courtesy of the NFSA

Publicity portrait of Phyllis,
from around 1927.
Courtesy of the NFSA

Above Isabel, Paulette, and Phyllis on board a ship.
Courtesy of the NFSA

Left Paulette in the 1920s in the garden of Drummoyne House.
Courtesy of the NFSA

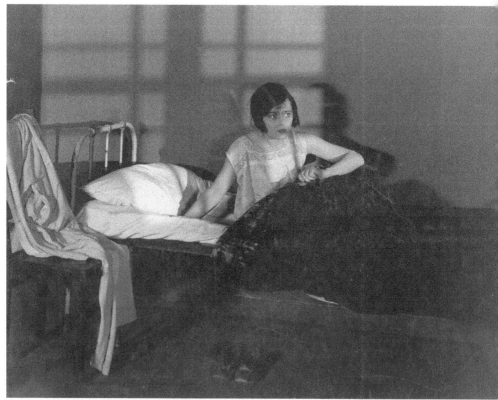

Above A scene from *Those Who Love*.
Courtesy of the NFSA

Top left Beach party scene at Tamarama Beach from the sisters'
first feature film, *Those Who Love*, released in 1926.
Courtesy of the NFSA

Left Isabel in a scene from *Those Who Love*.
Courtesy of the NFSA

Cinema lobby card for *The Far Paradise*, released in 1928,
with Isabel billed as Marie Lorraine.
Courtesy of the NFSA

Gaston Mervale, Marie Lorraine, and Arthur McLaglen from *The Far Paradise*.
Courtesy of the NFSA

Paulette directing lead actor Paul Longuet for a scene from *The Far Paradise*.
Cameraman Jack Fletcher is behind the camera.
Courtesy of the NFSA

Marie Lorraine as Cherry Carson in a scene from *The Far Paradise*.
Courtesy of the NFSA

A scene from *The Cheaters*, released in 1930, with
Marie Lorraine as Paula Marsh, about to crack a safe.

Courtesy of the NFSA

Paulette directing a scene from *The Cheaters*, with cameraman
Jack Fletcher and two unknown actors.
Courtesy of the NFSA

A scene from *The Cheaters*, with Josef Bambach and Marie Lorraine.
Courtesy of the NFSA

Marie Lorraine as Denise and Frank Bradley as General
Gresham in *Two Minutes Silence*, released in 1933.
Courtesy of the NFSA

Paulette directing a scene from *Two Minutes Silence*.
Courtesy of the NFSA

Campbell Copelin and Marie Lorraine in a scene from *Two Minutes Silence*.
Courtesy of the NFSA

5

ORPHANS
(1924–1925)

At the age of twenty-five, Isabel accepted her sudden elevation to the head of the family with a maturity and aplomb that belied her youth. After all, she had been nicknamed 'Googie' by her friends and family (slang for a hard-boiled egg), which suggests that on the outside she may have looked sensitive and fragile, but on the inside she was firm. Even though Phyllis and Paulette were only one and two years younger, they, along with the other siblings, automatically turned to their older sister for motherly care and advice. Isabel calmly attended to all the banking, correspondence, and running of the house. She enrolled Anita and Paula at Kincoppal College, where she, Phyllis, and Paulette had enjoyed so many happy years. The two weekly boarders returned on the weekends to Drummoyne House and the preferred company of their older siblings. It's possible that Aunt Mary assisted with the steep school fees.

Still, after the death of their mother, money was again tight. One day, Phyllis, resourceful as ever, noticed an advertisement in the paper for singers. She auditioned for an opera at the Majestic Theatre in Newtown and, with a talent inherited from her honey-voiced father, secured a part in the chorus, appearing under the pseudonym Gloria Grant, a combination of her middle name and her grandmother's maiden name. She went on to appear in three subsequent productions at the same venue. While there, she also teamed up with old friend and fellow singer Gertie Purcell, who'd entered fancy dress competitions with Phyllis when they were children, and together they formed a routine that would be featured as an entr'acte in theatres before the screening of a feature film.

Later, Phyllis teamed up with JC Williamson vocalist Betty Vane to appear as a duo at the Lyceum Theatre. Throughout the 1920s, it was common to have theatrical acts – singers, jugglers, magicians, tank divers – as an additional attraction at any silent movie showing, and so Phyllis and Gertie briefly became part of the thrilling, raffish world of greasepaint and footlights.

Through her theatre connections, Phyllis also secured a job as art director for the company of the influential British West End actor-writer-producer Seymour Hicks and his wife Ellaline Terriss. They arrived in Australia in February 1924 with sixteen tonnes of scenery and seventy baskets of costumes. Once on Australian soil, Hicks stated to a journalist that he was on the lookout for Australian talent. The company opened at the New Palace Theatre in Melbourne with the comedy, *The Man in the Dress Clothes*. After the first performance, it received thirty curtain calls and a bouquet of flowers tossed by Dame Nellie Melba. They moved on to Sydney and opened the same play on 24 May at the Grand Opera House to similar acclaim.

Theatre promoter Hugh Ward, who'd brought the company out from London, was planning to reap profits with short runs and quick changes in theatrical material. It is probably at this point that Phyllis got the opportunity to design and create sets for the farce *Broadway Jones*, the comedy-drama *Old Bill, MP*, the one-act *Scrooge* and the three-act *Sleeping Partners* – also mounted at the Grand Opera House. One review of *Broadway Jones* singles out the stage design for praise: 'The farce was nicely produced, the café scene at the close being beautifully arranged and artistically produced'.

Now that they were orphans, the three older sisters were fiercely protective of the younger children and went to great lengths to spare them the details of any problems the family faced. At home, they were as strict as any Mother Superior supervising a convent. Until the three younger children were of a certain age, they were forbidden to socialise with adults and, continuing a McDonagh family tradition, they were expected to take meals at a separate table from the four older siblings. Though they considered themselves good Catholics, the sisters didn't feel the need to attend church; ironically, they were strict about imposing rules on their younger siblings, but they did not wish the rules of Catholicism to be imposed upon them.

It seems that Anita Junior felt the brunt of their mother's death the most. Described by the youngest, Paula, as the misfit of the family, Anita was in an invidious position. She was not old enough to be part of the adult, close-knit group formed by Isabel, Phyllis, and Paulette, but she also wasn't keen on the company of the younger Grant and Paula. She often goaded Paula into misbehaving, such as bashing Grant with a broom, and resisted Isabel's attempts at discipline.

Her rebelliousness was not confined to the home. At Kincoppal, the sixteen-year-old made a habit out of teasing the old gardener, Mortice, who lived in the basement beneath the school's playroom. At lunchtime she would don a floppy hat and, while Mortice sat inside eating his sandwiches, Anita would lurch back and forth just outside the open door, mimicking him and calling him insulting names.

At night, however, she would unwittingly reveal her vulnerability and the overwhelming grief at the loss of her parents. Once lights were out in the dormitory, students were forbidden to talk or, indeed, to make any sound at all, with transgressions resulting in immediate expulsion. There was no caning at Kincoppal; students were simply expected to live up to the ideals of the school, and any girl who refused to do so was automatically expelled. One night, soon after the lights were out, the girls suddenly heard the tinkling of a mechanical music box. Immediately alert to an obvious digression from the rules, all of them strained to find the source of the melody. The overhead lights suddenly blinked on, and a nun appeared and began to pace the aisle between the beds. Soon the source was found, and the nun exclaimed, 'Anita!'

Over the sound of the tinkling, Anita burst into tears, explaining through her sobs that the only way she could get to sleep at home was to play the music box. There were no consequences for Anita's wrongdoing. As another schoolgirl in the dormitory that night observed, 'Only a McDonagh could have done it'.

As a disgruntled teenager, Anita often ran away from home. She also began running away from school and managed to get both herself and thirteen-year-old Paula expelled from Kincoppal permanently. Marginalia of the Kincoppal registry at the end of 1924 states that they were 'both asked not to return'.

Exasperated, Isabel took the two girls home and enrolled them in nearby Drummoyne Grammar, a day school. Anita's rebellion, however, continued unabated. She was violent towards Paula – hitting and slapping her frequently and inexplicably – and continued to wag school, forcing Paula to do the same. 'Anita would take me to a park seat', said Paula, '... and read a book all day, and I'd just have to sit there. Instead of going to school. And then we'd go home, you know, at three o'clock ... I felt dreadful about it, but I was-- she had me bluffed. I wasn't-- I was too frightened to tell the girls'. Later, Isabel would try almost any alternative to ensure Paula's education, including tutors and governesses.

⋆⟻⟾⋆

Isabel closed the convalescent home but continued to care for Aunt Nellie, who remained bedridden with rheumatoid arthritis. Isabel, Phyllis, and Paulette were not remotely interested in pursuing careers in nursing. They thought 'it was beneath them' and believed they were destined for greater achievements. At the age of twenty-three, John continued to invite new friends home for teas and meals. The older sisters, however, remained fiercely clannish and did not appreciate the actions of flirty female visitors trying to attract the attention of their adored little brother. Their solution to this threat was to mock the table manners and speech of any girl who tried to get too close to John – and it always worked. 'This familial closeness', observed Paula, 'was like a disease'.

Today, this so-called disease has a name – enmeshment – but it is often used to describe an unusually tight bond between a parent and a child. According to Dr Kenneth M Adams, enmeshed family members become so involved with each other's lives that any individual who desires some autonomy experiences feelings of guilt and disloyalty. Enmeshed family members also become so dependent on one another that partnerships outside the family are collectively discouraged, and obligations towards each other are prioritised over any other considerations, romantic or otherwise.

Curiously, even the siblings' names are a Gordian knot of enmeshment, with one using the interchangeable name of Pauline or Paulette, another named Paula, and the female lead of their third feature film, *The Cheaters*, is called Paula Marsh. One brother was named Grant, another John Norman Grant, and Phyllis used the stage name Gloria Grant. One of sister Anita's middle names was Marie, which would be later adopted by Isabel as the first part of her stage name, Marie Lorraine. Paula's middle name was thought to be Leonora, which in the 1930s Grant would shorten to assume the literary pseudonym Leon Brock. The main character of Grant's only novel is called Julian Marsh, a name that the sisters had used in *The Cheaters* in the form of Bill and Paula Marsh, also a crook and embezzler. Even their handwriting reveals startling similarities: Isabel, Paulette, and Grant had an almost identical style, an ornamental, almost Gothic script without any discernible slant.

Enmeshment is usually a consequence of having experienced great trauma, when the natural development of a younger person is cauterised by shock. There is no doubt that losing both parents at such a young age bonded the seven siblings in curious and unexpected ways. On the one hand, it would prevent them from forming close attachments with partners outside the family for many years and powerfully affect the next generation of offspring. On the other hand, if it weren't for the imaginative and emotional entanglement of the older sisters, their astonishing feature films would never have been made.

Four years after the death of their mother, a journalist would detect their intense closeness after only a brief observation: 'The clannish trio speak of "we" that and "we" this, and all-for-one and one-for-all idea, that fits their chumminess admirably'. She also noticed that one sister could not accept a compliment without immediately crediting the other two. Paulette would repeat this habit for the rest of her life: whenever she received praise for her filmmaking, she would always retort that she didn't make those films, that they were, in fact, produced by the McDonagh sisters. This clannish habit would also extend to the next generation of the family: after Isabel's death in 1982, Paula wrote to Isabel's three middle-aged children in London, expressing her condolences, and praising the trio for never having left home, and for never having left the side of their mother. The second son, Charles, was almost insulted by the remark. He wrote back to Paula that it wasn't they who had never left their mother, it was their mother who had never left them.

⊷⊏⊙⊐⊶

For recreation at home, the sisters invited guests over for games of bridge, which would continue all through the night, with the players only ever going to bed at dawn. In the late afternoon, the sisters and their friends would rise, a game would recommence, and they'd play on throughout the next night, and the next. In general, even when they were not playing cards, the sisters wouldn't rise until about eleven or twelve o'clock.

Perhaps influenced by the Gothic atmosphere of old Drummoyne House, the McDonaghs and their friends would sometimes turn down the lights and conduct a séance at night. By this time in their lives, they had an abundance of departed relatives with whom to try and make contact: all four grandparents, their great Uncle Dean Grant, their father, their mother – not to mention old Captain Wright, who'd built the house, and the widowed Elizabeth Hordern, who'd died upstairs only five years before. Paula was convinced that during one séance with her sisters, a dining room table rose from the floor and floated up the staircase.

In early 1925, Paulette purchased an autograph book with a pink tortoiseshell cover, which today still contains the ghost-like inscriptions of friends and relatives long since passed. The first to write in it was teenage sister Anita. It was a ditty about keeping secrets, a telling decision on Anita's part since at the time she was withholding information from the sisters about regularly wagging school. Paulette would keep the book for the rest of her life, collecting poems, aphorisms, and messages, as well as beautifully detailed drawings and cartoons.

Throughout the 1920s, both modernism and bohemianism were largely realised in Sydney through the boom in newspapers and magazines and the popularity of Hollywood-style cinema. In both respects, the sisters were at the vanguard of changing social and artistic trends. In late 1924 and early 1925, Isabel appeared in the F Stuart-Whyte feature *Painted Daughters*. At the same time, Phyllis combined her interest in cinema with her desire to make money as a freelance writer by researching and writing an article for the *Sunday Times* about bit-part actresses trying to find fame through film. Narrated in the third person, it reads more like a short story than a news report and suggests that she shadowed Isabel through every moment of her participation in the making of *Painted Daughters* – from spotting the advertisement in the paper for extras, to turning up for and recording a dreaded screen test, to passing the test and receiving her first call. Following that, there was the demand that she supply her own clothes on the set the following day: 'Bring an attractive dress – a garden party – or evening dress – a ballroom scene'. Phyllis then captures the thrilling intensity of a working film set: 'The preparations, the sense of unreality, the bustle and movement, the director's voice, the click of the camera, the snap and sizzle of the great arc lights'. The story ends with the hungry bit-part actress collecting her pay and creeping home 'wearied in every limb, but ineffably happy. Her objective has been attained – she is at last a part of that gigantic machination – the Picture Combine'. Even as extras and journalists, Isabel and Phyllis were learning more and more about writing, producing, and acting in silent films.

In June 1925, the estate of the deceased Pat O'Connell, no doubt executed by Aunt Mary, sold Drummoyne House to two men, Richard Lonergan and John O'Brien. Since the new owners permitted the McDonagh orphans to live in the mansion indefinitely, it's safe to assume that the new buyers were friends of the family who could absorb the costs of such a dubious investment. After the death of Mrs McDonagh, and the closing of the convalescent home, it's obvious that widowed Aunt Mary wanted her husband's money back. Did her authoritative manner and Victorian ideals of femininity begin to cause a rift between her and her three ambitious nieces, who valued artistic expression over marital intention?

If Aunt Mary ever did try to control and manipulate the sisters by pulling at her purse strings or encouraging them to marry well, she failed miserably. Soon after the sale of Drummoyne House, she and her money moved out of the mansion and settled into a rented cottage in Rose Bay.

Five years later, Aunt Mary would continue to reveal her preference for tradition, and her incomprehension of what the sisters were trying to achieve, when she wrote in Paulette's autograph book: *Girls' dreams are always of the man / they are going to marry – boys of what / they are going to be. / When a man's dreams are over / he has begun to die, but when a girl's dreams are / over she has begun to live.*

6

LIVING AND BREATHING
AS ONE

(1924–1926)

Now that the sisters were free of any form of authority, they pursued their creative interests with flourishing curiosity and passion. It was the middle of the roaring twenties and the exuberant jazz age. They had no parents or relatives to nudge them into suitable marriages and suburban homes. Instead of planning engagement celebrations and assembling trousseaus, the sisters cut and bobbed their hair, learned to drive, and began enjoying the occasional cigarette at parties. By asserting their independence, they were enacting roles they'd admired from the Hollywood screen, transforming themselves into modern women who rejected domesticity in favour of artistry.

Paulette signed up for an American correspondence course to learn how to write silent film scenarios. Of the three sisters, it was Paulette who was most obsessed with filmmaking in general, and directing in particular. The girls had always gone to the pictures together as much as they could, afterwards discussing and dissecting the acting, directing, and production until they were all in agreement. But while Isabel and Phyllis were happy to see a given film once, Paulette would grab herself a Sargents pie for lunch, and a cup of coffee, and return to the theatre to a subsequent session and study the film in detail. She would repeat this routine on a single day until she'd seen the film three, four, or even five times. Paulette explained,

> Now I saw that where they took a close up, where they took a middle shot, where they took a long shot. And what that meant to ... to get it real. They didn't even try to do that here ... And I'd take that whole thing in, and I'd watch and watch it ... And anybody, anybody in that film that I loved when they came to the close up I'd see what they did with that close up. What it meant. To give them that close up ... And then to move away to the middle shot and the long shot. And I learnt how to do films by that way.

However, Paulette was not only studying filmmaking techniques but also the dramatic potency of international films. One film, *Sorrell and Son*, had a particular impact. Directed by Herbert Brenon, it tells the story of a husband who is deserted by his wife and left to raise their infant son alone. One of the themes of the first three McDonagh films was that family loyalty should always prevail over individual desire, and the film *Sorrell and Son* deeply embodies this trope. Paulette insisted she never copied the plots of other films but was inspired by the art and craft of superlative writers and directors. She always wrote her scenarios longhand and numbered each scene, gluing the pages together once she'd arranged the scenes in a preferred order.

Phyllis was similarly absorbed in her literary practice and, following her mother's death, she developed a creative routine that she would sustain for the next fifty years. Instead of working on a version of a nine-to-five schedule, Phyllis would settle at her desk only after the sun had set and would not complete the writing session until the early hours of the morning.

She also maintained her voracious habit of reading. One book that entranced her was the jazz-age novel *The Green Hat* by Michael Arlen, which froths with verbal witticisms, post-war cynicism, and a femme fatale who speeds around London and Europe in an ostentatious yellow Hispano-Suiza. Phyllis adored the book so much that she wrote an admiring letter to Arlen, who replied with a similarly enthusiastic letter and a signed photograph. In 1928, the novel would be adapted into an MGM feature film, *A Woman of Affairs*, starring Greta Garbo and John Gilbert.

Moreover, Phyllis and Paulette also took up painting, mostly in watercolours. Phyllis became so accomplished in technique that her teacher, Brock, believed that she could become a professional painter if she so chose. And while Paulette would keep up her practice as a watercolourist for most of her life, the sisters' talent for creating beautiful and meaningful imagery was about to be funnelled into a more contemporary and modern visual medium.

In the meantime, Isabel was cast in a major role in the silent film *Joe*, adapted from two short story collections by Henry Lawson: *Joe Wilson* and *Joe Wilson and His Mates*. As the family story goes, Isabel and youngest sister Paula were walking down a city street one day, when silent film director Beaumont Smith, suddenly beguiled by the sight of Isabel's beauty, stopped and asked her if she'd ever considered starring in a motion picture. Without a shred of envy, the other sisters would confirm the undeniable truth of Isabel's striking good looks: 'we'd just stare at her for ages and think: "Is she our sister?" We were so proud of her'. By this time, Smith had already directed other features, including *The Man from Snowy River*.

The day following Smith's approach, Isabel turned up at the studio for a screen test and, after completing it with muted flair, she was offered the role of Barbara, who is Joe Wilson's sister-in-law. In the test, which survives at the NFSA, it's obvious that the camera fell in love with her mesmerising presence. But her full abilities as an actress would not be revealed until she was under the scrupulous direction of her younger sister.

The plot of the comedy centres on Joe Wilson (Arthur Tauchert), a painter, and a young housekeeper at old Black's Station, Mary (Constance Graham), who marry and take up farming together. After Joe leaves on a business trip to Sydney, he becomes embroiled in the mishaps of his sister-in-law, Barbara (Isabel), who has inadvertently destroyed an expensive dress belonging to her employer. Joe compensates the employer for the dress and insists upon taking the wayward Barbara back to the farm with him. Once there, she is introduced to Harry Black, old Black's son, who has recently walked away from a failing marriage. The happy ending is assured when Barbara and Harry fall in love.

The film was shot in June 1924, only three months after the death of the sisters' mother. One of the locations was in the Burragorang Valley, west of Sydney, and the climax of the plot featured a raging bushfire. The interior scenes were filmed at the Rushcutters Bay studio of Australasian Films, while the ball scene was recorded at the Ambassador's Dance Palais over a continuous fourteen-hour shoot. Throughout the filming, Isabel absorbed more and more about the art and craft of acting, and the making of motion pictures, which she would share with her sisters when she arrived home at night.

Also in the cast of *Joe* was silent film actor Gordon Collingridge, twenty-one, who became deeply infatuated with Isabel, four years his senior. According to Collingridge, when Isabel first appeared on set, she had no idea how to express emotion in front of the whirring camera and, before the shooting of each scene, Collingridge would have to shake her violently to loosen her up. It was his opinion that, at first, she didn't appear to be a natural actress. But he also admitted that Isabel – with her large, wide-set hazel eyes and heart-shaped face, was the most beautiful woman with whom he'd ever acted. Alternatively, Isabel and her sisters did not think much of Collingridge's acting and, despite a close friendship, would avoid casting him in any of their films.

Paulette also learned how to write film treatments – a narrative that tells the story of the film in present-tense prose, and includes dialogue and action, with background information about each character as well as their motives and character arcs. In September 1925, she registered for copyright her first film treatment, *Those Who Love*, but it differs from the first film they would produce the following year, which shares the same title. However, certain themes and patterns that would define their cinematic oeuvre were there from the very beginning: an ingenue in danger, an unreliable father or father figure, emotional incest, moral ambiguity, the desire for revenge, mistaken identity, and father–son or father–suitor rivalry. As with every other film written and produced by the McDonaghs, the setting for a romantic interlude is always by the water. In this treatment, love is nourished and grown by its proximity to a pond on the property of a lavish mansion, and a lake in the countryside.

The plot of Paulette's first treatment unravels thus: Sylvia Carson is a pampered socialite with a six-year-old daughter, Lila, whose rich husband stakes all his money on an expedition to the Antarctic. During the trip, the boat sinks, and when Carson's attorney, Austin, opens the safe at home, he finds, like the outcome of Dr McDonagh's death five years earlier, that Carson has left the family broke: 'Austin, as Carson's attorney, has but one truth to tell. Carson is penniless, wiped out, the very home and effects no longer hers. Sylvia in a fresh outburst swears she'll kill herself rather than face poverty'.

Sylvia eventually accepts a Faustian bargain with the womanising married attorney: he will keep her as his mistress in the luxury to which she's become accustomed, but only if she sends away daughter Lila to a boarding school in another city.

Twelve years pass. During this time, Lila has grown into a beautiful teenager who is still devoted to her mother, but who knows nothing of her mother's arrangement with the opportunistic Austin. One day, Sylvia arrives home to find Austin waiting for her. Austin is happy because his divorce is complete and his ex-wife is moving to England. Sylvia is relieved that she no longer has to live in sin and can now live respectably with Lila beside her. But Austin informs her that their affair is over and that he no longer has any need for her. Sylvia is crushed but orders him out of her life. She collapses on the settee and sobs.

Lila is summoned from school after receiving word that her mother is gravely ill. When she arrives home, the nurse warns her that Sylvia has been hovering between life and death for days. Again, Paulette uses their experience of suffering and grief in the narrative: 'Lila waits for no more. Flying up the stairway she is arrested by a weeping maid who endeavours to stay her entrance, but sweeping her aside, she stumbles through and closes the door behind. The nurse hurrying up, goes to enter, then hesitating, takes a nearby seat, deeming it merciful to leave Lila alone with her Awakening. Whilst behind the closed door Lila in frantic realisation finds her mother already dead'.

Lila discovers by the bedside a framed photograph of Austin inscribed affectionately to Sylvia. She also finds a letter from her mother, explaining the poverty in which Lila's father Carson had left her, and the only option she'd been able to take – to live with Austin. Lila realises the hand that Austin has played in her mother's premature death and vows to seek revenge. Overwhelmed, she runs hatless from the house and ends up resting, hours later, on a park bench. A policeman mistakes her for a vagrant and marches her off to a hostel for destitute women. Lila is horrified by the hostel and the matron who runs it, so she escapes through a back door and down a lane, the policeman and matron in hot pursuit.

She runs into an open square and takes refuge in the back seat of an empty, parked car. A young man in evening clothes emerges from a club and spots the policeman, who asks him if he's seen a girl. The man is Peter Strang, Austin's son. Peter says, 'No', climbs into the car and drives away.

When Peter reaches home – a mansion – he parks, switches on a light to find some parcels in the back and discovers Lila asleep. He is amazed by her youth and beauty and realises she is the fugitive that the policeman had been looking for. In a burst of pity, he carries the limp Lila into his home. He places her on a divan and sends the butler in search of his widowed aunt, Mrs Farson. She arrives and tries to revive Lila, and questions Peter, who tells a lie on Lila's behalf, saying that his car has hit her. Mrs Farson is shaken by the story and tells Peter to carry the unconscious girl upstairs. Peter is already infatuated with Lila.

The rest of the story is complicated by the return of Peter's father, Austin. Even though he's already proposed to a French dancer in another city, he instantly falls for Lila as well, unaware that she's the daughter of his dead mistress. But Lila recognises him immediately and, even though she's now falling in love with Peter, sacrifices that love for the sake of revenge: to entice Austin to propose to her so she can leave him at the altar and humiliate him as much as he'd humiliated her mother.

The story reaches a climax when a wedding announcement appears in the papers, along with a photo of the engaged couple, Lila and Austin. The French dancer happens to see the photo and travels to the city in which Austin lives, also intent on revenge. Lila confronts Austin in his office, flaying him with scorn and contempt. She tells him that she is in love with his son. Austin weeps and Lila briefly regrets her harsh words. She is about to forgive him when a gunshot fires through a window and kills Austin. The French dancer is charged with the crime, leaving Lila and Peter to eventually reconcile and marry.

Of all the treatments and scripts created by the McDonaghs, this first incarnation of *Those Who Love* contains the most autobiographical detail, which raises the question: could the McDonaghs have produced such emotionally complex stories without suffering the losses of their parents, their home, and their expected inheritances? Certainly, the sisters were influenced by 19th-century theatrical melodrama and Hollywood Cinderella stories, but it could also be argued that the plots of their own lives infused their filmmaking with a depth and verisimilitude rare in Australian silent motion pictures.

In late February 1926, Paulette registered for copyright yet another treatment for a film, *The Greater Love*. Ironically, there are no extant treatments or scripts of the films that the McDonaghs eventually produced; the only ones that still exist are Paulette's treatments of their unproduced motion pictures, which would bear striking similarities to the films they would eventually make.

In the treatment of the year before, a father lusts after the orphaned daughter of his dead mistress but is shot dead by his current mistress, leaving the daughter to marry the dead man's son. In *The Greater Love*, the pattern is reversed: a noble rich man, named Orde, sacrifices his love for a French woman so his best friend can marry her and move to France. The wife gives birth to a daughter, Jaycenth, and later dies. When Jaycenth is eighteen, her father dies too, but not before he writes to his old friend, Orde, begging him to take her back to America and look after her. Before she leaves, she happens to meet Orde's much younger stepbrother, Lonny, a rakish and irresponsible racing car driver who falls for her. He is also a passenger on the liner transporting her back to America and pursues her affections. She reciprocates. After she arrives at Orde's mansion, Orde also falls in love with her. The rest of the story is an emotional tug of war between reckless Lonny, who is Jaycenth's age, and reliable Orde, who is old enough to be her father. After Lonny deliberately crashes his car and dies, the timeline cuts to a year later, when Orde and nineteen-year-old Jaycenth are cooing over their newborn son. With shining eyes, Jaycenth nestles in the shelter of Orde's arms, 'while in silent prayer, Orde Mordaunt thanks (his old friend) Leroux for his – wife and son'. Again, the roles of the orphaned daughter and the foster father are blurred due to the father's lust for his barely legal and innocent charge.

This is probably the reason why the first incarnation of *Those Who Love* and the treatment for *The Greater Love* remained unproduced: both were probably too histrionic to engage a general audience.

Every script produced by the sisters was a collaborative effort. Paulette would write a first draft, which was almost always overly melodramatic. Isabel and Phyllis would then help her to develop the plot and characters, taming the sensational elements and emphasising realism.

In both these treatments, Paulette's visualisation of the story – her framing devices and descriptive detail – is clearly in evidence. In the following scene from *Those Who Love*, for example, the writing suggests that Paulette is moving from a close-up to a medium shot, to a clear wide shot: '... drawing unsteadily to her feet [she] moves slowly backwards, step by step, til [sic] her fingers no longer clasp Sylvia's hand – then with an overwhelming cry of horror gropes for the door, and stumbles through and down the stairs'. In *The Greater Love*, Jaycenth's vulnerability and loss are conveyed in a simple and poignant image: 'A great [ocean] liner ploughs her way to a distant shore, while at the rail crouches a desolate figure in black, watching a beloved France fading into the mist'. Here, the writing is sharp, succinct, and supremely cinematic.

By March 1926, the sisters had three scenarios to choose from for their first feature film, the third being a second incarnation of the title *Those Who Love*, which jettisons the foster father/daughter romance for a more conventional love story of boy meets/loses/ wins back girl. In this sense, the one that they all agreed to produce was also the most commercially viable.

Writing treatments and scenarios were not the only experiences that the sisters sought out. In 1925, Paulette appeared as an extra in a ballroom scene in Arthur Shirley's directorial debut *The Mystery of a Hansom Cab*. No doubt she yearned to experience filmmaking from the other side of the camera, to witness the creative synergy that rose between director, actor, and cameraman. She was particularly interested in how lighting design affected a scene. As a teenager, she'd openly despised the way sets in Australia had been built and shot, with outdoor stages lit only by harsh sunlight, and theatre-like painted flats and backgrounds hand-held by trembling assistants. It all looked so primitive and stagey, and she knew that the way to photograph interior scenes and achieve an acceptable form of verisimilitude would be through artful lighting design and realistic sets.

The filming of *The Mystery of a Hansom Cab* began in February and took five months to complete. Many of the scenes in Melbourne were set on the steps of Parliament House, Fitzroy Gardens, and St Kilda Road. Interiors were filmed at a studio in Bondi Junction, Sydney, which was where Paulette became involved. It was the first Australian motion picture to run for ten reels, and one of the first to use the technique of double exposure, which Paulette would later employ in their second and third films.

Still, as an extra and an observer, Paulette was not impressed by Shirley's direction: '[I] only went out of sheer curiosity and to learn, to see what others were doing. That was the last time I ever did anything with Arthur Shirley, but my God I wanted to get up there and tell him what to do then. I only realized [then] he was a stupid man, what he was doing'.

For her part, as a female actor, Isabel admired and learned from the work of Hollywood star Mary Pickford, who under the direction of DW Griffith developed a subtle technique of acting that was perfect for the camera. The process was vastly different from that of stage acting: information and mood were conveyed on the screen by changing facial expressions, looks, gazes, and the briefest of gestures, reducing the reliance on intertitles (dialogue or information conveyed by a series of words printed on a single card) to explain the action. Pickford is also credited with having defined the 'ingenue' type in cinema – a girl or young woman who is endearingly innocent and naive, a type that Isabel would recreate with distinction in the sisters' first two features.

While Isabel, Phyllis, and Paulette were learning all they could about this new, ultra-modern medium, The Good Film League was launched at a special conference on film in Sydney. The local incarnation of the league was a product of the better films movement, based in New York, which had declared that its mission would be 'a conscious effort to encourage the production and exhibition of a high type of film by discriminating patronage at best'. The mission cascaded into affiliated national and local leagues and groups worldwide, to promote 'a movement for encouraging better cinema films and the use of educational films, and also for giving women more influence in the censorship of films'. In their pursuit of Hollywood aesthetics, rebellious female characters, and contemporary glamour, the sisters were in direct opposition to the aims of The Good Film League and of middle-class wowsers.

❖

Joe was released on 23 August 1924, but the credits did not feature the acting debut of 'Isabel McDonagh'. Instead, they listed the silent film actress 'Marie Lorraine'. The sisters were intrigued by Hollywood actresses who reinvented themselves by creating a new persona and changing their names. According to her sons, Isabel chose the surname 'Lorraine' because there was a singer named Violet Lorraine who had recorded with George Ruby the romantic ballad, 'If you were the only girl in the world and I was the only boy'. She selected 'Marie' in honour of her Catholic heritage – of Mary, the Mother of God, which was also sister Anita's middle name. Reviews of the film were generally positive, with the *Bulletin* claiming that it was 'a faithful reflection of the spirit of the pioneers, who battle in the open spaces, with a broad vein of humour running through it'.

Following the premiere of *Joe*, Paulette grew more and more frustrated with the standard of films being produced in Australia and declared to Isabel and Phyllis, 'We should make our own films'. All three sisters were fed up with the focus on the bush as the predominant site for Australian experience and identity. They were also dissatisfied with the intertitles of Australian silent films, which were often crude and grammatically incorrect.

'We were deeply critical of the Dad 'n Dave films being turned out', noted Paulette, 'and felt there was a genuine need for social themes along the American pattern'.

'They felt there was a need', concurred Paula. 'An opening for something different.'

Statistics collected later in the decade confirmed the sisters' conclusions: of the 721 motion pictures screened in Australia throughout 1925, 676 had been produced in Hollywood. Attendance at Australian cinemas was among the highest in the world – roughly eighteen films for every resident; two-thirds of the attendees, however, were young, independent women. These trends reinforced what the McDonaghs had already realised: the mostly female audiences were bored by the heroic masculine tales of outback Australia and yearned to view films that reflected their own experience as sophisticated urban dwellers.

The sisters reached a consensus. They would form a film production company, but they also agreed that they knew so little about the actual process that they would need to educate themselves with whatever resources were available in Australia at that time.

In addition to taking a scenario-writing course via correspondence from America, Paulette signed up for a three-month film acting course with an industry professional named PJ Ramster, who ran a school on Oxford Street, Paddington, and featured his students in his own motion pictures. Through Ramster, Paulette assumed she would attain all the skills necessary to produce and direct her first feature. '... he was a very pompous gentleman', said Paula. 'I don't think he had much ability. That was a weakness with the girls. They could be taken in very easily, because they would become enamoured of a person, or a thing, and they wouldn't quite trace it through to find out how genuine it was.'

Paulette also became deeply interested in German Expressionism, particularly the work of FW Murnau and Fritz Lang, both of whom created moody, shadowy scenes with a pattern of themes that included psychological conflict, paranoia, fate, and moral ambiguity.

After the success of *Joe*, Raymond Longford approached Isabel and offered her the lead in one of his next films. The offer, however, contained a caveat: in return for the role, she would allow him the use of Drummoyne House as a set. Perhaps Longford's keen interest in both Isabel and Drummoyne House made the sisters realise that they already had in their possession the necessary elements to produce a successful motion picture: a beautiful star and an elegant home that could double as a studio. In answer to Longford's offer, Isabel merely smiled and shook her head: 'We're saving the house for our own films'.

The sisters decided that if they were to produce films, they would do so without any recognisable Australian setting, which would make the stories relatable to audiences of any country. Later, Paulette would further explain the motivation and reasoning behind their intention to form a film company, MCD Productions, and why they felt the primitive Australian industry, with its celebration of the bush and its clichéd blokey characters, needed fresh and feminine creative input: 'We felt that we could improve upon all previous Australian efforts. We were satisfied that if we were to succeed we would have to cut out the bush, the Melbourne Cup, the wealthy squatter's son, the Sundowner and Dad and Dave. We decided to meet the Americans on their own ground, and if the picture is not Australian in that sense, it is certainly Australian-made'.

Hollywood producers were also coming to the same conclusion, that the survival of this nascent art form depended on engaging female viewers, as most men did not attend the cinema alone or in groups, but in the company of a date, a steady girlfriend, or a wife, who would invariably choose the title of the movie she wished to see. 'The kinema [sic] must please the women or die', declared British film critic CA Lejeune in 1926. And in 1924, back in Australia, the clever trio of sisters had already figured out the same strategy for success in cinema. 'The three of us talked and talked', said Phyllis, 'and decided if Australia was going to compete overseas we'd have to meet overseas standards by making *interior* films, technically difficult then'.

They agreed that they would write and produce stories that they, as avid female film-goers, would want to see on a Saturday night at their local picture theatre. Their female characters would not be stuck behind country stoves or be mere foils for brave and brawny leading men; they would instead crack safes, break and enter buildings, and dance the Charleston with abandon. But while the female lead characters of their first three films were daring and subversive, they would always come from the lower classes because, according to the sisters, 'it created more sympathy for the woman in the picture'.

The classical fairytale of 'boy meets girl, boy loses girl, boy gets girl back', dates back many centuries and permeates various cultures, but in the mid-1920s, popular culture and modernism promoted storied romance in the form of the wireless, the gramophone, and the cinema, refiguring the fairytale into radio dramas, songs recorded on records, and, of course, silent pictures. With such a powerful medium as film, the McDonaghs had almost immediate access to the latest hairstyles, fashions, and cosmetics to imbue their leading female characters, their cinematic Cinderellas, with an international and stylish flair.

Right at the time that the McDonagh sisters were stepping out as confident 'new' women intent on self-determination and creative freedom, dress hemlines around Australia mimicked their growing independence by rising from calf-length to just below the knees. A contemporary dress of the mid-1920s, such as the McDonagh sisters would have worn, was usually crafted from silk crepe de Chine, and the most popular colours were monochromatic creams, greys, blues, and whites. Similarly, the tight-fitting cloche hat became all the rage, replacing wide-brimmed headwear fussy with flowers and veils hailing back to the Edwardian era. Paulette can be seen wearing one of these popular hats while directing *The Far Paradise*.

The sisters embraced this stylistic and sartorial example of the liberated woman by taking up their hemlines, applying make-up, and neatly trimming their flappers' bobs so that by the time they began to make their first feature film, with their lower necklines and single strands of pearls, they looked like three glamorous versions of the Hollywood actress Louise Brooks.

Initially, they approached businessmen in the industry to invest in their venture, but the men 'scoffed at the idea of girls succeeding where others had failed'. The sisters gritted their teeth and decided to proceed on their own. Their friends and relatives tried to discourage them from throwing away precious financial resources on what was assumed to be a passing whim, but the confident and stubborn sisters would not be discouraged. And if anyone underestimated these young women because of their stunning good looks, they were in for a rude awakening. Separately, each sister possessed a unique talent that the other two didn't: Isabel was empathic and intuitive; Phyllis was charming and assertive; while Paulette was a visionary and accomplished storyteller. Together, they transcended the sum of their parts. As Phyllis later observed, 'We practically lived and breathed as one'.

The standard myth surrounding the McDonagh sisters, promoted by fiction writer Phyllis, is that just before his death, their father left them 1000 pounds to produce their first film. In reality, he had left them virtually penniless. The sisters realised that a story of the supposed support and encouragement of their father, still so respected in theatrical circles and high society, would carry greater prestige in the eyes of the press and the public than the unvarnished and unpoetic truth.

About a year after their mother's death, the family solicitor contacted Isabel with the sensational news that Ernesto Amora, their Chilean great uncle, and brother of their criminal grandfather, John Horatio, had recently died and left the seven orphans some money in his will. The children had barely heard of their distant

South American relative, let alone met him, though they did remember their mother writing to him regularly, and the promise to name her youngest child after him if it had been a boy.

Amid grief and great personal challenges, salvation did not descend from the respected McDonagh side of the clan but from an unknown benefactor whose brother had brought shame upon the extended family. The sisters accepted the money gratefully but asked no further questions about their Chilean ancestry.

They had just inherited a staggering 8000 pounds (the average price of a Sydney house at that time was just over 1000 pounds). In this sudden and thrilling turn of events, their lives were assuming the qualities of the Hollywood melodramas that had enthralled them for so many years.

7

CAMERA ROLLING
(1925–1926)

Now that they had enough money to finance any number of films, the sisters quickly decided to produce their first feature, *Those Who Love*, without further delay. Isabel would star in it, Phyllis would design sets and also source props and costumes, and Paulette would direct it. But first, they had to refine the scenario to bring it up to Hollywood standards.

'The actual making of the story of *Those Who Love*', said Paula, 'would have been a combination of the three, that's for sure ... They would take days fighting over a subtitle, the wording. "No!" Isabel would say, "That's ridiculous. You can't do that." Paulette [would say] "But you must do that!" And Phyllis something else, you know? They would thrash everything out'. To underscore this point, in 1927, the *Bathurst National Advocate* reported that Phyllis was 'a scenario writer of exceptional ability and it is by her that the story of *Those Who Love* was written'. In the completed film, however, it is Paulette who is credited with having written it.

This collaborative process would extend to the film set, but Paulette would always have the final say about how a particular scene would unfold. And it was she who most deeply identified with the characters, especially during the periods of writing and casting:

> In the difficult process of writing a scenario, every character becomes alive. It is something of a Dr Jeckyl [sic] and Mr Hyde business. One has to dissect their thoughts; to explore something of their mental makeup; to imagine how they would feel or what they would do in a given set of circumstances … In any case, it is not long before the characters in a story become real people – to oneself, at least, they are alive and intensely human. Because perhaps they are invested with such personal interest, the problem of casting is a fascinating one. It is also a most satisfying one – the job of searching for the characters of one's imagination and finding their prototypes in real life.

The McDonaghs employed a mix of well-known professional actors, as well as amateurs such as friends and relatives to fill in for minor roles and as extras. But the fact that Paulette cast the films independently, without the input of her sisters, suggests that she was the one who was most obsessed with the story, and who cared most deeply about their success as a company. And her scenarios were meticulous – not only did she write the action contained in the individual scenes, but she also included where, when, and how individual shots should be filmed, detailing emotional directions for each character.

The plot of *Those Who Love* mirrors the Cinderella story of lost love and steep class differences. Wealthy Sir James Manton is disturbed by his son's love of jazz, beach parties, and a flamboyant dancer names Bébe Dorée. But instead of disowning him, he offers a bribe to Bébe to disappear from his son's life, and insouciant Bébe breezily accepts it. When son, Barry, learns of the deal, he is so appalled by his father's actions that he decides to throw off his aristocratic background and vanish from his home and former life of privilege. He drifts through the streets for days, sinking lower and lower in mood and predicament.

After he walks into a seedy dockside bar, he encounters yet another cabaret dancer, the beautiful Lola Quayle (Isabel), and buys a drink. While there, he is appalled to see Lola's boss sexually harassing her. Barry automatically reacts by king-hitting the boss, causing Lola to lose her job and lodgings.

Feeling guilty, Barry invites her to stay in the spare room of his flat until she can find another job. He discovers that Lola is terrified of lightning when, after a raging storm hits, she rushes into his bedroom and into his arms, where he tries to comfort her. Lola senses his growing affection and the two begin to fall in love. Time passes and the couple eventually marries in a small ceremony.

Meanwhile, Sir James' solicitor, assigned with the task of tracking down the wayward Barry, finally discovers him at the wharves, where he now works. This leads the solicitor to the lower-class Lola and the shocking news that Lola is now Mrs Barry Manton. During a private conversation with Lola, he manages to intimidate her so much that, crestfallen, she runs away from Barry and the haven of his love and protection, not wanting to come between him and his rich family.

When he realises that he's been deserted, Barry suffers a breakdown and spends most of his time drinking alone in dockside dives. The resilient Lola, however, bounces back from misfortune by becoming a nurse's aide at a hospital.

Dissolute Barry eventually suffers an accident on the wharves and is rushed to hospital, the same one in which Lola happens to work. Reunited at last, a relieved Lola gently nurses Barry back to health and, once Sir James and Lady Manton witness the deep devotion between the two lovers, come to accept Lola into the family. This acceptance is further deepened when Lola presents the Mantons with her and Barry's son, who was born after she'd been forced to leave her husband.

In 1971, Phyllis admitted that the plot was a bit corny, 'but it had a human element that people wanted'.

The criminal underworld of wharf-side grog shops and brothels was not so far from the sisters' experience as one might imagine. Their father's best friend and business partner, Larry Foley, had grown up in The Rocks during the 1870s, leading the notorious Rocks Push gang in brawls against others from Woolloomooloo and Pyrmont. Like the McDonaghs, Foley was Irish, and he and his cohorts defended the dignity of Catholics against the Protestants from the dockyards on either side of The Rocks. Foley graduated from the rat-infested streets to become a legendary bare-knuckle fighter. Through their father's vast network of friends, the sisters were exposed to stories and anecdotes not only of the rich and the famous but also of the poor and desperate.

A few months before production began the sisters were mourning the death of yet another relative, this time their mother's sister, Nellie, who for years had suffered from paralysing rheumatoid arthritis. She passed away in the presence of the sisters at Drummoyne House in late 1925. Perhaps only too aware of how much responsibility Isabel had shouldered since the deaths of her parents, Nellie named Phyllis and Paulette as executors of her estate.

During pre-production, Phyllis boldly approached the bosses of department stores such as David Jones and Snows and told them about the film she and her sisters were producing. After quietly charming them, she requested clothes, furs, and costumes to use for free in the feature. Her strategy paid off because no department store director or manager could refuse her pleas to borrow the most glamorous garments available.

Production of *Those Who Love* began in the middle of May 1926, and immediately the sisters began attracting intense interest from the press. According to Phyllis, 'it was mainly doubt on the point of three inexperienced young girls succeeding where so many men had failed'. Their home Drummoyne House – still filled with their father's collection of tapestries, Venetian mirrors, antiques, ornaments, and gold-framed oils – was the main setting for the story.

In interviews, the sisters always claimed that the budget for their first film was 1000 pounds – a modest amount for a feature, even in 1926. In fact, two years before, when Raymond Longford and Lottie Lyell planned to produce the mystery/thriller *Fisher's Ghost* for the same amount, it was said to be 'unheard of', and those in the industry didn't believe it could be done, even though the film's length was only 5000 feet long, compared to the 6700 feet of *Those Who Love*. The budget did not include salaries for Isabel, Paulette, or Phyllis, or for the rental of lighting equipment. The sisters were able to further cut costs by using their home as a set, and by anticipating and planning every detail of the production design. 'There was nothing haphazard in our approach to film production', wrote Phyllis, 'we had one fixed rule – only to use the best'. All the other main characters were played by leading professional actors and were paid award rates.

On the first day of shooting, it seemed as if all the residents of Drummoyne were standing out on Wrights Road to take in the spectacle of a cumbersome film camera, klieg lights and reflectors, and a group of costumed actors with faces shellacked in thick make-up. In fact, the cast and crew often attracted so much public attention that they would pretend to pack up the equipment and lights so that the crowds would begin to disperse. Only once the set was cleared would they again begin shooting their scenes. Often, this pantomime would be repeated up to four or five times a day.

'We were utterly determined and took every mishap in our stride', said Phyllis. 'At the outset the three of us agreed to abolish the word *No* from our vocabularies.'

It was fortunate that the sisters made a group pact to never give up during the production process, because the challenges they would face, without the support of a studio system, would severely test their patience, resources, and stamina.

The sisters wisely hired cameraman Jack Fletcher, who'd previously worked in Hollywood at Paramount Studios, and upon his return was filming for PJ Ramster during student productions. Fletcher came from a wealthy family who'd made its fortune in Australia designing and manufacturing cast iron stoves, with a foundry in Edgecliff and a store in Oxford Square. Fletcher's father encouraged his son's keen interest in filmmaking by buying him his first camera and paying for the construction of a laboratory in the backyard that doubled as a dark room and editing room. In those days, there were no light meters, which meant that Fletcher would have had to gauge the correct lighting with his own eyes, and the speed of the recording with the velocity of his right hand as it cranked the camera's handle. Most cameras exposed eight frames per turn of the handle. This resulted in two revolutions a second, which produced sixteen frames per second. While working with the McDonaghs, Fletcher used an American Bell & Howell Model 2709 camera, well known at the time for its superior design.

Paulette initially secured the services of her mentor, PJ Ramster, as technical director, so she could acquire more confidence in transforming her scenario from the page to film. Since she'd written such a detailed scenario – describing every shot, angle, and movement – Ramster did not have much to do except follow her instructions.

For the dockside cabaret scene, supposedly set in a maritime workers' watering hole, Phyllis was unable to find the right venue, so she designed and built a set in a Bondi Junction studio run by Australasian Films, one that could reveal the emotional and psychological truth of the hard-luck characters. Exteriors included the suburb of Rose Bay, Mort's Dock, Prince Alfred Hospital, and the Italianate mansion, Rothesay, in Bellevue Hill.

Another landmark exterior scene was shot at Tamarama Beach. By the mid-1920s, sunbathing and surfing were becoming as popular with the Australian public as rollerskating and movie-watching. But at the time, most Australian beachgoers remained clothed as they cavorted on the shore, while the more faint-hearted sheltered beneath trees and wide umbrellas. During the shooting of *Those Who Love*, however, the McDonagh sisters boldly broke with this Victorian tradition by dressing the cast in modern bathers. Bébe Dorée, Barry Manton's beautiful yet frivolous girlfriend, wears a scant swimming costume with a court-jester design and dances a spirited Charleston across the sand to the music blaring from a nearby gramophone. Her friends are delighted and soon jump up and join in. No other cinematic image so encapsulates the wild, bohemian hedonism of the jazz age in Australia.

Paulette would rehearse the actors mercilessly: their actions, their facial expressions, their eye movements, their gaze, their soundless dialogue, the latter of which would be repeated on a title card. Not a moment could be improvised, or a gesture reinterpreted.

Forty years later, she admitted that she would have attempted a different directing approach had she been working with experienced film actors. But in 1926, with only stage actors and amateurs available, she had no qualms about dictating the actors' every expression and movement, which she'd do by calling out instructions while Fletcher cranked the camera. After all, her process saved the precious commodities of time and money, as she wanted every scene to be recorded in a single take.

Paulette credited her ability to direct actors from closely watching Hollywood films, noting how much more subtle and underplayed the action was compared to the histrionics of stage acting: '... when I got them they started to act their heads off. And they were so hostile, they wouldn't take any notice of me. So I said, "All right, I don't want that. You're going to do it this way".' When the actors refused to tone down their performances, Paulette merely shot the overly dramatic acting, had the film developed, and the following day showed the actors the rushes: '... and they were shocked. There they were, jumping and leaping. After that, they took every bit of direction I gave them'. Paulette became an advocate of what Alfred Hitchcock would later call 'negative acting': the ability to express and communicate emotion by doing virtually nothing. As the master of suspense proclaimed, 'the best screen actor is the man who can do nothing extremely well'.

Later, Paulette would reflect on her status as one of the very few female film directors in the world during the 1920s:

> At first there was an instinctive feeling that, being a girl,
> men would resent encroaching on their masculine fields.
> But when I actually met and had dealings with them,
> I realised just how absurd this was; on the contrary, I
> learned to value their camaraderie and good fellowship –
> it had helped us over many a difficult patch.

Brothers John and Grant acted small parts in *Those Who Love*, and John, who by this time had dropped out of medical school, often assisted as a sundry crew member.

Paulette never lit sets and scenes herself but rather told Jack Fletcher the effects she wanted to create, and he would make the adjustments according to her brief. But the harsh lights required to illuminate the set caused problems for the cast and crew.

'After a day of shooting your eyes were raw and watery and you couldn't see much at all – like someone had thrown pepper into them', said Phyllis. 'Not long after shooting began we all came down with klieg eyes. We just had to lie low for a couple of days, which meant a complete hold up with the shooting schedule.'

But even greater challenges lay ahead. Once they'd all recovered from klieg eyes, cameraman Jack Fletcher came down with a virulent strain of influenza. 'The poor man was in a terrible way', related Phyllis, 'shivering and sweating, and as the day wore on Paulette and I literally held him up at the camera to get through'.

The exhausted sisters put him to bed in Drummoyne House and alternated nursing shifts, sitting up with him all night and ministering hot lemon drinks and Aspro. The following morning, groggy and weak, reliable Fletcher was back behind the camera, cranking the handle.

Another setback, however, was about to beleaguer them. 'One morning we had to shoot a hospital sequence', Phyllis observed. 'The walls of the bedroom we'd adapted were reflecting too much light. Every single person on the film worked like demons repainting the whole room in their lunch hour.'

Teenage Paula used to tag along to their shoots and observe the filmmaking process. During the hospital scene, the sisters asked her to play one of the extras by getting into a nearby bed and acting as a patient. Nervous Paula refused, until ultimate family authority, Isabel, took charge, commanding Paula to get into the bed before the cast and crew lost any more time. No one, it seemed, could refuse gracious and persuasive Isabel anything.

One day, around dusk, the council rang to inform the sisters that the suburb of Drummoyne had been plunged into darkness because their klieg lights were using up all the electricity. The sisters were amused by the unintentional mishap, and their tolerant neighbours did not complain.

The final scene during the shoot of *Those Who Love* was filmed in the Australasian studio in Bondi Junction and was one of the few scenes that Paulette shot out of sequence. It was the underworld cabaret scene during which the male lead, Barry Manton, first encounters the beautiful yet exploited Lola Quayle. The scene also incorporated seventy extras, costumed in the Apache style of Parisian gangsters, men wearing peaked caps, striped shirts and baggy pants, and women garbed in loose blouses and wide skirts, who 'danced and made merry to the strains of a three-piece slapstick orchestra'. One myopic film critic would later complain that Sydney did not contain such 'doubtful public resorts', obviously not realising that the sisters were deliberately trying to create a universal story in a non-specific setting that could be applied to virtually any western city in the world. *Those Who Love* and all their subsequent films would trenchantly avoid recognisable Australian settings, characters, and dialogue.

For centuries, beautiful and talented women such as Isabel have been cast in acting roles, and for almost just as long, others like industrious Phyllis have worked behind the scenes. But Paulette's role as a female director at the time was comparatively unusual – in Australia or anywhere else in the world – and people would frequently ask her what it was like to direct a film. 'At first it is something of a strain', she admitted. 'The nervous tension and responsibility are tremendous. But afterwards, there is no real feeling at all. Soon, it is possible to make decisions and advise quite coldly and deliberately. Sleep and the thought of food become almost impossible when actually on the job. At the end of the day we are all physically exhausted. But tiredness, somehow cannot reach you. Always there is the knowledge of something fresh to create on the morrow. The thought has an amazing and stimulating effect.'

According to the McDonaghs, the main requisite in making a film is ordinary practical common sense. Each night, after shooting, the sisters and crew would watch the rushes of that day and felt intuitively that they had a good film. At the end of the production schedule, they were also proud of the fact they were able to shoot *Those Who Love* in only four weeks. The three of them collaborated on writing the intertitles, which were always, fortunately, grammatically correct.

During the era of silent films, cameramen were expected to not only light and shoot the scenes but also to develop the negative, print the film and, in concert with the director, edit the story. The processing of film in the 1920s involved 'the rack and tank' method, whereby the undeveloped film was looped up and down around pegs on a square frame roughly four-and-a-half feet (1.4 metres) high, which was then submerged in a tank of developer. Once the film was deemed fully developed, the rack was immersed in fixers and washes. Later, the racks were dried outside in the sunshine on large revolving drums. Fades and dissolves were achieved by simply dipping the requisite frames into a bucket of bleach, or by the cameraman winding the negative backwards and re-exposing it with new action over the old.

Jack Fletcher developed *Those Who Love* in the studio that had been built into the backyard of the large home owned by his parents in Waverley. The 6000 feet of footage was edited by Jack and Paulette, according to the way Paulette had already 'cut' the film in the scenario, and the way she had chronologically numbered the scenes, which had been primarily shot in sequence. '... we sat there in the studio and with a light behind and put it and glued it together,' said Paulette. 'Because we didn't have to test it, because I knew I had put ... in everything I shot'.

Working with the versatile Fletcher, however, had its downside for the sisters. '... he was a very dangerous man, with women', said Paulette. She hinted that it was challenging to collaborate with such an openly libidinous man – but a man whose cinematic skills they depended upon: 'he was a lecherous creature ... ugly little man, you know'. Fellow cameraman and friend Jack Bruce, with whom

Fletcher had travelled to Hollywood, confirms that Fletcher had a lascivious roving eye, which at times landed him in dangerous and compromising situations. For example, an older millionaire once approached him and invited him to sail around the world on his large private yacht. All Fletcher had to do in return was to film footage of the millionaire and his much younger wife in various locations around the globe. Fletcher accepted the offer and the yacht set sail. It wasn't long, however, before the millionaire walked in on Fletcher in bed with his wife and unceremoniously dumped him back in Sydney.

On the other hand, Fletcher's parents were the epitome of old-world charm and hospitality, and whenever Paulette was working with Jack in the studio, the mother would invite Paulette to stay for lunch. She remembered them being very wealthy and very old, and that their son completely took them for granted. Paulette adored the parents and appreciated their warmth and generosity.

Phyllis, like Isabel, was shy in public, but in her role as production manager and publicity agent, she was remarkably gutsy. She took control of the film's publicity before *Those Who Love* had even premiered, creating an atmosphere of suspense about the mysterious McDonagh sisters. Already a seasoned fiction writer who'd started writing at an early age, Phyllis began exaggerating and sometimes inventing statements about themselves and their film. In June 1926, an article appeared in the *Daily Telegraph* to promote the upcoming release of *Those Who Love*, describing Paulette as an experienced Hollywood screenwriter: 'Paulette has written four scenarios which have been accepted in America'.

Furthermore, in August 1926, the sisters began creating a romantic mythology around the film's inspiration: 'The scenario is founded upon the story contained in some old documents found when clearing out a cellar at Drummoyne House. ... It deals with a fascinating romance depicting the joys and sorrows of [a] proud old family'. Since this claim is never repeated in any other article about the sisters, we can assume that the three of them made it up.

During this pre-publicity blitz, it was reported that friends of the McDonaghs had thrown a surprise party for the sisters to celebrate the successful completion of *Those Who Love*. Sixty people were invited, and the guest list included actress Kate Trefle, who'd played the role of Lady Manton. Since the 'surprise party' was staged at the sisters' own home, Drummoyne House, it's likely that they organised the event and invited the press to garner more publicity for the release of the film. The strategy worked as the party and the title of the finished film was publicised in the Society column of the Sydney *Sun*, attracting more and more anticipation for its eventual release.

Almost two weeks after the party, on 16 September, the McDonaghs prepared for the premiere of the film. For the occasion, they booked the Prince Edward Theatre and invited 200 guests from Sydney society and the Australian film industry to attend the first screening. 'We sat in the dress circle, side by side, so nervous we couldn't breathe', said Phyllis. 'Then we relaxed a bit, reassured by that quiet which always settles in a theatre when the audience is being held. Halfway through, Paulette nudged me and whispered, "Look at the governor." He was sitting fairly close by. We saw him hold a handkerchief to his eyes.'

Music was a vital part of the silent film experience in cinemas. Even travelling showmen screening films in primitive conditions such as bush sheds and tents admitted that they had no show if they didn't have a pianist or at the very least a gramophone recording to accompany the action flickering across the screen. Accompanying *Those Who Love* at its premiere was the famous American organist Eddie Horton, dubbed 'the Wizard of the WurliTzer', who chose to play, at crucial moments of the film, the tear-jerking, popular song of the day, 'Always', written the year before by Irving Berlin as a wedding gift for his wife, Ellin Mackay. During the era of silent films, theatre organists were as feted as much as matinee idols, as were conductors who wrote the scores for the orchestras that accompanied films from the theatre pit.

As the end credits of *Those Who Love* began to roll, the sisters were greeted with thunderous applause and a standing ovation. When the governor, Sir Dudley de Chair, was leaving the theatre, he assured the sisters that he would encourage his wife and daughter to attend a screening of the film once it was released to the public.

Their excitement and relief were palpable. That night, they rushed out to buy the late edition of the *Sun* newspaper and glimpsed the headline: 'The Best Film Made in Australia That I Have Seen'.

Later that week, the positive reviews continued to roll in:

'... excellently produced, both photographically, and from the point of view of artistic presentation.'

'... a wonderful triumph ...'

'... a picture decidedly above the average ... well acted, well produced, and well presented. Story, acting, and photography give it a place which no other Australian production has beaten.'

Other press reports were equally ecstatic about the quality and depth of this new Australian film, comparing it favourably with the best of any Hollywood effort. At the time, 'Australian Film' was still considered by many as an oxymoron, and one critic even addressed the reluctance to pay money to watch one by stating,

'Certainly Australia has never approached the standard this film has set'. The reviewer at *Sydney Smith's Weekly* wryly warmed to the sisters' project of modernising and urbanising Australian narrative film: 'Search as you will, you cannot find even a shadow of a Hayseed, a suntanned young squatter, or a Man They Could Not Hang'.

At first, the sisters tried to negotiate with American companies to release the film, but to no avail. When they tried to secure a distributor, they were met with bemusement and told, 'Go home, little girls'. Eventually, five copies of it were made and *Those Who Love* was released in Sydney in late 1926 by JC Williamson Films, on a rental basis. During the first week of its run, it took more at the box office than Charlie Chaplin's *The Gold Rush*. The company then went on to sublet the copies to individual exhibitors around the country. However, despite the outstanding post-premiere reviews the film received, exhibitors were still reluctant to lease a film made in Australia, due to the many shoddy precedents. After a delay of six months, it was finally screened in Melbourne and, after a further six months, it opened in Adelaide. The bigger theatres employed orchestras to perform pre-selected classical music and jazz to accompany the film, while the smaller ones installed a single organist or piano player to provide a sympathetic soundtrack.

Eventually, the patience and resilience of the sisters paid dividends. The circuit manager of Hoyts Theatres in Victoria rapturously praised the McDonaghs' first foray into filmmaking, claiming that the picture 'had received the best public reaction of any picture he could recollect in the past fifteen years'. Earlier, the same publication had praised Isabel in particular: 'Marie Lorraine is a Sydney girl whose histrionic ability is remarkable. Her portrayal of the young wife is a splendid performance and ranks with some of the best characterisations ever given to the screen by the world's greatest stars'.

Following the successful release of *Those Who Love*, the sisters were approached by a representative of Fox Films in America, who offered to take them to Hollywood as a single producing team. At the time, there were many American studio-based companies marketing films in Australia, but Fox was the only one to express an interest in the local film industry. From 1919, it had periodically filmed Australian news items and edited them into the international *Fox Movietone News*.

The representative who approached the sisters was most likely Stanley Crick, an early Australian film producer who, in 1922, had become managing director of the distribution company Fox Film (Australasia) and introduced revolutionary administrative changes. Two years later, Crick visited America and returned with 'a trunk full of systems and data', which he implemented into the company. Crick was studious and highly organised and would not have made the offer if he were not completely convinced that the sisters could make a big mark in Hollywood.

They were naturally flattered and excited but needed to discuss the implications of the offer with each other, and their younger siblings, before making such a life-changing decision. There was no doubt much deliberation in the McDonagh home that night, with the two brothers and five sisters weighing up the pros and cons of emigration to America. After all, there were indeed precedents to inspire such a dramatic move: Louise Lovely, for example, along with Enid Bennett, Sylvia Breamer, and their own cameraman, Jack Fletcher.

Had their parents been alive, perhaps the sisters would have felt free and confident enough to have taken such a risk, but at the time, the younger siblings, still teenagers, were very much reliant on Isabel for emotional and physical care. The sisters also suspected that in Hollywood they would be overshadowed by the plethora of famous actors and directors who lived and worked there. Their prospects in Australia, however, were growing day by day. For example, managing director of Hoyts Theatres, George Griffiths, declared, 'We are prepared to find the money for them to do as many more pictures as they like on the same standard'.

After a long and gruelling deliberation, the sisters finally decided to remain in Australia with their younger siblings. They reasoned that they still had enough funds from Uncle Ernesto's inheritance to establish their ultimate independence in Sydney and their authority within the Australian filmmaking industry. In March 1927, Isabel and John, as the eldest sister and brother, purchased Drummoyne House from friends Lonergan and O'Brien and began to develop their next film, *The Far Paradise*, which would again be partly shot in their home, the perfect film set that they now owned outright.

But before the sisters plunged into the heavy work of producing another feature, they wanted, at last, to have some fun.

8

WILD AND CAREFREE

(1926–1927)

After the success of *Those Who Love*, the sisters celebrated the dizzying turn in their lives by throwing lavish parties at Drummoyne House. Paulette was usually the instigator and would design and hand-paint up to fifty individual invitations. The dress code was white tie and tails for the men and formal evening gowns for the women. And the guest list not only included friends from the film and entertainment industries, but also business leaders, solicitors, and doctors. In their own way, they were reviving the traditions set by their father in the late 19th and early 20th century, such as the grand soirées on Sunday evenings that the girls had witnessed from the sidelines. But instead of appreciating light opera and classical music, as Dr McDonagh and his guests had, the sisters now danced the Charleston to fast jazz and ragtime, the hems of their silk dresses whipping around their knees. The wind-up gramophone, thought of as an amusing curiosity before the war, had become wildly popular with young people.

Paula, Grant, and Anita, now teenagers, were forbidden from the parties and reduced to eavesdropping on the celebrations from the top step of the staircase. Housekeeper Lucy also liked the parties. When they were winding down late at night, Paula noticed that she would go to each room and knock back the dregs of the guests' discarded glasses.

As Paulette would remark decades later, shortly before her death: 'We ... lived a wild, carefree life, throwing parties and entertaining friends'.

Throughout the 1920s, the house party was the preferred way of socialising for artists and theatre people, enhanced by fancy dress, alcohol, and modern music. It was a time when Sydney was an industrious port city with a ceaseless ebb and flow of international commerce and ideas that began to define cosmopolitan modernity, and the McDonagh sisters were at the vanguard of these post-war changes.

At a private party, guests were free to dance with abandon, drink liberally from the punch bowl, and pursue romantic longings in candlelit corners without being asked to leave. The only limit to a house party carrying on for days was the level of tolerance exercised by disgruntled neighbours. For young women such as the McDonaghs, the flourishing bohemianism of the 1920s offered the opportunity for self-reliance and independence at a time when their roles in society were limited to marriage and motherhood. In Sydney, bohemia was realised not through high art such as painting and opera, but within popular products such as newspapers, magazines, novels, and films – all of which the McDonagh siblings embraced with gusto. The force behind bohemia was against nationalism in all its forms, embodied in the swerve away from bush poetry, realist outback fiction, and the corny Dad and Dave films so loathed by the McDonaghs.

These shifting social and artistic mores had been unwittingly assisted by laws drafted to change the social habits of the working people. In 1916, for example, legislation was passed in New South

Wales to close pubs at 6 pm, and the loss for pubs was a gain for moving pictures. After the hotels slammed their doors shut at six o'clock, the rest of the evening could be passed pleasantly at the local picture palace. In the same year, a Public Instruction Amendment required the attendance of children between the ages of seven and fourteen for two hours in the morning and two hours in the afternoon every school day. This increased the literacy levels of the average child, who, nine or ten years later, was able to read and enjoy the title cards that appeared at intervals throughout all silent films. In addition, the modern, reduced working week entitled workers to take off Saturday afternoons, allowing for increased leisure time that could be spent at the pictures.

Meanwhile, liberated working Australians were gaining a reputation for their ability to relax and enjoy themselves. Film critic Beatrice Tildesley reported that 'Quite recently a criticism from a foreign quarter was made about Australians that they cared for nothing but amusement. Whatever justification there may be in that, it is certain that Australians are better able than people elsewhere as regards money and leisure to indulge a taste for amusement'.

While the sisters were throwing raucous parties and collaborating on their next film, their friends from school were selecting wedding gowns and planning honeymoons. Already, former fellow debutante Peggy Smith had married Charles Coffey, and another, Ethel Trimnell-Ritchard, had wed Vincent Goldrick. In September 1926, Phyllis's best friend from Kincoppal, Estelle McDermott, married John C ('Bud') Macken, a grandson of retail magnate Mark Foy, in a large society wedding at St Mary's Cathedral. Even Phyllis's showbusiness sidekick, Gertie Purcell, who'd performed with her in a vocal act, wed James Russell in 1925.

In contrast, the sisters did not seem remotely interested in protracted romantic entanglements – unless they were imaginary ones that could be adapted into a film scenario. If one sister was invited out on a date, at least one other would tag along and chaperone, or turn it into a double date. A frustrated young friend named Aiden would inscribe a poem in Paulette's autograph book, lamenting the necessity of a third person on a date: 'Two's company; three's more / the extra one spoils all the fun ...' The pleasure that the sisters experienced in each other's company was more powerful than that offered by any random man, and they were fiercely protective of their intense closeness. In fact, over the years, the sisters resisted so many offers of marriage that it's possible they may have formed a secret pact.

As the popularity of silent films soared, Sydney's taste for amusement was sated by the construction of four purpose-built cinemas, based on the plush and palatial American picture palaces. The apotheosis of this grand high style would be the State Theatre, on Market Street. The Managing Director of Union Theatres, Stuart Doyle, was the brains behind the design and planning: 'He determined to put into his theatre every conceivable idea of showmanship that could ever be thought out, and he toured the world and picked ideas from every successful theatre he came across'.

But in the months following the release of *Those Who Love*, the sisters remained haunted by certain mysteries from their past. In June of 1927, for example, they noticed a photograph of a handsome man in the newspaper who was the image of their younger brother, Grant. The man's name, they noticed, was Efrem Zimbalist, and he was touring the country as an internationally celebrated violinist. At once, the sisters' romantic imagination kicked into overdrive: Zimbalist was possibly the son of wayward

Aunt Annie, who'd run off with the married man, moved overseas, and given birth to the legendary child musical prodigy. Isabel and Phyllis, convinced that they'd at last found their long-lost cousin, rushed down to the Sydney Town Hall, where Zimbalist was giving his first recital, and later met him backstage, where they gushed out their story. A bemused Zimbalist let them down lightly: he'd been born in Russia to Jewish parents Maria Litvinoff and Aron Zimbalist, the latter of whom was a renowned conductor.

At home, rebellious younger sister Anita was tired of being excluded from the intense camaraderie shared by the older sisters, especially now that they had begun to make motion pictures. She was envious of their flourishing careers and longed to appear in films as well. But she was too young, too inexperienced, and too different temperamentally to fuse with the tight-knit trio, who lived more as a single entity than three individuals. This is perhaps why Anita always claimed that her older sisters did not provide her with a stable home life, when in fact Isabel had exerted every effort to discipline Anita and keep her in school.

At the age of eighteen, Anita ran away from home for the final time, eventually surfacing at the Rose Bay cottage of her former nanny, Stella, and Stella's husband, Willy, who took her in and looked after her. 'The girls couldn't forgive Stella for that', said Paula. The sense of betrayal ran deep and wouldn't be healed for a very long time.

Anita lived with Stella and her husband until she was able to earn her own living. Not long after settling in, she fronted up to St Margaret's maternity hospital on the corner of Elizabeth and Cleveland streets in Chippendale and was admitted into the nurse's training course.

During her training, Anita was asked to submit a copy of her birth certificate (which, of course, didn't exist) to keep on file for her graduation. Later, Anita maintained that she was indeed able to produce a birth certificate for the hospital, but the document stated that her true age was two years younger than that which she'd claimed when she'd begun her training, and the hospital refused to endorse her nursing qualifications. But it's also possible that Anita was practising the McDonagh habit of fictionalising the past, and that the real reason why she was unable to graduate as a nurse was because she was unable to produce a birth certificate at all.

Crestfallen, Anita withdrew from St Margaret's program and enrolled in the one offered by St Vincent's Hospital in Darlinghurst, where she began her training all over again. There, she became a popular member of staff. Of all the sisters, it was Anita who looked the most like Isabel, who shared the same heart-shaped face, wide-set hazel eyes, and cascades of thick black hair. In fact, according to Paula, Anita was apparently so good-looking that 'the patients used to ring their bell to bring her into the room to show her off to visitors'.

In a curious twist of fate, Anita's behaviour was beginning to mirror that of Lola Quayle's in *Those Who Love* (a girl who runs away from home and reinvents herself as a nurse), and life began to imitate art in a most mysterious way.

The three older sisters continued to thrive on the thrill of self-expression. By July 1927, Isabel was in Melbourne, appearing nightly on the stage of the Hoyts Deluxe Theatre, introducing the screening of *Those Who Love*. Paulette, in Sydney, was about to join her. By this time, she had acquired the nickname 'The Tigress' due to her assertiveness and volubility on the film set. Two years later, their close friend, cartoonist Syd Nicholls, would draw a detailed picture of a predatory, striped, big cat in her autograph book and entitle it 'La Tigresse'. In the mid-1920s,

Nicholls created the wildly popular comic strip 'Fatty Finn', which inspired the Sydney-based 1927 film comedy *The Kid Stakes*. He'd also drawn art titles for Raymond Longford's *A Sentimental Bloke* and many other silent films. Moreover, he would draw a large, detailed pen and ink picture of the three sisters, depicting their beauty and grace, which now hangs framed in the home of their nephew, John Dornan.

While in Melbourne, Isabel was courted by businessman Frank Graham, who at the time was working as the circuit manager for Hoyts Theatres. They no doubt met while Isabel was appearing on the stage of Hoyts during her pre-screening introductions. Possessive Paulette acted as chaperone and somehow Graham was able to charm and befriend her too, writing in her autograph book in August 1927: 'To Paulette – A charming chaperone / A little lady / A perfect pal'. After the sisters returned to Sydney for pre-production of their next film, Frank Graham began making regular trips from Melbourne to spend time with Isabel, and to ingratiate himself with the rest of the siblings at Drummoyne House.

Graham was charming, had a great sense of humour, and was reportedly very amusing. According to Isabel's son Charles, he used to put a lampshade on his head and sing to her. About nine weeks after meeting Isabel, Graham resigned from Hoyts and joined British Dominion Films to head up their sales team, which would conveniently require even more travel to Sydney.

At the same time, Phyllis was in rehearsals as a member of a group of twelve female singers who would appear in the Australian premiere of the operetta *The Student Prince*. Also part of the production were twelve ballet dancers, twenty-eight male singers, and an orchestra of twenty-three led by Australian conductor Fred Quintrell. Phyllis adored her German-inspired costume of *The Student Prince* so much that, while wearing it, she had herself photographed professionally, and for over four decades would use it as a publicity shot. The press was equally impressed by the fashion design: 'the ladies of the chorus glitter in costly costumes in the palace ballroom'. Knowing full-well that her parents, had they been alive, would never have approved of her being 'a chorus girl', Phyllis appeared in the production under her pseudonym of Gloria Grant. As her younger sister Paula observed, 'Phyllis had a bland exterior, but she was a rebel at heart … She had tremendous courage … because she was, by nature, shy … the fact that she made herself do things, she was really a very gutsy woman'.

The original New York cast for *The Student Prince* was imported for the production and included veteran actress Daisy Belmore, younger sister of Lionel Belmore, who'd been a close friend and patient of Dr McDonagh and who had, years earlier, gifted the doctor with an engraved silver cup as a token of appreciation.

Another McDonagh–Belmore friendship was born. The now middle-aged Daisy Belmore was a progressive thinker who embraced the vitality and strength of the 'new woman', which the McDonagh sisters embodied. In an interview with the *Daily Telegraph,* she bemoaned the restrictions of her own youth, when she'd been forced to wear corsets, bustles, and bodices, and 'didn't have half the chance to enjoy life as the modern girl has'. The interviewer suggests that the Victorian clothing not only cramped the female body, but also the female mind, and Belmore heartily agreed: 'The modern girl … has plenty of freedom – and she knows how to use it in the proper manner. I think she is delightful in every way and does not deserve any of the black and mysterious things that are said about her'.

The interview took place in Belmore's dressing room, between scenes during a performance of the operetta's first week, but Belmore is forced to cut the interview short because she must rush off to the stage to perform her 'big scene'. It would be difficult, if not impossible, for a regular journalist to secure an interview with an actress backstage during a live performance, and more than possible that the writer of the uncredited article, who suggested that Victorian clothing cramped women's minds as well as their bodies, was none other than liberated Phyllis herself.

The Student Prince was a hit with audiences and enjoyed a run of thirteen weeks, closing in Sydney on Saturday 8 October 1927. Now that Phyllis was free of greasepaint and costumes, the three sisters started pre-production of their next motion picture, which would propel them to the heights of national acclaim.

9

THE SISTERS SHOULD ALWAYS GET WHAT THEY WANT

(1927–1928)

The romantic subject matter of the McDonaghs' first film, coupled with their glamorous portraits splashed all over the Australian press, led to the perception that the sisters were merely society girls indulging a hobby, or three vivacious flappers out for a bit of fun. But one female journalist of the day sensed the sisters' serious intent and artistic infallibility: 'In the great rambling home at Drummoyne the girls had long dreamed of the time when they could prove the ability of their sex in the making of films'.

In the spirit of this keen observation, two weeks before shooting their second feature, *The Far Paradise*, the sisters appeared as guests of honour at a feminist club. In the 1920s, such clubs were popular with middle-class and professional women, continuing a tradition of feminist ideals that had begun with the granting of votes at the turn of the century. Isabel gave the first address, explaining the methods of film production. She said that, in her opinion, the cinema industry would not be successful here unless the government and the public both gave hearty cooperation.

Many Australian industry professionals were still extremely dissatisfied with the dominance of Hollywood motion pictures in Australia. Any cinema that wanted to screen Hollywood films had to sign a contract to block-book them up to a year in advance, sight unseen, essentially sidelining Australian and British films. If a cinema owner refused to block-book, he or she would be denied access to the latest Hollywood hits. By then, American films made up 93 per cent of those imported into Australia. Following the First World War, American companies had gained the monopoly on film production and distribution, and the system of Hollywood storylines, glamorous stars, and soaring publicity budgets came to dominate the experiences of the cinema-going public. As historian Jill Julius Matthews has observed, 'Posters, stunts, tie-ins, fan and romance magazines, product sponsorship, radio programs and a vast array of other star publicity developed in Sydney people the movie habit'.

Those who objected to this cheap form of entertainment relegated moving pictures to 'low-brow' culture, preferring the 19th-century pleasures of opera, live theatre, and classical music. But like their father before them, who attempted to lift the amusement of rollerskating into a new recreation enjoyed by the elite, the sisters also tried to transform the perception of motion pictures, and the stories of cinema, from those of farmers and outback battlers to melodramas of sophisticated urban dwellers.

Their strategy was executed at a time when public interest in cinema was growing exponentially, defying social, religious, and class barriers. Records reveal that during the silent era, Australia's population of six million people attended the cinema a staggering 110 000 000 times annually. After all, the cheapest seats at a live theatre were at least double the price of those at the cinema.

On the other side of the camera, in the year following the release of *Those Who Love*, the Australian film industry provided employment for approximately 20 000 people. But from the end of the First World War until the beginning of the Depression, only ninety-seven features would be produced in Australia, compared to over 7000 in Hollywood.

A small-budget, independent feature like the one the McDonaghs had produced would have had trouble competing with the American product, as theatre managers were prohibited to screen Australian-made films that were not a part of the package determined by companies such as Union and Hoyts. As one manager complained, 'it is not so much a matter of choosing programmes as taking what we are given'.

However, Australian producers began calling for government tariffs, taxes, and quotas to protect British and Australian films. At the same time, other lobby groups were agitating the government for stricter censorship for all films screened in Australia – no matter the country in which they were made.

Due to so many concerns from so many sources, a Select Committee was appointed on 3 March 1927. In May it was converted to a Royal Commission on the Moving Picture Industry and heard testimonies from 253 witnesses: cameramen, producers, exhibitors, managers, and representatives from various women's organisations from all state capitals and numerous country centres. Although the McDonagh sisters were yet to experience the full effects of the American monopoly, they certainly would in years to come.

The story of the McDonaghs' second film, *The Far Paradise*, begins with the image of a train crossing a bridge above a wide river. A young woman, Cherry Carson, along with her puppy, is returning home to Kirkton and to a father she barely knows. She has just graduated from college, and her mother, long separated from her father, has recently died. During a stop in the journey, she loses control of the dog leash, and her puppy runs across the platform. Young and handsome Peter Lawton, who is also returning home, catches the puppy and returns it to her. On the train, the two sit together and become fast friends.

In Kirkton, Cherry's father, criminal James Carson, lives in a luxurious mansion where his illegal activities are carried out under the cloak of respectability and wealth. His partner-in-crime is the scheming and paranoid Karl Rossi. And while Carson is not happy about his daughter's imminent arrival, Rossi argues she could be a good front for their criminal activities.

Cherry arrives at the family mansion and greets the old butler. Her father is not there to meet her but is expected to join her at dinner. In the meantime, Peter's father, Howard Lawton, the Attorney General of Kirkton, throws an extravagant dinner party to welcome home his son. Peter's closest friend, Lee Farrar, is one of the guests.

Cherry dines alone that night, but she is so sad and disappointed she's unable to eat. Her father finally arrives, staggering through the room and very drunk. He gives Cherry a cursory kiss on the forehead and collapses into a chair. He can see that Cherry is unimpressed and accuses her of being just as judgmental as her mother. Cherry begins to weep and asks to be excused.

Later, Peter Lawton collects Cherry in his convertible, and they cruise along a road that hugs a shimmering, romantic coastline. They pull up and walk hand in hand across the rocks, admiring the surf and sea. Peter turns and lifts her into the air. After he puts her down, they lean in and kiss. In the meantime, sidekick Rossi warns Carson that Howard Lawton (Peter's father) is onto their scheme.

Peter soon visits the Carson mansion but is told by the butler that Cherry is not at home. Instead, he meets her father, James Carson. Peter introduces himself, explaining that he met Cherry on the train. Carson tells him that he has no desire to know the son of Howard Lawton and forbids him from entering his home again, and that his daughter no longer desires to continue her acquaintance with him.

Back at home, a downcast Peter tells his father what has happened. Lawton Senior explains that Carson is a scoundrel and currently under investigation by the police, but there's not enough evidence to convict him yet. Peter confesses that he is in love with Cherry.

Lawton Senior explains that twenty years ago he too was in love with a woman, but that Carson then came along, swept her off her feet, and married her. However, Carson made the poor woman's life a living hell, and so she left him so that their daughter, Cherry, might not suffer as she had. He fights back tears and dissuades his son from taking the romance any further.

At the Carson mansion, Cherry can't understand why Peter has made no further contact with her. She picks flowers in the garden while her father eats breakfast on the veranda. The butler delivers the mail to the table and Carson spots an envelope from Peter Lawton. He quickly hides it in his pocket. A disconsolate Cherry approaches the table and asks if there is any mail for her. Carson shakes his head.

To throw off her unhappiness, Cherry decides to attend a masked ball. She arrives wearing a blonde wig and pompadour ball gown, accompanied by her father. Sidekick Rossi is dressed as a masked pirate, but Cherry doesn't recognise him and agrees to dance with him. Soon she starts to feel uncomfortable and breaks away, fleeing to another room. Rossi follows and tries to seduce her. She pushes him away and another masked man enters the room. The stranger asks her to dance and spirits her away.

In the lobby, Cherry removes her mask and the stranger removes his: it's Peter Lawton, and they're both thrilled to be accidentally reunited. She reveals that she's waited a long time to hear from him. Peter explains that he has tried to visit her and write to her. The two lovers fold into each other on a couch. Cherry holds a single flower to her lips, then presses it against Peter's lips.

Carson enters and is horrified to see his daughter and Peter together. He reminds Peter of his earlier warning to stay away from her. Cherry pleads with her father, explaining that she's in love with Peter, who has asked her to marry him. Carson dismisses her feelings and tells her they're going home. Cherry reluctantly obeys him. On the way out, Carson and Rossi get into a fight and Carson accidentally kills him. As a result, father and daughter are forced to flee the city for the country.

A year passes. At the Lawton house, Peter is still obsessed with Cherry and her unexplained disappearance. His father encourages him to pull himself together, and to take a trip to ease his loss.

Peter's best friend, Lee, is holidaying at Paradise Lodge, a country tourist and hunting resort. Nearby, Cherry collects flowers, which she sells to support herself and her father. She is startled when Lee bumps into her, causing her to drop the flowers. He laughs at first but is beguiled by Cherry's beauty and helps her retrieve the flowers from the ground.

Peter arrives at Paradise Lodge and runs into his old friend, Lee. In Peter's room, Lee notices a framed portrait of Cherry and announces that he has just seen a girl identical to her in Paradise Valley. Hopeful, Peter spends the next few days searching the valley for her. He pulls up in his car in front of the Carson shack. He knocks, but there is no answer.

Cherry, forlorn, is carrying firewood into the yard. She picks up a bucket and begins pumping water into it. In a close-up, a man's hand grips the handle of the pump. Cherry turns, looks up and recognises Peter.

Peter is relieved, but Cherry suspects that he's trying to track down her father. She pleads his innocence and wrings her fingers nervously against the material of her dress, which fades to a flashback of her fingering the single flower at the masked ball the year before.

Cherry turns her back on him, but he comes up close behind her, confessing that he's searched for her everywhere, that he'll never give her up. He also tells her that her father is a trickster and a criminal and that he's deceived her.

Peter gets back in his car and drives away. Cherry is torn as she watches the car disappear down the driveway. Inside, her father has passed out drunk in his chair. Cherry enters and her father stirs. She tells him that Peter Lawton is in the valley and that he has told her everything about his (her father's) criminal past.

Carson staggers to his feet. Cherry says, 'I have been blind, a fool. Oh, how could you deceive me when I trusted you so?' Carson experiences a vision and is frightened: the image of his daughter fades into that of her mother. He reels back in horror and collapses.

Cherry waits out the night, alone and afraid. Her father's unconscious body is on the bed. She begins to weep and gazes out the window at dark clouds obscuring the moon. Her father's eyes open briefly and then they suddenly freeze. She kneels beside him and picks up his arm: it's now limp and she realises he has died. Cherry stands up unsteadily but faints beside the bed.

In the morning, Peter arrives at the shack, hesitates, then knocks on the door. There is no answer, so he opens it and glimpses Carson's corpse lying on the bed. Seeing Cherry passed out on the floor, he collects her in his arms and carries her to the nearby chaise longue. She stirs and wakes slowly. He's holding her hand and gently kisses her on the cheek.

After Peter returns from his trip, Lawton Senior greets his son, thrilled to have him home. Then Cherry appears in the room. Peter announces, 'Dad, meet Mrs Peter Lawton'. The father processes the news and says, 'My dear, you have given back to me a very beautiful memory. I am glad you have come home'.

Since Isabel played the lead in all the McDonagh films, the writing of the scenarios had to be crafted from a female point of view, with the heroine being the focus of the unfolding story.

The classic romantic narrative of boy meets girl, boy loses girl, boy regains girl had to be reversed so that the audience identified with the plight of the young woman rather than that of the man. Paulette could write to exploit Isabel's strengths as an actress and direct close-ups that revealed her character's vulnerability and emotional complexity. By expressing mood and emotion through the gimlet eye of the camera, Paulette had established a convincing female gaze.

Although she was crafting original material for Isabel as a female lead, Paulette also freely borrowed from a stock character of literature and theatre – the ingenue – a young woman who is fresh, innocent, and lacking in self-interest. She is also beautiful, vulnerable, and virginal, and finds herself in either emotional or physical peril. The ingenue usually lives with her father or a father figure, and she sometimes mistakes the villain of the story for the hero. Usually, there is a romantic subplot that involves the ingenue and an equally naive and innocent young man. Isabel's favourite female actor, Mary Pickford, refined the role of the ingenue in early silent films such as *Poor Little Rich Girl*, *Rebecca of Sunnybrook Farm*, and *Daddy Long Legs*. A real-life ingenue was the sisters' mother, who by the age of thirteen was the eldest daughter of a motherless family, living in poverty with her wayward father, who would grow up to meet her well-off hero in the form of Dr McDonagh.

Phyllis would later write, 'Though the newspapers made a big play of the novelty of three sisters going into the movie business, it never occurred to us that we were doing anything remarkable – only we were doing our own thing. Our first step was to gather the best cameraman and technicians available. In casting we followed one unfailing rule – to engage professional actors to fill the role. To this, I think we owed our success'.

Their flighty 'flapper' reputation began to wane, and some of the sharper journalists began to sense the depth of their commitment. While the sisters were shooting their second feature, a writer at the *Bulletin* observed, 'So many mushroom film companies, self-watered with their own glowing prospectuses, have sprung up and shrivelled lately that it is good to record the persistence of the McDonagh sisters'.

This persistence was given greater force by Phyllis's practice as a painter, which contributed to her aesthetic precision in production and set design. The sets were not only artistically beautiful but also intrinsically meaningful, with the various design elements expressing the class of the given characters, the mood of the scene, the time and place, and often a certain character's state of mind.

In *The Far Paradise*, the placement of flowers underscores an almost Catholic reverence for divine beauty and balance. Cherry's fragile innocence is reinforced when she is seen picking them in the garden before her father cruelly lies to her and hides Peter's letter. Later, a drunken Carson knocks over a vase of roses from the table to the floor, signifying his destruction of Cherry's hopes and dreams. In Paradise Valley, Lee unwittingly repeats the same accident, when he bumps into her, causing the collected flowers to drop to the ground.

Earlier, the criminal father's iron authority is established in the Kirkton home through heavy furniture and the bulky chair in which he sits at the head of the table. In his office, a large tapestry of a roaring tiger in a jungle hangs on the wall, while an open-mouthed tiger skin stretches across the floor. The inference is that Carson and his right-hand man are driven by base, animal instincts, rather than refined human ones, while the sunny office of Peter Lawton's father is decorated with billowing lace curtains. In the scene where Carson confronts Peter, a thick pillar stands between father and suitor, suggesting an insurmountable obstacle between the two. Later, an image of entrapment is masterfully created as Cherry stares through the vertical and horizontal frames within a windowpane as the moon floats in an intense, cloudy sky. It could be a scene straight out of a Bergman film, and all three sisters contributed to its poignancy and beauty. By now, Isabel had mastered the technique of containing visible emotion, and in her internal wrestle to control them, the overall effect is far more powerful.

The plot of *The Far Paradise* – two old enemies, one bad, one good, who once were in love with the same woman – repeats that of the earlier treatment, *A Greater Love*. The 'good' enemy relinquishes his love for the woman, who goes on to marry the 'bad' one and bears a daughter. As young adults, the offspring of the two enemies fall in love. This dynamic also anticipates the plot of their third feature, *The Cheaters*, which is further complicated by mistaken identities and a secret adoption.

Because the sisters were so close, and because they almost thought as one, the writing, directing, acting, and set design of each film had a single, unified vision, where it is almost impossible to see where one sister's contribution ended and another's began.

The Far Paradise went into production in March 1928. Paul Longuet was cast as the male lead, Peter Lawton; and PJ Ramster was again hired as technical director. When shooting commenced in Drummoyne House, however, Paulette was horrified to realise that Ramster was directing the actors and cameraman without paying attention to what she had written, as if he hadn't read the script at all and was merely making up instructions as he went along. 'He was the worst cheat and amateur I've ever seen in my life', said Paulette. '... And I wouldn't take it, and I had to stop everything he did by the side'.

Paulette quickly realised she had nothing to learn from Ramster and that he could, in fact, learn a thing or two from her. She soon grew tired of quietly overriding his directions from the margins of the set and eventually fired him. 'I told him to get out. I said, "I'm doing this anyhow I've done it all along".'

Later she would feel the need to publicly clarify Ramster's role in a press release: 'We have been asked to state that Mr Ramster had no connection whatsoever with the production of "Those Who Love" or "The Far Paradise" ... He was technical director for the continuity, and under personal supervision of Paulette McDonagh'.

For the next three weeks, they shot interiors at the Australasian studio at Bondi Junction. But the sisters found it almost impossible to hire authentic props and had to ransack their own home for antiques and furniture. 'For the picture', said Phyllis, 'we turned our old home into a studio; but we were very much more settled in Bondi Junction, where all the latest lighting stands and necessary conveniences had been installed. True, dear old Drummoyne House was almost bare as a barn when we had robbed it of its treasures, but we had the satisfaction of knowing that the interiors would be furnished with genuine antiques, giving the picture a background of solidness and an "air"'. One of the big scenes shot at the studio was the fancy dress ball, which contained 200 extras.

Exterior scenes were shot at St John's College at Sydney University, Watsons Bay, Farm Cove, the Macquarie Lighthouse at South Head, the old Como rail bridge that crosses the Georges River, and a rambling farmhouse with dogs and chickens in Donnybrook, Victoria. Phyllis also managed to secure for free the entire property of Royal Sydney Golf Club at Rose Bay, which closed for a day to allow the sisters to shoot important outdoor sequences.

Another vital exterior for the film was the glen that would represent the cinematic 'Paradise Valley'. According to a press clipping in the McDonaghs' scrapbook, a favourite pastime was long-distance walking, and in 1928 they and a couple of friends set out to walk the sixty miles from Wentworth Falls to the

Burragorang Valley. Most likely the group was on a reconnaissance trip to pinpoint possible locations for the film.

Curiously, this valley had been in the news the year before because a young boy named Allan Crago had gone missing in the area for over a month. He'd sheltered alone in a hut there for five weeks, after having been accidentally shot by a pea gun. When he was finally discovered, running a high fever, he was placed in a cane chair and carried out of the valley by six men, accompanied by his mother and uncle. The missing Allan Crago, and his dramatic rescue, had gripped the public's attention for weeks.

At the time of the sisters' sojourn, it was winter of the following year and, according to the clipping, the party got lost for days in the very same valley. They allegedly slept on a haystack one night, out in the open on another, and during yet another night in the shack 'once occupied by Allan Crago when he was shot'. Far from being traumatised, the sisters seemed to enjoy the life-threatening adventure. But what is telling about this article is that – unlike Crago's – their own disappearance was never reported to the police, and the only reason that this drama ever appeared in newspapers was because the sisters were engaged in pre-publicity for *The Far Paradise*. The story of the walking tour, of getting lost for three nights, and of sheltering in the same hut as Crago's, reads like fiction, or at least an exaggeration, to engage the public's imagination about their colourful personalities. Film historian Graham Shirley remembers Paulette mentioning to him that they did indeed get lost in the valley, but for only one day – not three nights.

Phyllis's personality was on full display when she went to work as production manager on their second film. There was one pivotal scene that was to be shot at Central Station that would require the exclusive use of a train carriage. The sisters did not have access to or the budget for such an extravagant inclusion, and so Paulette sent Phyllis down to negotiate with the Chief Commissioner for Railways, a Mr Fraser. Phyllis explained their filmmaking background, the plot of *The Far Paradise*, and their need to secure the use of a railway carriage for an important sequence. Fraser was fascinated by the story of the sisters and their motion picture enterprise. He agreed to help but made no promises, and so Phyllis continued to plead with him for a further three weeks, after which he finally capitulated and offered up the state premier's private train, organising for it to be moved into a siding at Central Railway Station for an afternoon of shooting. The original notice of permission from Fraser is still pasted into the McDonagh sisters' scrapbook:

4 April 1928: TO ALL CONCERNED

Authority is hereby given to Miss McDonagh and party to carry out a picture film act on No 13 Platform today between 11.30am and 3pm adjacent to Empty Car train which will be placed at that platform, and also to be permitted to the entire observation portion of Premier's Car in Eastern Shed after arrival to complete the scene.

Naturally, the shoot ran overtime, and when the premier and his entourage arrived to begin their railway journey into western New South Wales, the cast and crew were still filming. Rather than becoming impatient, the premier observed the lights, the camera, the actors, and was instead fascinated. 'Don't even worry – go ahead with your scene', he said. 'This is the first time I have ever seen a picture being made, and we'll enjoy watching'. A love scene between the hero and the heroine was completed as the premier looked on and the sun went down. The cast and crew ended up gathering on the platform and, after the premier and his assistants boarded the train, the whole company gleefully waved them off on their journey.

Paulette was full of praise for her sister: 'Phyllis went to store managers for settings, to salesroom people, to politicians, even to the governor. She'd go for whatever we wanted – a car, a mink fur, permission to film. It all paid off. We'd have never got things done as quickly without Phyllis'. After interviewing Phyllis in June 1928, a Sydney journalist observed: 'With their unusual personalities the McDonagh girls should always get what they want'.

Not all filmmakers were as successful at securing cooperation from government bodies. When Beaumont Smith tried to book the Sydney Town Hall for a scene representing the Artists' Ball in his 1923 film *Prehistoric Hayseeds*, the town clerk curtly refused. Instead, Smith had to build an avant-garde set at Australasian studios and shoot it there. In general, filmmakers of the silent era 'received little co-operation and much bureaucratic obstruction from authorities in New South Wales'. But not so when it came to clever, classy, and persistent Phyllis.

Due to his experience in Hollywood, cameraman Jack Fletcher had developed an aesthetic that embodied 'a striking use of shadows, depth of focus and backlighting'. He and Paulette even employed the diaphanous quality of direct moonlight as a way of recreating the romanticism of the European films that she so admired. They also experimented with special effects. For example, the identity of the villainous Rossi is only revealed during a masked ball when his mask dissolves momentarily under Cherry's gaze; and during Peter's first visit to the ramshackle farm, the fact that Cherry's coldness conceals embarrassment is, as Graham Shirley notes, 'adroitly conveyed by a shot of her overworked hands dissolving to the same hands toying with a rose during the ball'.

In the McDonagh imagination, family loyalty must always be prioritised over the lure of romantic love, just as it was in the context of their own inseparability. For example, the heroines of both *The Far Paradise* and *The Cheaters* have fathers who are criminals, yet despite romantic overtures from highly respectable suitors, the daughters choose to remain devoted to their corrupt relatives, which could be interpreted as another example (and projection) of the McDonagh family enmeshment.

Towards the end of the shoot, with only ten days available to record all the scenes of the hero played by Longuet, the company was working day and night to meet their deadline. On the final day, Longuet insisted that he had to leave for Melbourne to fulfil a previous engagement. The only problem was that there was still one scene to shoot, and Longuet was preparing to depart. Paulette was unable to persuade him to stay and so the entire cast and crew jumped into their various cars with lights and camera and followed the actor to Melbourne, over 500 miles away, where Longuet's last scene was filmed. Some exterior shots, such as Flinders Street Station, were also photographed in Melbourne, and production was completed in May 1928. The sisters were nothing if not spontaneous.

10

TWO DECENT PROPOSALS

(1928)

Isabel's beau, Frank Graham, was still commuting between Melbourne and Sydney, juggling his business interests with romantic ones. In early February 1928, he managed to isolate Isabel from her sisters and chaperones to the extent that he proposed with a diamond ring. Isabel accepted and the engagement was announced in the press on 9 February. She had previously accepted proposals from other men, but this was the first time a betrothal had been published in the press. Frank Graham obviously wanted the world to know that the hand of the beautiful, desirable silent film star Marie Lorraine belonged to him, and him only.

When the siblings learned of the news, however, they were absolutely devastated. They all looked up to Isabel as both a mother and father figure. But their hostile reaction was even more complex, more to do with 'the disease of closeness' that broke out whenever John brought home girls and the sisters alienated any possible future fiancée by mocking their speech and table manners. Two years later, when Paulette fell in love, she too would suffer the same fate.

The siblings weren't the only ones who were jealous of Frank Graham. Gordon Collingridge, who'd appeared in *Joe* with Isabel three years before, and who'd also been briefly engaged to her, became increasingly possessive of his former fiancée. Whenever Graham visited from Melbourne, he stayed at Drummoyne House, along with many other friends of the McDonaghs, and his presence enraged Collingridge, who would often stay over in one of the other rooms.

Even though the engagement was to be a long one, and no wedding date had been set, Collingridge would fly into drunken rages, arriving at the house late at night, or early in the mornings, banging on doors, even bashing them in, and challenging Frank Graham to a fight. For her part, Isabel was deeply embarrassed, but by then she'd become accustomed to Collingridge's inappropriate behaviour, especially when he'd been drinking heavily. Previously, a wealthy man named Sydney Snow, head of the department store Snows, and later to be knighted, had taken a keen interest in Isabel and escorted her, Phyllis, and Paulette out for an evening's entertainment. It's likely that Snow became acquainted with the sisters after Phyllis requested items from his department store for the shooting of *The Far Paradise*. At the end of the night's festivities, when Snow dropped them back at Drummoyne House, an enraged Collingridge was waiting on the steps and, according to Paula, 'put on the most dreadful act'. Sydney Snow never showed his face again.

In an ironic coda to Collingridge's behaviour, his drunken stunt turned out to be a blessing. The sisters and Collingridge did not know that, at the time of the outing, forty-year-old Snow had been married for thirteen years, and with his wife was now raising a son and two daughters. He'd conveniently tucked his family away in a large, remote home, Bonnie Brae, in the north shore suburb of Wahroonga, hours from the city centre where he worked.

⊹⊱══◉══⊰⊹

In early 1928, an article about Drummoyne House and its planned sale appeared in the *Labor Daily*. The article had no byline, but it was most likely written and submitted by Phyllis to gain free advertising for the sale and possibly secure a price higher than the deteriorating home was worth.

In the months leading up to the article, Isabel had become aware that the mansion was in urgent need of roof repairs and rewiring. For a while, she was forced to either sell or hock her mother's treasured jewellery – expensive gifts from Dr McDonagh to his wife – but soon even the income from this alternative stream reached its limit. By now, the money they'd inherited from Uncle Ernesto had been exhausted and, to keep the family afloat – let alone produce another feature – the sisters had been forced to take out a loan against the value of Drummoyne House.

The article waxes lyrical about the history of the home, playing on the imagined mythology of convict labourers creating secret, subterranean passages for rum smuggling along the Parramatta River. It also poeticises the residency of the McDonagh sisters and their filmmaking careers: 'Its ballroom has known soft candlelight, the delicate lilt of a minuet, the rustle of wide, silken skirts. And later the glare of movie studio lights, the blare of jazz, the tapping of high heels … It will be used for another movie and then (the) owners intend to sell it'.

For the premiere of *The Far Paradise*, the sisters once more organised a private screening at the Prince Edward Theatre on the morning of 19 June 1928, and again invited the governor and his wife; high-society friends such as Elizabeth Foy (wife of retail magnate Mark Foy); the managing director of Hoyts, Stuart Doyle; old family friend and rollerskater Jim Bendrodt, now a famous impresario; and tenacious Frank Graham, who was trying to ride out the veiled hostility of the McDonagh siblings over his engagement to their sister. Again, musical accompaniment was expertly provided by Eddie Horton at the WurliTzer organ.

Isabel enjoyed the fact that during the shooting of every feature, each of her male leads briefly fell in love with her, and she with him. Despite being engaged to Frank Graham, during the shooting of *The Far Paradise*, she and Paul Longuet had held hands one night, but she was surprised when he was not remotely interested in taking the romance further. During the premiere of *The Far Paradise*, however, Isabel found out why: a few rows ahead of her at the theatre, Paul Longuet was sitting in the company of three sailors.

The feature was hailed as an even bigger success than *Those Who Love*. *The Film Weekly* praised the 'highly capable acting ... careful direction and first-class photography'. The *Sunday Times* noted the 'expert lighting and make-up', and the *Sun* declared that the McDonaghs had produced 'a thoroughly convincing and really entertaining screen play', while the *Labor Call* rhapsodised, 'It will burn its appeal into hearts and rouse the slumbering emotions as no other drama in screen history'.

After the thrilling reception of *The Far Paradise*, the sisters finally felt vindicated by all the challenges they'd faced and the risks that they'd taken. It was programmed for two weeks at the Regent Theatre in Sydney, along with the docudrama *The Battles of Coronel and the Falkland Islands*, which was part of the British Empire quota system, introduced in 1927 to curtail the dominance of Hollywood films in Commonwealth countries. A lavish stage show was also part of the entertainment, with Strella Wilson and James Hay offering Gilbert and Sullivan operatic selections, and the Regent Ballet delivering a spirited sailor-girl routine. *The Far Paradise* went on to equal the box office success and soaring popularity of the double bill, at the same theatre, of Charlie Chaplin's *Circus* and Fritz Lang's *Metropolis*, though due to the distribution deal, not enough profits filtered down to MCD Productions to fund their next feature. The McDonaghs were accomplished creative collaborators – in directing, acting, design, and writing – but the business side of their ventures would always be their Achilles heel. Essentially, they were their father's daughters, seduced by the siren call of 'Art', without calculating the cost of such a complicated affair.

A few days after the release of *The Far Paradise,* perhaps due to Frank Graham's connections, Hoyts contracted with British Dominion Films to distribute all their films in 1929. In late July, the film transferred to the Piccadilly Theatre, and then on to Melbourne, Hobart, and regional areas. As John Tulloch notes in his book *Legends of the Screen,* an ongoing war between Hoyts and Union probably contributed to the staggered releases of the motion picture around Australia.

The publicity for the film swelled into the hyperbolic, and in one advertisement it was hailed as, 'Australia's greatest movie', while Hoyts promised audiences that the film 'holds the spectator enthralled from start to finish'. *Those Who Love* had been considered by the press and public as a bit of a fluke, but *The Far Paradise* confirmed the sisters' reputation as serious and successful filmmakers who more than met the high standards set by Hollywood studios.

Since the film took place in a fictional city, the press and public now accepted the fact that the McDonaghs were deliberately avoiding 'Australian' settings and stories and aiming for a more universal cinematic experience. Still, reviewers were beguiled by the breathtaking photography of recognisable places of natural beauty, such as The Gap at Watsons Bay, Farm Cove, the Burragorang Valley, and the Georges River.

With Isabel framed by Paulette's flattering close-ups and illuminated by subtle, indirect lighting techniques, the actress wooed audiences and critics alike. Forty years after its release, film historian Graham Shirley was still impressed by the effect:

The scenes showing the deteriorating relationship between father and daughter ... are the most emotionally potent of the Australian silent film. All of these scenes play against inherent melodrama with their restraint and attention to personal detail. In the best of these, as the father conceals the boyfriend's letters, the despair of Cherry, the daughter, is beautifully underplayed as the camera lingers on her face. In this scene and others, Paulette used her camera and editing to build an emotional pattern of the kind that had moved her in American films.

Before the start of each screening, Isabel would again make a brief appearance on stage to introduce the film and attract even more publicity. Innately a shy woman, she found the experience nerve-wracking and confronting. Acting in front of a camera in the company of her sisters and Jack Fletcher was one thing; appearing on stage, unscripted, in front of hundreds of strangers, was quite another. But during the film's tour, she gradually grew into a poised and accomplished speaker, and charmed audiences around the country, from sophisticated Sydney to outback Orange. On stage, she would appear in a vintage dress that was featured in the film: 'Her pink pompadour frock against the black stage and the blue and gold curtains make for an admirable setting for her Dresden china beauty'.

In the meantime, the results of the Royal Commission on the film industry had been tabulated. The commission had spent nine months travelling to every state and heard evidence from 253 witnesses. Common claims were that Australian films were not up to international standards, that independent Australian films could not compete in an industry monopolised by the American block-booking system, and that censorship of all films, either Australian, British, or American, was either too harsh or not harsh enough. When Isabel appeared before the committee, she stated that she and her sisters believed an overseas market was essential for Australian films and suggested that 'at the start we should confine our production to simple stories. The more ambitious productions will come later ... Australian audiences would soon get tired of the ordinary bush story'. She also lamented that Australian audiences were still prejudiced against paying to see locally made films and, that if a quota were to be introduced, a board should be established to weed out inferior products. In a feisty nod to feminism, she also argued that at least one woman should be appointed to the Censorship Board.

At his appearance before the commission, Gayne Dexter, the proprietor and editor of *Everyone's*, complained about Australian film actors and their plainness, dowdy dress sense, and lack of sophistication, compared to their counterparts in Hollywood. And even though the films of the McDonaghs were an antidote to these portrayals of national crudeness, with critics praising the sartorial elegance of the characters and the natural confidence of their gestures and physicality, they could not compete with the block-booking system that favoured American films.

Louise Lovely proved to be at her visionary best when she suggested to the commission that the Commonwealth government should begin subsidising the industry: 'It would not be a bad idea for the Government to advance money to producers to be paid back later'. Since the 1970s, this has been the most effective support that the government could offer national film production, but in 1927, the idea was dismissed as fanciful. At the end of the study, the commissioners concluded, inexplicably, that there was no evidence to suggest that a covert combine of Australian and American distributors was dominating the market.

Despite impassioned pleas from hundreds of individuals for more strategies to support Australian cinema, the commission determined that 'there is no American combine in existence in Australia exercising a stranglehold over the motion picture industry'. It recommended, instead, a quota system such as the British had implemented, but failed to pass the legislation that would have implemented the recommendation. The only assistance offered to Australian filmmakers was an annual cash prize for the winner of a national film competition. With their next feature film already being written, the determined McDonagh sisters set out to scoop the award.

After the success of *Those Who Love* and *The Far Paradise*, Frank Thring Senior approached the sisters and asked to read the outline of their next planned feature, *The Cheaters*. In 1918, Thring, a former conjurer and projectionist, had become the managing director of JC Williamson Films. And in 1926 the film company merged to become Hoyts, of which Thring was appointed managing director. After reading the scenario, he was so impressed by it that he offered to distribute and exhibit the film and publicise it through his vast connections within the Hoyts network. Thring was a shrewd and highly competitive operator, and he had a reputation for relishing 'the wheeling and dealing, and the startling amounts of money that it could generate'. The fact that Thring made such a generous overture to the sisters is a solid confirmation that they were highly talented and had the potential to attract superlative profits for both Hoyts and MCD Productions.

The McDonaghs, however, were suspicious of the offer and suspected that Thring was trying to take advantage of them. They returned to his office with a counter-offer, proposing that they be advanced 250 pounds per week during a five-week shooting schedule, against the profits that would be made from the eventual release. A bemused Thring flatly refused. He did, however, urge them to reconsider his original offer, and guaranteed that if they accepted it, he would 'send them to Hollywood and sit them on golden thrones'. Paulette later surmised that he'd been insulted by the sisters' rejection and could not understand why they would choose to remain completely independent.

Forty years later, Paulette would admit, 'It was the greatest mistake of our lives'. She also mused that even if Thring had failed to introduce them to Hollywood, he would have, at the very least, employed them in the company he would establish a few years later, Efftee Film Productions.

But was this regret well placed? As head of his own company, Thring would develop a reputation for being a cinematic dictator, appearing on set and often contradicting the notes given by the director and repeatedly undermining his authority. Moreover, he developed a habit of claiming credit for the direction of a film when his input had been negligible. It's hard to imagine outspoken Paulette experiencing any creative satisfaction while being dominated by such a megalomaniacal boss.

The other proposal for the sisters to consider – the offer of marriage to Isabel from a smitten Frank Graham – was also collectively rejected, particularly after they learned that he'd been twice divorced. The possessiveness of the siblings, coupled with Paulette and Phyllis's desire to continue producing films, also contributed to the broken engagement. Graham would go on to take a third wife, but throughout his three marriages, as the sisters later learned, none of his wives ever fell pregnant. Over the years, Paulette, perhaps trying to justify her intervention against Isabel's wedding to Graham, would often say, 'I'm so glad you never married Frank Graham. If you had, you wouldn't have had your three kids'.

Moreover, their decision to reject both offers would have been influenced by the extraordinary success of their second feature, and the almost universal praise of Isabel as an actress:

We would like to say that Miss Lorraine has a screen future here: she would if the future of Australian production was not so far away. Any girl in Hollywood who showed such form in relation to other girls ... would be worked constantly ... [with each role] developing and carrying her closer to stardom. Our conditions are such that so far Miss Lorraine has done only two productions in about eighteen months. There's the pity of it.

In April 1928, the sisters told a Melbourne journalist that after they'd completed two or three more pictures, they intended to travel to England and America and market the films personally. There is no doubt that the McDonaghs – especially Paulette – daydreamed about embarking upon such an independent venture. After all, there had been precedents set by other Australian women who'd found success across the Pacific. But these inspirational women were working in traditional roles as actresses, not directors. And even if there had been opportunities in Hollywood or London for the sisters, it would have been almost impossible to take advantage of them. For one, due to the unfair distribution deals for their first two films, they did not have the funds to finance three sea voyages around the world, on top of hotel accommodation and sundry expenses. Secondly, the youngest of the McDonagh siblings, Paula, would require their care and attention for at least another five years. Thirdly, although they didn't know it in 1928, the window of time that was allowing women film directors to work in Hollywood was slowly starting to close.

By the late 1920s, the only female filmmakers to survive in the industry were those protected by companies managed by men in general, and their husbands in particular. 'Women were allowed to flourish to a certain point and no further', claims writer and historian Helen O'Hara. 'Men controlled the industry, men made business decisions ... Much of the longevity of [Lois] Weber and [Alice] Guy's careers owed to the fact that their husbands were, essentially, their front men.' In England, accomplished scenario writer and film editor Alma Reville, in her mid-twenties, was inundated with career opportunities after her marriage to a young director named Alfred Hitchcock. Even Australia's Louise Lovely depended on her husband and collaborator, Wilton Welch, to co-produce, co-write and co-direct their 1925 silent film, *Jewelled Nights*. No woman in Australia or America was attempting to do what independent Paulette had already done. But there would be consequences for her stubborn refusal to accept that she and her sisters were living in a business world monopolised by those of the opposite sex.

Unlike Lovely, Weber, and Guy, who directed films in the 1920s, Paulette had no colleague to protect her interests and finances, or to promote her talent in a rapidly changing industry dominated by men. There was no one to advise her on the economic side of film production, exhibition, or distribution in Australia and overseas. Had the sisters accepted the professional offer from Frank Thring, or the personal offer from Frank Graham, they might have felt unsatisfied, but they also would have avoided treading the long and difficult road ahead, which was pot-holed by mounting bills, bankruptcy, and the sudden appearance of Hollywood 'talkies' that would transform the filmmaking process entirely.

To pay off their growing debts, in August 1928 the sisters proceeded with the sale of Drummoyne House to Walter John Simpson, and reluctantly relinquished the one asset that they'd ever owned. But what to do with all their father's furniture, art, and memorabilia? As a temporary measure, they again decided to move the collection into a storage unit until they could find a new and permanent home. During that time, the storage unit caught on fire and the siblings lost some of their father's precious collection, including the silver cup affectionately inscribed to the doctor by one of his former patients, Hollywood actor Lionel Belmore.

But there was another reason why the sisters were hesitant to leave Australia and pursue a career in Hollywood. By October 1928, their rebellious younger sister Anita had fallen pregnant out of wedlock.

11

MAGIC AND MIRACLES
(1929)

By the end of 1928, the siblings were waiting for a house in Darling Point to become available, suggesting that yet again they were the recipients of a generous and charitable friend who would allow the family to live in their home for free, or at a greatly reduced rent. While they were waiting for the house, the siblings moved into Carisbrooke, a new apartment building in the art deco style on Springfield Avenue, Kings Cross, and just a ten-minute stroll from where their mother had been born in Woolloomooloo.

The accommodation provided two bedrooms and a narrow sunroom, plus a combined living and dining room, kitchen, and one bathroom. John and Grant would have occupied one bedroom, and the three sisters the other. There, again sharing one bedroom, the heated all-night discussions between the sisters continued, so much so that the downstairs neighbours initially assumed the arguments were becoming violent and wondered if they should call the police.

Teenage Paula, like her sister Anita before her, was exercising typical teenage obstinance. As usual, it was left solely to Isabel to exert a stabilising parental influence and persuade her to enrol in yet another boarding school, this time in Potts Point.

'I went through that rebellious stage of where I wouldn't have my schooling at all, and it upset her badly', said Paula, full of regret. 'And it was only my appreciation of what she – how much she loved me, that I agreed to go to boarding school. Only for her sake. I wouldn't do it for my own, or for anybody else's'. Paula promised Isabel that she would stay at the school for one year, but at the end of that year, Paula, to her dismay, realised that she loved boarding at the school, and ended up staying for a further two years and matriculating. 'It was the making of me', she admitted. St Vincent's boarding school was just around the corner from the McDonagh apartment, at the northern end of Victoria Street.

While the sisters were involved in the pre-production of their next film, Anita and her boyfriend, Gregory Blackall, married in a hasty wedding before her pregnancy began to show. The couple had met a few years before, at Drummoyne House, as Gregory had been a schoolmate of John's at Riverview. We do not know if the McDonagh sisters attended the ceremony, but there was no announcement of the wedding in newspapers, and no commemorative photographs were taken of the occasion.

In the 1920s and early '30s, Kings Cross began to assume the bohemian air of Paris's Montmartre, or London's Soho, or New York's Greenwich Village, boasting flower stalls, bookstores, and cafés by day, and raffish nightclubs and sly grog joints by night. It was close to the National Art School in Darlinghurst, and a ten-minute walk to the city. It was cheap; it was handy; and it was just what the McDonagh sisters needed after the loss of their home, to live among fellow modern artists who lived for their work, rather than for the securities of suburbia.

By the time they moved in, many of the colonial-era mansions of the area had been demolished to make way for high-rise art deco apartment buildings such as Birtley Towers, Cahors, Macleay

Regis, and Franconia, some of which provided bellboys, porters, and even their own restaurants. But Carisbrooke employed only a caretaker to attend to the needs of its residents. Smaller homes such as terraces were being subdivided into flatettes and bedsits, attracting single working-class people, and struggling writers and artists to the area, including poets Christopher Brennan, Mary Gilmore, Kenneth Slessor, Ron McCuaig, and Douglas Stewart; aspiring actor Peter Finch; royal biographer Hector Bolitho; prose writers Steele Rudd and Sumner Locke Elliott; journalist and professional bohemian, Dulcie Deamer; and the infamous eccentric, Bea Miles. As Cam Bone recalls in her memoir, *Knock Around the Cross*, 'rents were low and one could starve much slower in the Cross than anywhere else in Sydney'.

During the time that the McDonaghs lived on Springfield Avenue, John briefly moved out and into an apartment on Womerah Avenue, a five-minute walk from Carisbrooke. While there, he secured a job as a labourer.

The shifty criminal element, so present in the scenario the sisters were currently developing, also pulsed through Kings Cross and Darlinghurst. Just months before the McDonaghs moved in, Frankie 'The Little Gunman' Green, accompanied by 'Big Jim' Devine (first husband of infamous brothel owner Tilly Devine) shot one man dead in the Strand Hotel and seriously wounded another in an ongoing gang war just around the corner, on William Street.

With the opening of the California Café on Darlinghurst Road in 1929, an artistic atmosphere blossomed through the Cross and into coffee shops such as The Arabian and The Willow, where locals gathered, surrounded by hand-painted murals and live music. At the time, Kings Cross was the most lively and tolerant place in Australia, and the focus of all that was new and modern, including architecture, food, music, writing, technology, and design. The sisters would have been attracted to the area for its cheap rents, for the thrill of all things modern, and for the company of fellow creative misfits. As Cross resident of the '30s, Lydia Gill, observed of the tenants in her building:

> There was Selena who made junk jewellery from glass beads and copper fuse wire, Nancy who believed in the curative powers of carrot juice and who worshipped her cat, the lass who took university extension course, and one who travelled with a circus and was cut in half at every performance.

Also living in Carisbrooke was a Houdini-type fakir named Rahman Bey who had been travelling the world performing stunts such as hypnotism, walking through fire, and being buried alive. Bey shared his apartment with his manager, Bruno Valletty, and Valletty's father, who acted as valet and cook in the home. Throughout the 1920s, variety theatre would showcase dwarves and giants, sword swallowers and fire eaters, tightrope walkers, tank divers, song and dance duets, crooners, tap dancers, novelty musicians, jugglers, and exotic magicians. But Bey wasn't just another vaudevillian doing the rounds. In fact, he proudly claimed to be an 'Egyptian Miracle Man', having once sealed himself inside a metal coffin that was submerged in Sydney Harbour for fifty minutes, perplexing attendant doctors. The trio arrived in Sydney in early 1928 and had been performing sold-out shows at the Stadium and the Tivoli.

Paula was later under the impression that the McDonaghs only met Bey and Valletty after they'd moved into Carisbrooke, but as early as 12 March 1928, when shooting of *The Far Paradise* began, Valletty had written a romantic inscription in Paulette's autograph book, in Italian, praising her gifts as an artist:

Come il Poeta, il Pittore, il Musicista
e gli artisti in generale, l'Arte
risveglia la Mente ed il genio progredisce
Paulette, un Genio raro
del secolo 'moderno', ben meritato
sia sempre suo perenne successo.

[Like the Poet, the Painter, the Composer
and all the artists, Art
awakes minds and genius progresses
Paulette, a rare genius of the modern century:
well-merited be her perennial success for ever.]

Unlike Australian male friends who in the book had mocked Paulette's role as a director with their ditties and cartoons, Italian Valletty admired and honoured her abilities and was not shy about celebrating them. Obviously, the two groups had met much earlier than during the residency in Kings Cross, when the McDonaghs were still living at Drummoyne House, throwing wild parties, dancing, and drinking champagne. The sisters would have been attracted to Bey's unabashed theatricality, his penchant for fancy dress and for playing a role as an exotic and mysterious magician. Both the McDonaghs and their neighbours were involved in the showbusiness of illusion and make-believe.

On Sunday afternoons, the sisters, Rahman Bey and Bruno Valletty would drive down to St Vincent's boarding school and smuggle boxes of cakes and biscuits over the fence – not only for Paula but for the entire school population. Even though the habit transgressed the strict Catholic school rules, the nuns invariably turned a blind eye.

⤙✦⤚

Rahman Bey inevitably developed strong feelings for Isabel. To express them, he once gifted her a pet rabbit, which she named 'Ramona', a feminine form of her beau's stage name. Bey had smooth olive skin, penetrating dark eyes, a moustache, and a goatee beard. He was slim; his limbs were skeined with muscles, and he wore a turban. Essentially, he was tall, dark, handsome – and oh-so mysterious: the complete antithesis of Isabel's former love, businessman Frank Graham. Bey began romancing Isabel, double-dating with Paulette and Valletty. An October 1928 article described the effect of Bey's persona on women when he was socialising at a Sydney nightclub:

> One of the best publicity stunts round town is being staged by Bruno Valetty [sic], who now again brings his Egyptian, Rahman Bey, to Romano's for all the girls to see. The Bey, perfectly tailored with natty red velvet millinery, sits there quietly and has only an occasional dance, so that the illusion of Bedouins, hot sands, and Miss Edith Hull's romance is not entirely shattered.

The 'romance' the reporter refers to was Hull's popular 1919 novel, *The Sheik*, which in 1921 was adapted into a silent film of the same name, starring matinee idol Rudolph Valentino. Like Valentino, Rahman Bey was Italian and, while performing, he always wore, as did Valentino in the film, flowing white robes and a traditional white cotton headscarf, called a *keffiyeh*, held in place by an *agal*, a strong, knotted cord. By aligning himself visually with the handsome and arresting Valentino, Bey attracted more and more attention from smitten and adoring women.

Bruno Valletty, who spoke with a strong Italian accent, was the opposite of the inscrutable Bey: garrulous, happy, and full of fun. 'Oh, he was a lovely bloke', said Paula. 'We all loved him.' While Bey and Isabel developed a crush on each other, Bruno fell even harder for Paulette, and the headstrong film director, to her dismay, also found herself falling in love with him.

The sisters, John, and Grant would take Rahman and Bruno out for weekend drives, on boating trips up the Hawkesbury River, and on picnics. Photos of the group during one such outing reveal the sisters playfully teasing Rahman Bey by pretending to worship him as if he were the second coming of Christ. Good-natured Bey plays along with the ruse. A group shot of the picnic reveals all the McDonagh siblings, except Anita, along with Valletty, Bey, Valletty's father, Phyllis's lifelong friend, Gertie Purcell, and John's friend, Hugh Foster, who in the 1950s would go on to become the Mayor of Woollahra.

Even though Bey and Valletty were from another country and culture, they had much in common with the McDonaghs: they lived by only their wits, in the fickle entertainment industry, and without any fixed address.

Rahman Bey first appeared in public in London in 1926, just months after the death of the world-famous Houdini. He'd arrived on a plane (it was not reported from where) and was swiftly followed by the arrival of another mystic/fakir named Tahra Bey. Rahman claimed he was a delegate from the Egyptian Psychic Union, that he hailed from Eritrea, and that he was twenty-six. He also claimed that his mystical practices caused him to refrain from alcohol and meat, though in another article he admits to eating meat and other Egyptian dishes; and in a photograph snapped by one of the McDonaghs, he can be seen in Hyde Park smoking a cigarette. In terms of inventing a public persona that would attract free press, Bey was a master and could have taught the publicity-generating McDonaghs a thing or two about creating a sensation.

On 28 December 1928, *The Jazz Singer* opened at Union Theatre's Lyceum Theatre, Sydney, featuring a synchronised recorded musical score, lip-synchronous singing, and speech in several sequences, including six songs performed by its star, Al Jolson. The part talkie had been released in Hollywood the year before by Warner Bros with its new Vitaphone sound-on-disc technology. In the intervening months, filmmakers around the world collectively began to panic: Was this 'synchronised sound' a passing fad or was it here to stay? How did Warner Bros develop the sound technology, and could it be copied or appropriated by other companies?

At the time, there was no technology available in Australia to make a 'talkie' feature and, at the end of 1928, most filmmakers were content to proceed to produce their films in the traditional way, even though the first talkie film to screen in Australia ran for over six months, breaking all former box office records. For the McDonaghs and other filmmakers, the popularity of *The Jazz Singer* set a chilling precedent and put pressure on the industry to develop the necessary technology to add sound to their features.

In February 1929, no doubt influenced by Paulette's obsession with filmmaking, and the entertainment revolution of the 'talkies', Valletty registered a motion picture production company, Triumphant Films, located on Castlereagh Street in Sydney. It's more than likely that Valletty and Paulette were planning to go into business together, with him as a producer and her as writer and director.

Paulette continued to work on film storylines with Phyllis, developing plots and characters, after which time the former would spend months formally writing the scenario. At the end of that process, Phyllis re-joined her sister to co-write the dialogue into intertitles.

In conceiving *The Cheaters*, Paulette and Phyllis again exploited Isabel's strength as an actor by focusing the scenario on a sole female lead character, one who boldly cracks safes and breaks into buildings, but who can just as easily settle into the embrace of a moon-eyed lover.

The elements of earlier McDonagh treatments and films are reworked into their third feature: the poisonous and misplaced need for revenge; mistaken identity; romance blossoming against a background of water; and an ingenue caught in the clutches of a corrupt father figure, who tries to come between her and her own true love.

The plot of *The Cheaters* again involves two fathers who are also old enemies: the first, Bill Marsh, is sent to gaol, and the second one, John Travers, is responsible for his arrest and imprisonment. Marsh swears that he'll eventually exact revenge on Travers, and so when he is finally released from gaol, he kidnaps Travers' baby daughter, Paula, and raises her to be a charming, beautiful jewel thief who becomes a vital part of his slick crime gang. Marsh's criminal headquarters is a remote, imposing mansion complete with a flashing warning device on his desk to alert him of approaching visitors, and an enormous, circular secret vault in a wall.

The opening sequence shows a rich, middle-aged woman and her attractive daughter gazing at jewellery inside a luxury store. The younger woman spots an expensive necklace and begs her mother to buy it for her. When the mother hesitates, the daughter pleads, reminding her that her father would relent and purchase it, if only he were here and not so busy at work. His office is nearby, and the young woman asks the manager to allow her to leave with the necklace, and present it to her father for approval, after which she'll return and arrange for payment. The manager is wary until the mother presents her visiting card, stating that she is a 'Lady', and offers to wait in the store as collateral until her daughter returns. The manager can see no harm in the proposal and allows the daughter to leave with the necklace.

Time passes as mother and manager wait for the daughter's return. Finally, the door bursts open and two policemen arrive, spot the mother, and immediately arrest her. The startled manager demands an explanation, and the policemen announce that they've been tracking this woman for some time, that she's a member of an elaborate crime gang. They wrestle her out the door.

Inside Marsh's lair, the policemen, mother, and daughter laugh about their latest heist and proffer the necklace to Marsh. They are all part of his gang, with adopted daughter, Paula, his most prized member.

Next, Marsh sends Paula to a luxury hotel on a solo residency to rob rich idle women of their precious jewels. She arrives at the hotel and checks into a sumptuous suite. But instead of performing her usual, subtle crime spree, Paula meets a dashing young man named Lee and the couple spend two weeks together. They motor through the countryside and spend tender moments beside lakes and fountains. Lee is the adopted son of her father's arch-enemy, Travers, but Paula remains ignorant of this connection. Eventually, Lee proposes marriage, but Paula, keenly aware of her 'father' and his criminal empire, feels she is unable to break free of her past. Instead, she leaves him a brief note and disappears. After she returns to Marsh's headquarters, she despairs at the desperate lives that she and Marsh lead. 'Cheaters, cheating life!' she cries.

Lee, confused and sad, retreats to the rooftop of his apartment building in the city. In the background stand the two arches of the almost completed Sydney Harbour Bridge, which are yet to meet at the summit, a visual representation of his sudden separation from Paula. Lee's head in the foreground fills the space between the arches, as if he is mentally trying to join the two sides.

Softening towards his trembling adopted daughter, Marsh promises her that once she performs one final planned crime, they will pack up and leave their sordid ways behind. Paula finally relents and, wearing a veiled hat, breaks into the mansion that Marsh has indicated and begins to crack the safe, while her father's sidekick waits outside as a lookout. While doing so, she is disturbed by a resident, who discovers her trespass and attempted robbery. She's shocked to realise that the resident is, in fact, her lover, Lee, and that she is burglarising his family's home. She tries to explain to him, and a disgusted Travers Senior, that she did not know they were the owners of the home, but she and the sidekick are arrested and taken away.

Marsh eventually exacts his ultimate revenge by summoning John Travers to his headquarters and revealing the truth – that the wanton thief who attempted to rob his home is, in fact, his own daughter, stolen as a baby and raised as a common criminal. Travers is naturally mortified by the revelation. Hearing police sirens, Marsh realises that his sidekick, now in goal, has reported his address to the authorities, and that he is now trapped with no way out. He gulps down a pre-prepared poisonous concoction and dies.

A shocked Travers Senior withdraws the charge against Paula, and the two reconcile in a beautifully underplayed scene. Paula, now untethered from her criminal past, is free to marry Lee, who also happens to be her adopted brother. Here, the main theme of the sisters' films – romantic love versus family loyalty – literally and figuratively collide, eventually resolving itself in a form of enmeshment that mirrored the one running rampant through their own family.

The film *The Cheaters* begins with an image of the Three Fates (a trio of elderly women spinning yarn in a gloomy cavern), suggesting that no matter how many unknown forces disrupt a life, one's destiny will always prevail. The sisters believed that their heritage as the daughters of a high-society doctor, who was himself the son of a doctor, had gifted them with the potential to overcome any obstacle, no matter how reduced their circumstances became. They also believed that the superior talents with which they'd been born would eventually be recognised by authorities in their field, just as Travers Senior recognises the innocent stolen daughter in the adult jewel thief.

Many contemporary viewers have compared the set of Marsh's hideaway to design aspects of Fritz Lang's German Expressionist crime classic, *Dr Mabuse, der Spieler,* or *Doctor Mabuse, the Gambler* (1922). Alfred Hitchcock's early work attracted similar comparisons, but, as one Jesuit critic has suggested, Hitchcock's admiration of the qualities of German Expressionism didn't manifest in a lightning bolt straight after watching the films of Lang and Murnau ... rather, it developed naturally from 'the religious and educational atmosphere of St Ignatius College (London) prior to World War One', which was 'heavily baroque and was congruent with the new wave of Expressionism'. The same could be said of Paulette's direction and Phyllis's design, and the pre-war influence of Kincoppal Sacred Heart School, with its embellished rituals, ornamental decoration, and Gothic stone chapel.

There was a specific reason why the sisters were working so hard on their next project. In April 1928, the Commonwealth had finally acted upon two of the nineteen recommendations from the Royal Commission that they were able to institute within the constraints of the constitution: a prize for Best Production, and another for Best Scenario. It was to be funded by increased duty on imported films. But if this action was an attempt to establish a quota system for Australian films in Australia, it certainly fell short. This was because federal and state governments had little motivation in curtailing the American dominance of the local film industry. And why would they, when they were receiving what amounted to incentives bordering on lucrative kickbacks. In 1927, the federal government received 140 000 pounds a year from duty on imported films and a further 37 000 pounds a year from an entertainment tax. Adding insult to injury, local film producers such as the McDonaghs were required to pay a high tax duty on raw imported film stock. Subsidies and quotas to bolster locally made feature films were in no way a priority, despite the thousands of jobs it provided for Australian workers.

The conditions of the prize allowed for entries from any Commonwealth country, which of course included England, with its studio system and superior resources. Still, the ever-determined sisters remained undaunted, vowing to produce a feature that would be so outstanding that it would take out the coveted first prize, which was 10 000 pounds. The deadline for the prize was 31 March 1930.

While he was at Riverview, John was friends with a fellow student who eventually became a close friend of the family, often visiting and staying over at night and on weekends. Neville Macken was the son of Sir Hugh Macken, and a grandson of HV Foy, of Mark Foy's department store fame. In March 1927, he sold his 'Mani' sheep station in the Cannock district of New South Wales and was yet to reinvest the funds. He'd also married a woman from Orange, who did not wish to continue living in the country, so the couple moved to Sydney and bought an historic property in Penrith, named 'Fern Hill'. At the time, Macken was thirty-four years old, bored, and felt as if he was far too young to put his feet up and retire.

Due to the flawed distribution deal the sisters had accepted for *The Far Paradise*, there was not enough profit to finance their next feature. Therefore, when John asked Macken if he was interested in financing the next McDonagh film, the cashed-up former farmer was more than enthusiastic.

Out of all the McDonagh siblings, Paulette was the one who impressed Macken the most with her intelligence, drive, and exactitude. 'Paulette was the brains behind the whole thing', Macken once remarked. 'She was an extraordinary girl.'

12

TROUBLE WITH TALKIES
(1929)

The six-month shoot of *The Cheaters* began in June 1929. Interiors were filmed at Australasian Film Studio, while the exteriors fanned out into several locations around Sydney, including Gowan Brae mansion in North Parramatta and the Ambassadors Café in the basement of Sydney's Strand Arcade, coincidentally the same site of the earlier ramshackle boxing stadium owned by their father's business partner, Larry Foley, and where the doctor himself had spent so many happy hours. The shooting of *The Cheaters* coincided with the screening of a number of American 'part-talkies' – films with songs and minimal dialogue – in Australia. But these films were still something of a novel oddity and the sisters decided to stick to their original plans to produce *The Cheaters* as a silent.

As usual, Paulette cast *The Cheaters* from a seat in a theatre. One night, when she was still writing the scenario, she watched Arthur Greenaway in the role of Richard III. 'And I sat and I watched and knew that this is my man', she said. 'He was a fantastic actor. So I went behind and I engaged him immediately ... He did a magnificent part in that.'

They employed more professional actors than they had in their previous two films, including twenty-three-year-old singer Josef Bambach as the young male lead, and Leal Douglas to play the Lady; silent film stars John Faulkner and Claude Turton were contracted into secondary roles. The younger siblings stepped in as extras: Grant played the doorman of the bank; John played the shop assistant in the jewellery store; and in a flashback sequence, Phyllis played the mother of Paula Travers as a baby.

All the interiors of *The Cheaters* were shot at a studio. The McDonaghs transported furniture from the storage unit and had a set built according to designs created by Phyllis and Paulette. In the scenes set inside the crime boss's cavernous hideaway, the sisters used some of Neville Macken's furniture, including an Italian oak table with atlases carved into the legs. Within the same set, a moveable staircase was built to lead up to a huge, round, walk-in wall safe, both of which were operated from behind by the younger McDonagh siblings. 'We knew what we wanted', Paulette claimed. 'You had to have exactly the set for your story. And we believed that we could do it.'

Editor Bill Shepherd was on set during the filming of *The Cheaters*. He distinctly remembered that between takes in the studio, there were a lot of heated discussions between the sisters before they finally agreed, and Paulette took charge.

During the shoot, younger sister Anita went into labour with her first child. The mother-to-be booked into a private hospital, Seacombe, on Wolseley Street in Drummoyne, only 400 metres from Drummoyne House. On 29 July 1929, she gave birth to a daughter, Ann. However, the baby's respiratory system was so compromised that Anita would spend the rest of her life caring for the fragile daughter whose conception had changed the course of her life.

The new parents moved to Glebe Point Road in Glebe so that Gregory could begin his studies in Pharmacy at Sydney University.

As Anita often remarked to her children, 'I put the white coat on your father's back', suggesting that his sudden elevation to fatherhood meant that he'd had to knuckle down, earn his degree, and begin to support his family.

Meanwhile, the three older sisters resumed production of *The Cheaters*. As usual, Phyllis was on hand to secure permission to use various locations. 'We had everybody that helped us', said Paulette. ''Cause I believed in something ... genuine. We weren't pulling any tricks on them.' Phyllis also had to secure a believable location to represent a prison. She explains,

> My man at the top in this instance was the Commissioner
> of Police, and I had a personal interview with him at Phillip
> Street headquarters. I asked for the correct layout [design]
> for a prison identity card ... and also the correct details in
> building a prison cell set, together with a prisoner's uniform.
> He was greatly intrigued by this somewhat unusual request
> and insisted on hearing all our story. Again, it worked the
> oracle ... not only did the Police Commissioner suggest
> bringing in our actors to police headquarters to have their
> photographs taken for inclusion on the required police
> identity card, but he arranged for us to go out to Long Bay
> [Gaol] and to photograph our scene in an authentic prison
> cell. Our chief character in this scene was also fitted out with
> an authentic prisoner's uniform.

The way that Phyllis tells this story suggests that when she first met the commissioner, she fully intended to secure the use of the authentic prison card, the uniform, and the cell, but through her restraint and charm, she'd made it seem as if it had been the commissioner's idea all along.

When Phyllis was required to locate a plush office for the set of a bank manager's office, she used the same modus operandi.

The best office building she could find was one that had been recently built in Martin Place:

> When I told the secretary I wanted to see the director on important business, he must have thought that I was about to deposit one million dollars. For, almost at once, I was ushered into the director's office and it was as I imagined an office de luxe. Deep pile carpet underfoot, handsome furnishings, and a magnificent polished desk that looked half-a-mile across. Here, again, I was to find, the story of our enterprise immediately caught the director's interest. He finally agreed to loan his office to us for one Saturday afternoon's shooting. There was an amusing sequel to this: when we arrived on the arranged date, with cameramen, technicians, and the company of actors, we were met at the entrance by an officer in uniform who kept us under surveillance with a revolver for the entire shooting of the scene.

Exteriors were shot at Centennial Park and Sydney's Royal National Park. Another location was the roof garden of the Austral Flats, on Macquarie Street, which managed to capture in the background the unfinished northern section of the Harbour Bridge, Sydney's monument to modernism.

The single camera used to film *The Cheaters* still required the use of klieg lights to illuminate the set, but, again, the intense radiance from the globes temporarily damaged the eyes of some of the actors and crew. They suffered from intense, burning pain and, halfway through the shoot, one of the male actors, probably inexperienced Josef Bambach, could no longer bear the agony. He stormed off the set and fled to his flat in Woolloomooloo, refusing to return. Ever-stubborn Paulette followed him home and found him sitting in the darkness, feeling sorry for himself:

But I could take it because I was determined that the film had to be done; you had to take everything. And he wasn't going to take it. And I sat with him for about an hour I guess it was and I talked and talked. I said, 'Now, you get over it ... I know the agony you're going through now, because I've been through it. And like the cameraman, all of us, but you can't give up. Once you get it you won't get it a second time ... You're halfway through and you'll [give] a magnificent performance ... Are you going to throw that away? ... I expect you on the set tomorrow ... If you don't you're going to lose one of the best performances of your life.'

No one, it seems, could resist Paulette's passion, grit, and perseverance. The next morning, the affected actor appeared on set, ready to complete his scenes.

Another of the actors was Kate Trefle, who'd previously played Lady Manton in *Those Who Love,* and who at the time was ascending Sydney's social ladder. It was she who helped the sisters attract the required upper-class couples to appear without pay in the film. Trefle also tried to persuade the sisters to accept invitations to the best and most exclusive events on the calendar. Predictably, the sisters were not interested in hobnobbing with the wealthy and powerful, and would invariably turn these invitations down, preferring, as usual, the familiar company of each other.

'We were so loyal', said Paulette. 'We were so close. We didn't need outside friends or companionship with any people.' When asked if they took any notice of what was going on in Sydney society, Paulette was dismissive. 'No, it didn't matter to us. Couldn't give a damn ... You're wasting your time if you worry about [other] people.'

The people with whom they did enjoy socialising were fellow artists and actors – ones who shared a similar sense of playfulness and fun. During the shooting of *The Cheaters,* the actor playing the handsome love interest, Josef Bambach, must have ended up socialising in the home of the McDonaghs because he got hold of Paulette's autograph book and composed a funny, affectionate ditty about Paulette's perceived ability to emasculate men, along with a drawing of her standing with a clipboard beside a camera, directing a film:

> To Dear Paulette – my would-be bloke
> that you've changed your spots
> To me's a joke
> Your heart's too big – to me you're Eve
> So pick up your chattel
> From this make believe
> Your feats accomplished – my would-be bloke
> to the fires of success.
> 'Cheaters' add more coke
> The works you've done – make blokes like me
> heave up their breasts
> with jealousy.

On another occasion, during the production of *The Cheaters*, the sisters drove over to the north shore to visit John Faulkner, who was also appearing in the film. When they arrived, they found Faulkner pleasantly drunk and joined him on the second floor of his home to also enjoy a glass or two. As the day wore on, Faulkner grew nauseous and threw up through the open upstairs window. Unfortunately, the projectile vomit also collected his upper false teeth, which fell out of his mouth and slid down the roof. A tipsy Paulette attempted to retrieve them by leaning out of the window with a fishing rod and casting the line out across the tiles.

In June 1929, the same month that shooting for *The Cheaters* began, Isabel exploited her charm, good looks, and reputation as actress Marie Lorraine to form a partnership with Belgian photographer René Pardon. Together, they opened a plush photographic studio in the city, just six doors down from the fashionable Ambassadors Café, with Isabel managing the booking and greeting of clients, while Pardon managed the photography and printing. As usual, the McDonagh gift for self-promotion and publicity was soon on display in the press:

> On calling here to see Miss McDonagh, we found her looking very pretty and efficient, sitting at a trim desk in the corner of a charming blue and gold reception room. She is looking forward to making a great success of the venture, and wishes it made known that clients are to make themselves quite at home here, and use the studio as a meeting place, where a quiet cigarette could be smoked amid restful surroundings while waiting for sittings.

At around the same time, Isabel became a sitter herself, making extra money by posing as a model for the painter Thea Proctor, whose studio on George Street, near Circular Quay, was only a ten-minute walk away.

Proctor was part of the modernist movement in art and design that gained momentum in the late 19th and early 20th century, and by the time Isabel had begun sitting for her in the late 1920s, Proctor's public profile was at its peak. Like her paintings and drawings, her studio was the embodiment of beauty and clarity: 'It offered a sense of keen and cool delight to the visitor ascending from the grime of the city streets'. Proctor had moved into it in 1921, soon after returning from her second residency in London. The light-flooded space was a work of art in itself, with paintings and objects of contrasting colours hanging against white walls.

Proctor was a contemporary of Margaret Preston, but unlike Preston, she was not enamoured of strictly Australian subject matter. In her 1923 watercolours, Proctor repositioned the gaze of the viewer away from representations of the bush and outback towns to a new and fresh image of urban contentment: the light-filled interior – and in their filmmaking, the McDonaghs were striving to do the same. These women deliberately created art from the sensation and thrill of living in the city. And they collectively grew to exemplify 'the new woman', in art as well as in life.

Just as the McDonaghs replaced farm horses with automobiles, and haystacks with chaise longues, Proctor jettisoned historical scenes for modern inventions such as aeroplanes, searchlights, and high-rise buildings, particularly in her fan paintings. In Isabel, Proctor had found the perfect model upon which to project her urbane and modernist sensibilities.

While Phyllis wrote and submitted articles and Isabel worked as a receptionist and model in the city, stubborn Paulette stayed at home with her brothers. She would not be enticed into the real world by finding work in a shop or, even worse, an office. To be fair, Isabel and Phyllis possessed talents that could be easily adapted to other occupations, such as journalism and modelling. But in 1929, there were no jobs available in Australia for a young, female film director.

Despite her full-time job in the photographic studio and part-time job in the painting studio, by October Isabel could no longer afford to pay the bills and was forced to declare bankruptcy. In the same month, a creditor's petition from Kenmore Ltd, directed at Isabel, appeared in the press. On 2 November, another bankruptcy notice appeared, this time in relation to unpaid taxes. Three days later, yet another petition appeared from Kenmore Ltd. Then, on 3 December 1929, Mr AG de L Arnold appeared for the petitioning creditors, but it was adjourned again, with a view to a settlement. But the matter wasn't resolved until February the following year when leave was given by the court to withdraw the petition. It suggests that the sisters had by then come to an acceptable settlement.

The final scenes of *The Cheaters* were shot in November, six months after the initial ones were filmed. The sisters used their social connections to their advantage when they invited the governor's daughter, Elaine de Chair, and many other socialites, to be extras in sequences shot at the Ambassadors Café. The extras were asked to wear their best finery, so the budget didn't have to accommodate costuming. Investor Neville Macken also played an extra, appearing in formal evening wear as one of the guests. In his scene, he was ushered to a table to meet his fiancée (Elaine de Chair), and her mother (Leal Douglas), who are furious with him for arriving late.

With her usual panache, Phyllis had arranged for the use of the club throughout an entire Sunday night for free. Paulette recalled,

> ... when they closed at 2 o'clock, I took over ... we moved in
> all our lights and we kept the staff on all night from 2 till 6
> the next morning. Worked all night with the original waiters
> ... it had to be original. It had to be true ... they were all
> real people. The waiter, the head waiter ... he belongs at the
> Ambassador ... Then the other men that had the – they were
> all staff. They were genuine ... the real people. Not made up.

The sisters cleverly created a fictional country hotel by combining the exterior of the Ranelagh Hotel in Robertson, the lobby of the Hotel Australia, the dining room at the Ambassadors Café, and sets at the Bondi studio.

Yet another all-night session was pulled on Friday 21 November, when the cast and crew had to shoot scenes inside the Hotel Australia. The first to arrive were the electricians, just after midnight, who were armed with yards of wire, cameras, and lights. An hour later, the cast appeared, about forty frisky extras dressed in tuxedos and glamorous evening gowns, masked in thick make-up, excited and laughing at the prospect of appearing in a film.

Next to arrive was Paulette, who beelined around the lounge, checking lights, cameras, and backgrounds. After announcing a few firm instructions, she choreographed the crowd into their places and told them what to do, and when. The sisters had invited a journalist from the *Sun* newspaper, who published a regular column entitled 'Topics for Women', and who succinctly described Paulette's brisk, authoritative directing style for her fascinated readers:

> 'Now, are you ready?' came her cry at last; 'We're really going to take it this time. Come along, Nancy and Jean. Walk quickly across. That's right. Now greet the women. Say, "So here you are!" and all walk off to the right. You three men over there, keep on talking. That's right. Now, Josef, say, "There's the lift, I must go". Come on, girls. That's your cue to cross over and leave the lounge.'

The shoot didn't end until 4 am. The last to leave the set were the cameraman, Fletcher, as well as Paulette and her exhausted siblings – even the youngest, Paula, who'd watched from behind the scenes with absolute awe.

In the same 'Topics for Women' article, the sisters claimed that *The Cheaters* would be 'Australia's first talkie', which they planned to release early the following year (1930).

At the time the sisters made this statement, they knew they were facing stiff competition from other companies keen to win the national filmmaking prize of 10 000 pounds. While they were shooting *The Cheaters*, Artaus Productions was producing the feature *Fellers*, starring Arthur Tauchert, about three friends in the Australian Light Horse Brigade during the Palestine Campaign of the First World War. It was saturated with mateship and slapstick humour, but set in the desert rather than the bush. The McDonaghs must have got wind of the fact that Artaus was scrambling to find a way to add dialogue and music to its film. The sense of competition would have been overwhelming for the sisters, who were regretting their earlier decision to produce *The Cheaters* as a silent film. They were now desperate to win that 10 000 pounds, which could finance up to six or seven future films.

13

THE CRASH
(1929–1930)

While the McDonaghs were racing to complete *The Cheaters*, and dodging bill collectors and court summonses, the rest of the world was collapsing financially. On 29 October 1929, the Wall Street stock market crashed, the day after the largest sell-off of shares in US history, which mirrored the crash of the London stock exchange only a month before. It triggered the Great Depression and, for the next few years, Australia and many other nations would struggle through poverty and stunted economic growth.

The imposition of talking pictures, coupled with the king-hit of the Depression, devastated the film industry. Unemployment soared and cinema attendance dropped. In Hollywood, studio bosses were thrown into utter panic. The president of RKO, for example, announced that unless radical changes were made, 'the industry would be bankrupt within three months', while at Warner Bros staff was cut drastically, as were the salaries of its most glamorous stars.

American films and their block-booking contracts continued to dominate Australian theatres, to the detriment of local film-makers. By the end of the 1920s, the distributor Australasian Films, which also ran Australia's only significant production company, and was allied to Union Theatres, still relied on Hollywood for 90 per cent of its product. Thus, many local films struggled to find a release, mostly because they were silent.

In Australia, Stuart Doyle had no choice but to liquidate Union Theatres and restructure his network of companies. In 1931, he would form Greater Union Theatres, and the following year stage a temporary partial merger with Hoyts. However, his power over the industry was greatly diminished and he would never regain his former influence.

The sisters had planned to release *The Cheaters* at the end of 1929 but, with the popularity of the American talkies growing day by day, decided to postpone the premiere until they'd added a musical score and three sound sequences to the film – the same formula employed in the final cut of the hugely popular *Jazz Singer*. Neville Macken offered to stump up the money for the sound conversion, but at that time, Australia still lacked the technology to produce a talkie.

The technical and financial challenges that came with the arrival of sound brought Australian feature film production to an abrupt halt. Some local cameramen and technicians were able to override overseas patents on sound-recording equipment, developing their own methods, but the process was complicated and expensive, putting even more pressure on independent companies that did not have the financial resources to absorb such costs. Neville Macken, along with Jack Fletcher's parents, funded Fletcher's experiments with sound-on-film at his Standardtone Laboratories behind his parents' home on Edgecliff Road in Woollahra.

For a while, the sisters contemplated sending the film to Hollywood for synchronisation, but before they could do so, they learned that a company in Melbourne, Vocalion, had recently imported a 33 rpm disc recorder for talkies.

Upon hearing this news, Paulette and Isabel immediately climbed into their car and drove all day and night, without a break, to Melbourne. Not only did they plan to shoot several scenes in sound, but they also intended to hire an orchestra to record background music to accompany the film. At the time, theatre musicians around the world were out of work, not only because of the crippling Depression, but also because the popularity of 'talkies' had made them redundant. 'Canned' scores projected from soundtracks had replaced live musicians playing from the pit of a theatre. Naturally, they were desperate, but Paulette presumed she'd be offering a small consolation to unemployed musicians by offering them studio work. But when she applied to Mr Trevelyan, the General Secretary of the Musicians' Union, to hire an orchestra, she was flatly refused.

Undaunted, Paulette went straight to the press and gave a frank interview: 'When we explained to Mr Trevelyan that we would be employing Australian musicians who were now out of work he said he was fighting canned music and would not let them play. We said we would go ahead with the work, and he challenged us to do so – we might try, [he said] but would not get musicians'.

Two years before, the Sydney office of the Musicians' Union had staged a war against a thirty-piece Italian orchestra performing at Hoyts picture house, while the Union's Melbourne office was attempting to eject a forty-two-piece Italian orchestra accompanying the Gonsalez Italian Grand Opera Company – all in the name of protecting the jobs of local musicians, who by all accounts were nowhere near as technically accomplished.

When it came to jazz music, Clause (q) of Section 4 of the union's rule book stated their vehement opposition to 'colored musicians', and Trevelyan had certainly been behind a concerted effort between corrupt Melbourne police investigators and the tabloid press to have a wildly popular African-American jazz band deported from Australia on trumped-up charges. Trevelyan's favourite justification for this form of musical xenophobia was what he called a matter of 'principle'.

Ironically, Trevelyan was one of the most unprincipled men in show business, and a failed flautist originally named George Sanderson. The mediocre musician reinvented himself as the manager of Belfast's Empire Theatre, married a local lass and fathered two children. On 11 July 1900, however, he faked his own death by drowning and afterwards secretly joined his lover, escaping to Scotland. Less than two weeks later, he and his lover boarded a steamship in Liverpool, bound for Sydney, under the names Mr and Mrs George Patrick Trevelyan.

The resolute sisters did not know of Trevelyan's background as a scoundrel, but they were determined not to be bullied by this ageing and mothballed bureaucrat. They needed a sixteen-piece orchestra immediately and, with only sixteen days to complete the sound version before the competition deadline of 30 March, had no time to waste. At once, they took out a large advertisement in *The Age*, requesting applications from orchestra musicians for the recording of sound-on-film and, perhaps with an extra dig at the uncooperative Trevelyan, emphasised that 'Unionists (were) preferred'. An affronted Trevelyan immediately shot back with his own press release the next day: 'Any member of the Musicians' Union who plays for or in any way assists in the making of mechanical music for films will be expelled immediately'. A public debate sprang up in the Letters sections of the Melbourne news-papers on the logic of the union banning unemployed musicians from accepting work.

Three days after the publication of the advertisement, and after having received over 200 enquiries, the sisters emerged victorious: 'We have had so many applicants', they stated to a journalist, 'that we hope to be able to choose an orchestra of 16 easily from among them ... We are already in touch with a conductor'. A disgruntled Trevelyan put the word out that members of the union intended to form a picket line outside the Vocalion studio on Bourke Street, but on the day that the recording began, there wasn't a protester in sight. The sisters had finally called his bluff.

Three new scenes with dialogue were shot at the Vocalion studio, including Paula singing a song to her lover, Lee. Jack Fletcher filmed the footage through a window from inside a small, soundproof wooden box with a Prestwich camera and synchroniser, invented by Sid Guest for Vocalion. The previously shot scenes of *The Cheaters* were completed with music on disc. A voice coach was secured to help Isabel transition into a 'talking' actress, but the coach was of the theatrical old school, emphasising the importance of enunciating certain words to reach the back stalls of a theatre rather than adapting to the naturalism of sound film. According to veteran projectionist Albert Wright, the sound-on-disc version was screened in the early 1930s at Melbourne's St Kilda Palais. Following the screening, however, this version of *The Cheaters* seems to have vanished from public view.

The Vocalion sound-recording equipment was still primitive and the results were disappointing, with voices out of sync with the lip movements of the actors. The sisters and Macken spent the last of their money correcting the imperfections before the 31 March cut-off for entry to the Commonwealth Prize. The judges were members of the Commonwealth Film Censorship Appeal Board, which included poet Mary Gilmore, hardly an authority on the structure and aesthetics of contemporary motion pictures.

The McDonaghs narrowly made the deadline and waited nervously for the results. They had staked the proceeds from the sale of Drummoyne House, and the last of their money, on winning the coveted 10 000 pounds. Inexplicably, however, no first or second prize was awarded that year. But Arthur Higgins and Austin Fay, who had also used the Vocalion sound studio to produce partial talkie and war film, *Fellers*, won the third and only prize of 1500 pounds in May 1930. Since that film would not be released until 23 August of that year, *The Cheaters* did end up being the first Australian part-talkie to be screened to the public anywhere in the world. However, the highly anticipated event was beset by embarrassing problems.

When the film premiered at the Roxy Theatre on Castlereagh Street on 1 June 1930 to a large contingent of trade and press representatives, the sound sequences jarred with the carefully crafted structure of the film, and the experience of watching it was compromised by bad sound monitoring. As Neville Macken recalled:

On that evening it died a horrible death. We had shocking trouble. All the film up to and around the dialogue was padded out with the music ... I was placed in charge of running the discs from the projection booth and in order to maintain a constant level Phyllis (McDonagh) was seated in the audience with a buzzer on the arm of her chair. If the sound was too soft, she'd buzz once and I'd turn the volume up. If it was too loud, then I'd receive two buzzes. The crucial dialogue scene arrived, the love piece on the terrace between the hero and the heroine at breakfast. At the height of the true heart confession Phyllis buzzed twice for the sound to be decreased and I, misunderstanding her, upped the volume – so that when one of them tapped an egg, it sounded just like the Anvil Chorus. In the midst of the love scene, where the women should be sobbing quietly and the husband should be trying to keep his emotions tight, there was a roar of laughter from no less than seventeen hundred people, and there was no keeping them quiet after that.

The critics were disappointed, and both the film and the sisters were savaged in the press: 'The Cheaters, frankly, is not a good film. It marks no advancement on previous efforts. The plot has one or two smart twists but it is unconvincing and bodiless'. This didn't stop budding journalist Grant McDonagh from publishing an article later that year that claimed *The Cheaters* was the first successful talkie to be made in Australia. At times, this family may have lacked good fortune, but they were never without a surfeit of chutzpah.

Six months later, the sisters attempted to make a second sound version of *The Cheaters*, employing the same sets, technology, and crew as the recently released talkie, *Showgirl's Luck*, which had been recorded with Fletcher's Standardtone sound-on-film process. Several sections were reshot with sound, while the remainder was dubbed with revoicing to picture, sometimes in combination with music. Many of the film's scenes were shortened, not allowing the film's narrative to 'breathe' as effectively as had been the case with the silent. But while Paulette was adapting as quickly as she could to this developing technology, and finessing three different versions of the same film over a period of eighteen months, the world of cinema was changing rapidly.

By October the following year, they were still trying to secure a distribution deal. In that month it was reported in a small paragraph of a film column that Charles Hardy of Celebrity Films had agreed to distribute the sound-on-film version, but nothing seems to have come of that premature announcement. Graham Shirley has speculated that the sisters' earlier rejection of Frank Thring's generous offer to publicise and distribute *The Cheaters* may have contributed to the silent version's difficulties in finding a commercial release.

Macken and MCD Productions had lost a lot of money financing three versions of the same film. Devastated by the reception of their first talkie, the McDonaghs wondered if they should revert to their original plan and re-release *The Cheaters* as a full silent feature. But by this time, women's dress fashions had changed radically, making the ensembles worn by the female characters look hopelessly out of date, and they decided not to release the film at all. '"The Cheaters" was at first a bitter experience', Paulette admitted in 1934. 'Later, we learned to accept it as a whim of fate.' The silent version, considered by critics to be vastly superior to the two sound versions, would not be screened publicly for another thirty-five years.

By embracing the crime thriller genre, and gangster characters in particular, the silent version of *The Cheaters* would display the influences of what would become known in the 1940s as American film noir: the exploitation of moody shadows, a strong depth of focus, and a concentration on the lifestyles of underworld figures. There is a vivid example during the first act when Marsh is in prison, and the shadow of gaol cell bars falls dramatically against the back wall, with Marsh's silhouette trapped within it. Towards the end of the film, the light on his desk begins to flash, alerting him to the fact that police are approaching. He glimpses the cars through the window and realises that his sidekick has ratted him out to the authorities. His hopeless predicament is reinforced by the vertical and horizontal wooden frames of the window. He is literally and figuratively incarcerated in his criminal lair, with no way out.

As noted previously, the film that influenced Paulette more than any other was the masterpiece *Dr Mabuse, the Gambler*, directed by Fritz Lang. While it was shot in 1922, it only screened at the Crystal Palace in Sydney in October 1924. In general, German Expressionist films aimed to reveal interior, subjective experience through external, objective details. They were also defined by highly stylised sets and performances, employing a fresh visual style that used contrasting dramatic lighting, deep shadows, and unusual camera angles. As her nephew, Charles. observed,

'She absorbed the whole milieu of the criminal underworld from Fritz Lang'.

Furthermore, because *The Cheaters* was the first MCD production to be filmed entirely in a studio, it is the most stylised and 'designed' of all their motion pictures, with sets that are meticulous in their symmetry and aesthetic. The best example is the first shot of the interior of Marsh's hideaway: his authority is established when we see him sitting in the middle of a heavy desk, his upper body framed by an arch in the wall, which also frames the outline of mullioned windows. Later, the maniacal crime leader's paranoia is expressed through a flashing warning device and a secret vault and staircase. Marsh's bulk is bracketed on each side by sculptures of wild, bucking horses. In the foreground is the figure of a snarling tiger about to pounce. A vase shaped like an elephant holds a bunch of wilting flowers. The criminal is literally and figuratively surrounded by animals.

Another example of the film's sophisticated mise-en-scène is when Paula travels to a luxury hotel to grift from wealthy guests. Her suite at the hotel mirrors Marsh's hideaway with geometric precision: a double bed is framed by a wall arch, which itself is flanked by two identical wall lamps. A third identical lamp completes the artful symmetry by being positioned in the middle, directly above the bed. Another reminder of the hideaway is the clutch of wilting flowers in a vase on a side table. The visual pattern is later repeated in the dining room of the hotel, where an arched doorway in the background leads to an indoor fountain, (with water being a visual shorthand in MCD productions for the presence of romance and love).

It is also in *The Cheaters* that Paulette most exploited her knowledge of film grammar: after a package is delivered to Paula in her hotel room, a series of beautiful dissolves reveals a puzzled, then interested, and then happy expression as she opens the box and reads the card. Similarly, when Marsh confronts Travers and reveals his true identity, we see Marsh's face from twenty years ago, and then, through a series of dissolves, we watch him age into the elderly man he is today, at which point Travers finally recognises him.

Besotted Bruno Valletty made it clear that he wanted to marry Paulette and take her back to Italy to meet his family and settle down, and she briefly entertained the idea. Sister Paula believed that Bruno was the only man who could have 'handled' her stubborn, bossy, older sister, who could tolerate her fierce individualism and varying moods.

But Paulette's Bronte-like enmeshment with her siblings eventually came between the couple. There was no way that the other McDonaghs were going to allow their cherished sister to marry an Italian who was going to sweep her off permanently to the other side of the world. 'Well, it was just taken for granted', said Paula. 'When you said a thing wouldn't happen, it wouldn't happen … Family-wise, you know?'

But it wasn't just family disapproval that put Paulette in a bind but also her ambition to continue directing films. Margaret Coen, who'd helped Isabel make the faux sweets from sunlight soap and flour in Yass all those years before, was now grown up and facing a similar dilemma. She'd just begun her career as a serious painter and did not believe that a satisfying creative life could be combined with marriage. 'I hadn't gone to art school for a husband', she observed, 'and I thought that if I married I wouldn't be able to be an artist'. Apart from the pressure from her siblings, it's likely that Paulette would have felt the same. 'It was a cruel thing for the family to have done', said Paula. 'But at that time it was the wrong time, with [the development of] *Two Minutes Silence*, you know, in view.'

Forty years later, Paulette would heartily approve of the choice she'd been forced to make. When a journalist noted that she'd never married, Paulette interjected: '... and thank God I didn't ... I don't believe in marriage. I always wanted to be my own woman'.

Not long after Paulette rejected Valletty's proposal, Rahman Bey returned to the apartment building in Kings Cross to find Isabel downcast and distant. Intuiting immediately that their relationship, too, was coming to an end, he gently announced, 'Isabel, you don't love me anymore ...'

Valletty, Bey, and the magic show soon left Sydney and the caravan moved on. But with the absence of Paulette in his life, the entrepreneur did not lose his enthusiasm for creating a film company. In July 1931, he was listed in the *Los Angeles Times* as co-director of the motion picture production company Triumphant Films, which he and two colleagues were floating on the stock market at one dollar per share. It's likely that Paulette's passion for filmmaking had influenced Valletty to invest in the new talkie industry, but sadly, nothing came of Triumphant Films and the new Hollywood venture was over before it had even begun.

In 1934, Bey returned to Sydney for a season at the Tivoli. The following year, he appeared as part of a vaudeville line-up at the Civic Theatre, Haymarket, the same theatre that would screen the next feature made by the McDonagh sisters, *Two Minutes Silence*. On 6 October of that year, Bey began a series of broadcasts over 2UW in Sydney entitled 'Mysteries of Egypt'. Listeners were encouraged to write to the station with any queries concerning love, work, health, finance, or any other problems, and Bey would predict their fortunes over the wireless.

In 1936, Rahman Bey again returned to Sydney, and later it was reported he'd given up show business to sell silk stockings. It was also reported that he'd tried to become a farmer in Australia but had failed miserably. Two years later he was back in London, performing his usual act. During the war, he disappeared entirely and did not emerge again publicly until July 1944, when he was listed at the very bottom of the bill for a show at the Tivoli in Newcastle, New South Wales, and merely described as 'a mystic', with no accompanying fanfare. After that billing, he disappears from the public record entirely. It is also not known what happened to Valletty after his failed bid to float his film company on the American stock exchange.

Following the failed romances with Bey and Valletty, the introduction of talkies, and the disappointment of *The Cheaters*, the sisters may have been down, but they were far from out. Isabel was about to meet the love of her life, Phyllis would enter a rollerskating competition against much younger competitors, and Paulette would explore a form of filmmaking she had never considered before.

14

⒜LWAYS DO WHAT YOU'RE AFRAID TO DO

(1930–1934)

On 11 November 1930, Isabel, publicised as the silent film star Marie Lorraine, stood at a stall on Castlereagh Street selling poppies to raise funds for war veterans.

In the nearby Usher's Hotel, a Scottish war veteran named Charles Stewart was in residence after completing a recreational fishing expedition on the coast of New South Wales. Since it was Poppy Day, he was celebrating at the time and, gleefully drunk, approached the attractive young woman and offered to buy the hundreds of remaining poppies from her. Realising he was inebriated, Isabel tried to get rid of him. Stewart briefly disappeared into nearby Hillier's Chocolate Shop and returned with armfuls of confectionary for Isabel and the other volunteers, but Isabel grew increasingly alarmed by his persistence. She said, 'We appreciate what you have done for us, but I refuse to [let] you stay here. [The] best thing to do would be to go back to where you're staying'.

But the swaying and besotted man continued to pester her. 'I'll leave you alone', he suggested, in his rolling Scottish burr, 'if you promise to meet me tomorrow'. To get rid of him, Isabel reluctantly agreed.

Following the day of their first meeting, Stewart turned up for their date sober and invited Isabel to dine with him that night at Usher's Restaurant. Isabel, still wary, agreed on the condition that another couple join them. After that first dinner, Charles would always carry a photo of a still from *The Far Paradise*, a beautiful close-up of Isabel wearing a headscarf.

In 1931, after the release of Norman Dawn's Australian talkie feature, *Showgirl's Luck*, Neville Macken and Jack Fletcher were enjoying moderate success with the Standardtone sound-on-film technology. Following that achievement, Macken wanted to exploit his progress by conceiving and financing several short documentaries, called 'reality films', to be directed by Paulette.

The first was *Australia in the Swim*, a documentary about Andrew 'Boy' Charlton and the Olympic Swimming Team, filmed at Manly Pool. Its cinematic innovations included underwater photography and slow-motion shots, for which Macken had to secure a special camera. Poet and journalist Kenneth Slessor, who was the same age as Paulette, agreed to write and record the narration for the short. 'Oh, I loved that man', remarked Paulette of Slessor. '... he'd come there to the studio, and we'd run it, and he'd sit there in the dark and watch it and we'd time it. And he'd look at it and make notes. And he had to synchronise, you see, the dialogue for that short ... But it was so brilliant his dialogue behind us'.

Another short, *How I Play Cricket*, was about internationally famous Australian batsman, Don Bradman. Forty years later, Paulette fondly recalled,

I made this glorious story up at his home. And (it) was beautiful. It's them there, for about two months. I went to Bell. I got my mountain ... And I shot down on the little cricket field he used to play on. And a shot down with height on the whole cricket field ... and then I shot to his home with his car pulling up and his old mother and father at the door, and he gets out to see his mother and father and going into a little weatherboard house, facing the cricket field which I started the shot with. And from there, I took to his backyard with a great big water tank. And showing him, which I made him do, against – he learnt how to play cricket against a water tank in his backyard. Every shot that made him a world famous man he learnt on that water tank ... I then took him over ... to the cricket field and I made him walk up and down, looking down to there and pulling his bat and tying up the shot, you know, to give the human interest.

Paulette also begged Bradman to allow her to film his wedding, but he was a very private man and wouldn't allow it. Still, she was immensely proud of the finished product: 'It was so wonderful, that film, it went all over the world'.

The other reality films directed by Paulette that year, under the Standardtone banner, included *Billy Bluegum* (about koalas, filmed at a koala sanctuary in Sydney's Pennant Hills), *The Trail of the 'Roo* (about kangaroos), and *The Mighty Conqueror* (about champion Australian racehorse Phar Lap). Of all the documentaries that Paulette directed, only *The Mighty Conqueror*, *Billy Bluegum*, and *The Trail of the 'Roo* still exist.

Following the multiple challenges she'd faced directing and producing three versions of *The Cheaters*, it seems that by making so many shorts in such a small amount of time, Paulette was trying to achieve several aims at once: to make some quick money, to adapt and develop her writing and directing skills for more commercial work, and to exploit iconic Australian subject matter in the service of attracting an international audience (and funding) for her future films.

Ultimately, none of these objectives was fulfilled. Paulette and Standardtone made no profit from the distribution of the shorts, she was offered no further work from other production companies, and even though the shorts were screened in England, it would take more than a few 'reality films' to secure international interest in her next feature.

One of the weaknesses of the sisters – just like their father's – was their inability to budget. When money was plentiful it was splurged on sumptuous parties; when it was scarce, they weren't quite sure what to do. Hock more jewellery? Buy goods on time payment? Unfortunately, due to their legendary lack of business sense, the sisters were disinclined to make deals with cinema conglomerates and would always organise film premieres themselves.

'See, we were so stupid', admitted Paulette. 'We were young, we had no one in charge of us. Had we a manager or somebody to tell us what to do, we'd have been on top of the world today.'

While Paulette was busy directing the reality films, Isabel was being swept off her feet by Charles Stewart, who had by now won her trust, and her heart.

His friends called him Bonny Prince Charlie, and he was born in 1885 in Ballinluig, Scotland, the youngest of seven children. As a young man, he was accepted into the Perth Academy and became a cadet in the Black Watch. After graduating, he secured a job at the Bank of Scotland, then was offered a job at the National City Bank of New York, where he excelled as an investment consultant.

In 1914, when the war broke out, he was visiting Australia. Rather than return to Scotland, he joined the 25th Queensland Infantry Battalion and was shipped off to the Middle East. Stewart was part of the disastrous second landing of Gallipoli and was wounded twice. In 1916, he was sent to Oxford for promotion to Commissioned Rank and won the Military Cross on the Somme.

After the war, Stewart left banking altogether and became a rubber broker. As his experience grew, he came to be considered the leading rubber broker in the world. Those who sought out his personal advice included Winston Churchill and Woolworths heiress Barbara Hutton.

At the age of forty-six, when he first met Isabel in Sydney, he was so wealthy and successful that he'd decided to retire and was planning to return to Scotland to purchase an estate in the highlands, Easter Tyre, where he could live out the rest of his life shooting grouse and catching wild salmon. But now those plans had been cast aside.

Isabel and Charles had been dating for seven months when the three sisters attended a theatre production of the play, *Two Minutes Silence*, by journalist Leslie Haylen. The Playhouse Theatre, founded by Carrie Tennant, had been established in the basement of St Peter's Church Hall in Darlinghurst the year before. *Two Minutes Silence* was a strident anti-war play, set in London on Armistice Day. During the traditional Two Minutes Silence at 11 am, four people recall, in succession, their heartbreaking experiences of the First World War, which are enacted sequentially on the stage. A French governess remembers being being abandoned by a German officer, after giving birth to his illegitimate child; a charlady remembers the time that she received the devastating news of her soldier-son's passing; a general recalls the split-second decision he made that resulted in the death of his platoon; and a butler relives the day, following the war, when a depressed ex-soldier committed suicide on the banks of the River Thames. 'As soon as the curtain came down at the end', said Paulette, 'I knew I had to produce it as a film'.

Since they'd been teenagers, the sisters had always felt great sympathy for returned soldiers. Following the war, their father had treated wounded and traumatised diggers in his surgery and private hospital, and from the windows and veranda of their home on College Street, they'd witnessed the abject poverty in which these brave men had been forced to live as they dossed down, homeless, beneath the fig trees of Hyde Park across the road. They'd held numerous charity events for them, and every year they helped to sell 25000 poppies to raise money for their ongoing care.

Paulette approached playwright Haylen, and the two agreed to collaborate on a film adaptation of *Two Minutes Silence*. But development was hampered by the economic privations of the Depression, and it would be a further two years before the project went into production.

In January 1932, with the aim of producing and releasing their first full-length talkie, the sisters and John formed a syndicate with their friend Neville Macken to rent the Standardtone studio, along with its accompanying sound-recording technology and studio equipment. The McDonagh siblings authorised Macken to negotiate a twelve-month licence from Standardtone, to be extended on a rental basis. As with most business matters associated with the McDonaghs, the terms of the agreement were vague, which would later lead to misunderstandings and an ongoing court drama.

In the meantime, the sisters still hadn't managed to raise the funds for their next film. Salvation eventually came in the form of Isabel's new beau, Charles Stewart, who offered the McDonaghs 1500 pounds to produce their next feature. Being a veteran of Gallipoli and the Somme, he would have been sympathetic to the subject matter and more than willing to help. Accepting the money, however, would have been difficult for the sisters – and Paulette in particular: in the eighteen months since their first meeting, Stewart and Isabel had fallen in love. Paulette herself had recently sacrificed the love of her life, Bruno Valletty, for the sake of her film career, and to keep the enmeshed siblings together. But in accepting Stewart's offer, she would hardly be in the same position, when the time came, to ask the same of Isabel and her generous paramour. It's possible that a deal was done – official or unspoken – that Stewart would stump the budget for *Two Minutes Silence* upon the understanding that this would be Isabel's last film. With his wealth and good taste, Charles Stewart would be able to return to Isabel the luxurious lifestyle she had enjoyed before the untimely death of her father.

The day before the grand opening of the Sydney Harbour Bridge in March 1932, Phyllis attended a 'monster carnival' that was unfurling through the streets of the city. She was not celebrating the anticipated ribbon-cutting that would change the skyline and the commuting habits of Sydneysiders forever, but taking advantage of the crowds by selling tin hats for the United Returned Soldiers' fund. She headed the committee that had organised the fundraising, demonstrating a deep commitment to the wounded casualties of war – and to the subject matter of the McDonaghs' next film – when most other young women of the day were plucking their eyebrows and picking out dresses to wear to parties.

In July that year, however, plucky Phyllis did attract attention when, at the age of thirty-two, she entered a popular skating competition at the Palladium Rink, held to select the annual 'Queen of the Harbour'. The contest was run more like a political campaign than a recreational tournament, stretching over several weeks and many social events, including bridge parties and dances, and was in aid of raising funds for the Royal Hospital for Women. By the third week of July, Phyllis was reported as leading the poll. Two days later, all the contestants participated in a one-mile rollerskating championship in front of an enraptured audience. By 21 August, contestants Maisie Bailey, May McKenzie, and Phyllis were neck and neck at the polls.

The 24th of that month was the 'Queen of the Harbour Gala Night', during which a final contest category would be staged, dubbed the 'Shapely Legs' competition, after which the winner with the most overall votes would be announced to the public and press. Not only was Phyllis beautiful, intelligent, gifted, and athletic, but she was also, apparently, in possession of a great pair of pins, because at the end the of the event, with over 2000 votes in her favour, she was crowned 'Miss Palladium, Queen of the Harbour' over much younger entrants, and awarded a prize of five pounds. The competition was ostensibly about popularity and charity, but when Phyllis was later interviewed by journalists about her win, she couldn't resist taking advantage of her sudden elevation into the limelight by publicising the title of the McDonaghs' intended new film, *Two Minutes Silence*.

By this time, the siblings had moved out of their apartment in Kings Cross and into a house at 66A Darling Point Road, Darling Point. A 1933 Census report reveals their ambivalence about the future and their general lack of direction. Both Phyllis and Paulette list their occupations as 'Home Duties'; Grant lists his as 'Journalist'; and John's occupation is merely left blank. Tellingly, Isabel is not listed on the form at all, suggesting that she'd accepted alternative accommodation by her generous beau, or was accompanying him on one of his many fishing trips to his favourite angling destination, New Zealand.

Paulette may have listed her occupation as 'Home Duties' on the Census Form, but once Charles Stewart forwarded the funds for the McDonaghs' fourth feature, she was firmly back in the director's seat. British cameraman James Grant was hired to shoot the film, with Jack Bruce to record the sound. Some of the sets would need to accommodate battle scenes and dugouts, and so former actor and singer Josef Bambach, who'd played the young male lead in *The Cheaters*, agreed to step in to design and construct them.

Isabel was duly cast in the role of the French governess. Original stage cast member Ethel Gabriel was retained to play the charlady. The other two major roles were filled by accomplished stage actors Frank Leighton and Leo Franklyn, who at first had no desire to be in the film, but insistent Paulette eventually persuaded them. 'This is going to be your first film', she urged. 'And it's going to make your names. From this film you're never going to look back.'

Before production began, Paulette made a pact with herself, one that would help her to deal with the troubles and challenges she knew she would face in making her first, full-length talkie: 'Always do what you're afraid to do'.

The filming took place in the Royal Agricultural Society's lecture hall on Cook Road, Paddington, which had been converted into a studio with sound and film equipment. 'We had to build a large asbestos box to enclose the cameraman', said Phyllis, 'with a narrow aperture provided for the camera lens. By some miracle it worked'.

During production, Paulette again experienced the same problems with overacting from her two male leads and resorted to her usual tactic of showing them the rushes to rein them in. The result, according to Paulette, was that Leighton delivered the best performance of his film career, especially when he was required to go mad in a battlefield dugout. Also acting in the film were Campbell Copeland, Frank Bradley, and Arthur Greenaway.

Paulette planned to stay within her tight budget by paying the actors only twenty-five pounds a day, for an average of about three days' work. The shooting of the film, however, would be plagued by personal betrayals and unforeseen setbacks.

On the morning of 2 July, the McDonaghs arrived at the Cook Road studio to continue filming when they discovered the padlock on the front door had been changed. Affronted, John accessed a saw, cut through the bolt, removed the new lock, and replaced it with the original one. He ushered his sisters inside and they all went to work.

The following Monday, the sisters and John arrived at the studio to find their friend and business partner, Neville Macken, lurking about behind the scenes, but thought nothing of it. The next morning, they fronted the studio to continue shooting when they found the lock on the door had been changed yet again. The frustrated siblings confronted Macken about what the hell was going on. They were about to shoot a vitally important scene that day, and precious time was running out.

Up until this point, Macken hadn't been entirely transparent in his actions. The McDonaghs soon learned that three weeks before, the solicitor for and director of Standardtone, Keith Manion, had telephoned Macken to announce that he was putting the company into liquidation and that Macken was to change the locks on the studio and refuse entry to any film producers.

When the sisters and John learned of the news, they naturally protested and told Macken that they intended to proceed with the shoot. Macken countered with a threat to interfere with the completion of the film unless the McDonaghs signed a document that would forfeit their right to use the studio equipment. Bewildered by Macken's demands, they flatly refused. Insult led to injury when they realised that Macken had removed from the studio all the books and records associated with the syndicate, essentially shutting the film down in the middle of production.

The McDonaghs had no other choice but to take Macken and Manion to court. On Wednesday 20 July, an injunction was granted, restraining Standardtone, and defendant Macken, from interfering with the McDonaghs' use of the studio and its equipment for two days, until Friday 22 July. On the 23rd, another injunction was granted, restraining both parties from using the building or its equipment until Wednesday of the following week. The result of that hearing was not published in newspapers, but the McDonaghs must have made headway because the following month, it was reported that they were still filming final scenes in the Standardtone studio.

Oddly, Keith Manion had for years been the lawyer for the McDonaghs and was considered a close friend of the family, as was Macken. And in a still from an earlier film, an advertising poster for 'Manion's Revue Co.' appears on the wall, which Paulette later revealed was an affectionate joke on their close associate. It is not quite clear what caused the rift between the two parties, nor why the McDonaghs had to resort to the courts to gain access to the studio and complete the film. The most likely scenario would have been a lack of cash on both sides, with the syndicate unable to pay the rent on the studio, and Macken going broke due to unwise investments and the economic fallout of the Depression. According to Macken's brother, Bud, Macken was 'practically broke' by then, and so he'd had no choice but to comply with Manion's instructions.

Now, the delayed and rearranged shooting schedule was tighter than ever. Lead actors Franklyn and Leighton were due to depart for New Zealand to appear in a play, and so the various scenes that remained to be filmed had to be shot in only two days. The cast and crew worked non-stop for thirty-six of the next forty-eight hours.

During the shoot, a journalist visited the set and described Paulette's directing style: 'She works like a machine, cold and sure. There is need for perfect judgement, exactitude and nerve. Miss Paulette has them all. Like the conductor of an orchestra, waving his baton, she waves her pencil this way and that. The pencil is part of her'.

Close to the end of the shoot, exhausted cameraman, James Grant, 'went berserk'. After all, he'd been stuck in an airless box for hours on end, at the mercy of time and Paulette's unrelenting perfectionism:

> Screaming wildly, he sprinted [down] the studio corridor.
> I pursued him. He had the door open. I grabbed him by
> the collar, slammed the door and shook him violently.
> I filled myself with air and yelled, 'Get back on that set!'
> He went pale and quietened down. I started talking to
> him. 'We've all been working our guts out. There's nobody
> on that set that wouldn't like to do what you've just done.
> But none of them have, because they want to get the thing
> finished. Unless you go back, they won't finish at all.' Then
> he followed me back to the studio. Everyone on the set was
> surprised to see him return.

But further setbacks came when Stuart Doyle, head of Union Theatres, refused to release and distribute *Two Minutes Silence*. The sisters assumed that Doyle's ambivalence about the film had something to do with them personally, but the reality was that, in 1933, Australia, like the rest of the world, was in the grips of a severe financial and psychological Depression. The perception was that audiences craved escapist entertainment – comedies and musicals – over serious dramas, especially those about the desperation and melancholia engendered by the First World War.

At the time, Doyle's Union Theatres were haemorrhaging money. A few years before, in an unspoken competition with his arch-rival Frank Thring, and unable to predict the stock market crash and consequential Depression, Doyle had invested huge amounts of money in opening the grand State Theatres in Sydney and Melbourne. The Sydney venue held between 2500 and 3000 people, and an expensive WurliTzer organ had been installed to accompany the screenings of silent films. It also featured an orchestra of twenty-four players under an imported conductor, singers, solo dancers, and a permanent ballet of sixteen girls.

By the time the McDonaghs had approached Doyle about distributing *Two Minutes Silence*, he had rashly overspent and was in a permanent bad mood. As director Ken Hall noted, 'On the one hand, he was an impatient, hard-driving dictator who believed that the way to get the best out of his staff was to scare the daylights out of them ... On the other hand, he was a brilliant showman, had vision ...'.

Because the sisters were not part of a combine, they were probably not aware of the disastrous economic climate in which cinemas were operating, being instead focused entirely on their own survival as filmmakers. Only two years before, in 1931, film returns across Australia had been at their lowest for five years. In the second half of the same year, Hoyts Theatres lost 18 500 pounds. By the time Stuart Doyle refused to exhibit and distribute *Two Minutes Silence*, Union Theatres and Australasian Films together had lost an extraordinary 48 012 pounds in a single financial year. Doyle had also begun to reduce salaries and retrench staff; the orchestras of the Sydney Capitol and the Melbourne State theatres had been dismissed; and male ushers at the former had been replaced by women on lower wages.

Paulette considered *Two Minutes Silence* to be the best film she and her sisters had ever made, and her opinion was bolstered by the fact that it was the first Australian feature to contain an anti-war theme: 'To my thinking, with each film I made I got better and better'. But how on earth was she going to negotiate a national distribution deal in the middle of a global economic crisis?

15

CINDERELLA'S CHOICE

(1933–1934)

Although Isabel had been engaged several times before, each engagement had been broken off in deference to the wishes of her siblings. There was also pressure from Paulette, who wanted to continue directing films, featuring Isabel as the lead actress. But after the exhausting process of making *Two Minutes Silence*, and the devastating disappointment of its non-release, Paulette was growing more disenchanted with the obstacles, and Isabel, now thirty-three, knew that if she didn't marry soon, it would be too late. She didn't want to make the same sacrifice as Paulette when she'd turned down the proposal of Bruno Valletty. Moreover, the youngest sibling, Paula, now twenty-one, no longer required Isabel's ongoing care.

Directly after production on *Two Minutes Silence* was completed, Isabel and Charles Stewart announced their engagement in the press on 15 September 1932. Even the public announcement was an expression of the private emotional tug of war being waged between Charles Stewart and the younger McDonagh siblings. Below an angelic portrait of the future Mrs Stewart is the usual announcement of an imminent wedding, but tacked on to the statement is the following declaration: 'Miss McDonagh, who has figured prominently in local film production under the pseudonym of Marie Lorraine for the past five years, intends to continue her work on films. In collaboration with her two sisters she has just completed work on "Two Minutes Silence", which will be released in Sydney in the next few weeks'. It's likely that blindsided Charles Stewart did not see the copy before it was sent to the press.

But not long after the announcement, Stewart won the tug of war, at least temporarily. The couple married at St Mary's Cathedral, while the McDonagh siblings sat in the pews and quietly sobbed. Paulette found it hard to let go of her adored sister and leading lady who was also her muse and best friend. 'That was the breakup', said Paula. 'When she married. Very tearful breakup, I can tell you.'

After the reception, the newlyweds drove to Canberra for the first leg of the honeymoon and booked into the Hotel Canberra. Back home, the six younger siblings sat about weeping most of the night, like abandoned children. 'And there was only one thing to do', said Paula, 'we all had to get in the car, drive to Canberra and see if Isabel was happy'. The six travelled straight through the night and fetched up to the hotel the next day.

Far from being outraged, new husband, Charles, accepted the family raid on his honeymoon with bemused serenity. '... he was a fantastic person – and he accepted us', said Paula. '... and we had dinner with them ... and then we came home as happy as can be, because Isabel looked so radiant!'

After the stint in Canberra, the couple set off on a round-the-world cruise to complete their honeymoon. During the trip, they disembarked in Singapore, where many of Stewart's old business colleagues hosted a dinner for the couple. During a toast, one of them declared, 'Well, it was a well-known fact that what Charlie Stewart thought in Singapore today, the London stock exchange thought tomorrow'. 'He was really a financial wizard', said Paula. 'A very wealthy man.'

The newlyweds later spent six months travelling throughout the United States, visiting major attractions such as Niagara Falls and the Grand Canyon, as well as capital cities including San Francisco and Chicago, the latter of which Isabel adored. After nine years of looking after her younger siblings, of battling mounting bills, bankruptcy, rebellious teenagers, predatory suitors, and unfair film distribution deals, Isabel must have felt more pampered and at peace than she ever had in her life. Her easygoing and devoted husband assumed responsibility for all their economic and practical necessities, and at last she could relax and enjoy her new role as a loving wife.

Isabel fell pregnant during the trip and decided that she wanted to give birth in London. After arriving in the UK, the couple settled in a luxurious home on Prince of Wales Terrace, Kensington. On 5 September 1933, Isabel gave birth to a son in a nearby hospital. He was baptised in Our Lady of Victory Church, Kensington, and they christened the newborn Alan Breck John Stewart, after the hero of Robert Louis Stevenson's novel, *Kidnapped*. In the early years of his life, they would refer to their firstborn as 'Breck'.

Also in 1933, Anita's husband, Gregory Blackall, at last earned his pharmacy degree and, due to daughter Ann's severe asthma, doctors suggested that they shift to the west of the state where the air was dryer. Gregory moved the family to the small town of Molong, northwest of Orange, and with his brother opened a pharmacy there on 17 October 1933. The opening outraged the existing pharmacist, JJ O'Connor, and initiated a rift within the town, along with an advertising blitz from the two competing businesses appearing in the local newspapers. A desperate Blackall was forced to lobby the local medical association for equal referrals from the nearest hospital, but still the rivalry continued.

For entertainment, the town provided one picture theatre, the occasional euchre party, regular meetings of the Country Women's Association, and sporadic musical programs staged by touring Salvation Army bands. The enforced move to a one-horse town with a sick baby must have been a cruel disappointment for beautiful and vivacious Anita, who still harboured dreams of becoming an actress like her older sister. There would have been many a lonely night when the young mother regretted her earlier impetuosity and rebelliousness, and her rejection of the advice and discipline offered by her older sisters. Isabel was now married to an independently wealthy man and had been cruising around the world on an extended honeymoon, while she was stuck in Australia's wild west, with hardly any money and even fewer prospects.

Back in Sydney, the siblings inherited the financial difficulties that Isabel had previously handled. Three years before, on 8 October 1930, the McDonaghs had made purchases on time payment from the Chartres Trading Company, which enjoyed an almost complete monopoly on the Australian typewriter trade. The company also leased furniture and ran a business school from Remington House at 169 Liverpool Street, Sydney. On 31 July 1933, a law notice appeared in the *Sydney Morning Herald*, summoning the sisters, including Isabel and brother Grant, to court on 3 August for failure to pay the balance on goods that had been purchased on time payment, which most likely had been a Remington typewriter so that Paulette could complete her scenarios and shooting scripts, and furniture to replace the antiques that had been lost in the fire at the storage facility.

Isabel, of course, was unable to appear in court as she was overseas and would not be returning for the foreseeable future. The hearing was adjourned and rescheduled for 31 August.

No record exists of the outcome of the hearing, but the obvious result was that the typewriter and furniture were repossessed and the McDonaghs lost their entire deposit. Still, if true, the arrangement had given Paulette the use of a new typewriter for three years for a fraction of its true worth. In matters financial and legal, it seems that the sisters had inherited their maternal grandfather's gift for bending the law when necessary.

Despite all these setbacks and challenges, Paulette, Phyllis, and John soldiered on. In November 1933, Phyllis was once again advertising in newspapers for young women to come forward and assist her in selling poppies to raise money for veterans. But instead of the usual wording, and perhaps influenced by the meeting of Isabel and Charles on Poppy Day three years before, Phyllis cleverly reframed the call for help as a one-time opportunity, not for the charity but for the volunteers: 'Each Poppy Day brings its share of romance. Cupid gets busy among the crowd of pretty girls who come forward each year to do their bit for the cause of the digger. Last Poppy Day saw quite a few romances in the making, and already two or three happy marriages have eventuated'.

In January 1934, still under the banner of 'the McDonagh sisters', the siblings announced that preparations for a short documentary about the city of Canberra, *The Heart of a Nation*, had been completed. At the time, Parliament House had only been open seven years, and the nation's capital was still in its infancy. Many Australians still considered the minuscule, regional city a needless white elephant, and the McDonaghs were hoping to exploit the natural beauty of the area and the romance of its early, art deco architecture, and interpose these scenes with personal messages from Canberra's leading personalities. Perhaps the press blitz about the upcoming featurette was an attempt to attract investment money from the ACT government. But if that was the case, the plan failed. The film was never begun, and the team returned its focus to their most recent feature, *Two Minutes Silence,* which was yet to secure a distributor.

To attract attention to the delayed release of *Two Minutes Silence,* Paulette wrote and published an article about the McDonaghs' film careers and being a female director. Glancing over it, the casual reader would have had no idea how challenging it was to be a female film director in Australia in the early 1930s, when the market was monopolised by two competing film combines that were themselves monopolised by American companies, making it virtually impossible for an independent company in Australia to survive. Instead of complaining, however, Paulette is gently encouraging of women to join the industry:

> Some of the best scenario writers in England and
> America are women. I think, perhaps, this is because
> they have an imaginative faculty – the power of make
> believe – more than men. In costuming, art supervision
> and the design of sets, a woman's touch is not only
> preferable, but necessary.

She then goes on to name some of her strongest female role models in film: 'the creator of one of the greatest films ever made, *Mädchen in Uniform* is a German woman; while in Hollywood, Dorothy Arzner has interpreted the scripts of some of the biggest stories ever told'.

The German woman to whom Paulette refers is Leontine Sagan, who was, in fact, an Austrian-Hungarian theatre director and actress of Jewish descent. She directed three films throughout her career, with *Mädchen in Uniform,* shot in Germany, her first and undoubtedly most successful. The film was groundbreaking for several reasons: it had an all-female cast, it treated the taboo subject of lesbianism with grace and sensitivity, and the company that produced it did so with cooperative and profit-sharing arrangements with the cast and crew.

Paulette's second inspiration, Dorothy Arzner, was a Hollywood film director whose career spanned from the silent era into the early 1940s. From 1927 until 1943, when she retired, Arzner was the only female director working in Hollywood. She directed a total of twenty films and was instrumental in launching the careers of several Hollywood female actors, including Katharine Hepburn, Rosalind Russell, and Lucille Ball. Furthermore, Arzner was the first woman to join the Directors Guild of America and the first woman in America to direct a talkie.

It's tempting to speculate on how Paulette's film career might have flourished and endured had she been born in Europe or America, where opportunities to be involved with cooperative filmmaking in Berlin, or the studio system in Hollywood, would have been able to match her talent, drive, and soaring ambition.

Two Minutes Silence had been sitting in the can for a year when Paulette and Phyllis, exasperated by the long delay, hit upon a new tactic to force Stuart Doyle's hand, or that of another distributor. They arranged for a free and private screening at the Capitol Theatre, Canberra, to engage the attention of prominent politicians and publicise their reactions.

For some unknown reason, Paulette and Phyllis did not wish to attend the screening themselves. Isabel was now long gone and perhaps it didn't feel right for them to be promoting the film without her. Or perhaps the herculean struggle to even get the film made had exhausted them both. Instead, they sent Paula and John as their official representatives, along with playwright Leslie Haylen. The drive down was complicated by heavy rain, thunderstorms, poor visibility, and blown tyres.

However, they arrived in time for the premiere on 18 October

1933 and found the theatre filled with curious federal politicians. As they settled into their seats, the lights went down, and the stage curtains parted. The film began with a dedication:

> This isn't a war play. It is a story of Rememberance [sic],
> the relic of a tragic peace, wherein four characters relive the
> twisted drama of their lives.

> It is dedicated as a tribute to the living who wear the scars of
> sacrifice; an epitaph to the fallen, who died that we might live;
> and as a scourge to the Aggressor, who would forget the price
> of peace.

> In blood and bitterness, in sacrilege and sacrifice, it is written:
> 'Lest We Forget'.

As a nervous young Paula observed,

> Well, I had to be the hostess ... but I got through it all right,
> because it was just a parliamentary screening, and then
> we gave them drinks and refreshments after it at the Hotel
> Canberra, and just talked to them ... I think they were all
> quite genuine, quite impressed, because it was a good film.

Former prime minister of Australia, Billy Hughes, by now a member of the United Australia Party under Joseph Lyons, agreed with Paula's assessment of *Two Minutes Silence*: 'Through the memories of Armistice, it presents the problems of today and the ideals of tomorrow. It gives Australia wider publicity. It is a message that the world would note, a gesture which the people in other lands will note'.

The unusual strategy of the sisters eventually worked, but the outcome wasn't quite what they'd envisioned. Five months later, due to the favourable public response from Canberra, Herc C McIntyre, head of the Australian branch of Universal Pictures, agreed to release the film, but not before his company recut the film to sharpen its dramatic tension. It was scheduled to be screened at the Civic Theatre in Haymarket, on the edge of the city centre, where the streets were badly lit and rumoured to be dangerous. The McDonagh siblings believed that the decision to premiere *Two Minutes Silence* in such an unsavoury part of town was not in the film's best interest. But still, they battled on, devising yet another idea to attract favourable publicity.

Before settling in London, Isabel had written regular letters home to her siblings, detailing her travels with her new husband and the exotic sites to which they'd travelled. On 1 March 1934, an article appeared in the *Sydney Morning Herald*, with the author listed as Isabel McDonagh (aka Mrs Charles Stewart), describing her impressions of her brief stay in Hollywood.

According to the article, she visited actor Lionel Belmore, who'd been a patient of her father when he'd performed in Sydney, and who'd had fond memories of 'Sporting Doc'. Belmore then ushered Isabel onto the set of the film *Night Flight*, and after the shoot, she was thrilled to meet the film's star, John Barrymore: '... he impressed me as an amazing personality. He has a low, rich voice, languid and tuneful in quality, and a gracious almost regal presence. I should say he is much more handsome off-screen than on – if such a thing were possible'. Later, the director of the film joined the conversation with Isabel and Barrymore, eager to know how American films were received in Australia. The following day she lunched with 'two of Hollywood's most odd and fascinating figures', Wallace Beery and Roland Young, at the famous Brown Derby restaurant, and found them witty and entertaining company. The next day she visited the set of *My Lips*

Betray, starring Lilian Harvey and John Boles. On her final day in Hollywood, she lunched with actor Victor McLaglen, brother of Arthur McLaglen, who'd appeared with Isabel in *The Far Paradise*. She was impressed by his multi-acre grand estate, with sweeping gardens and swimming pool.

In yet another example of the sisters' deep enmeshment, it turns out that it was not Isabel who'd written and published this article but freelance journalist Phyllis. From the tone of the piece, it reads as if Isabel has only just left Hollywood a day or two earlier, when in fact she and Charles had departed Los Angeles roughly a year before. But to attract publicity for the release of their new film, cunning Phyllis had adapted and condensed the material contained in Isabel's various letters and rewrote them in her own voice and style, before submitting them for publication under Isabel's name. The introduction to the article states that Isabel plays Denise in *Two Minutes Silence* and that it's 'the first Australian film with an international theme'. Paulette and Phyllis had obviously decided that aligning themselves with Hollywood and its brightest stars would be just the boost that they and their film required, especially now that they had lost their leading lady.

One curious aspect of Phyllis's article was that in her rewriting of the Hollywood visit, Charles is completely absent, as if Isabel had been travelling alone. Whether the omission was deliberate or not, it's possible that Phyllis and Paulette were still in denial about the success of the interloper who'd stolen away their adored older sister.

But in her letters back to Australia, Isabel also included what seemed to be subtle yet sensible reminders to her sisters about why she swapped the arduous work of filmmaking for the security of marriage. The article includes the following warning:

Yet most of the glamour one associated with Hollywood is
gilt and a great deal of its romance rather grim reality. There
are eighteen thousand people, I am told, on the casting
bureaus of Hollywood, yet only something like eight percent
of their number are making a moderately comfortable living
out of films. The remainder are either playing 'extra' or 'bit'
parts and eating when and where they can or serving in one
other of the innumerable small shops and cafes that abound
in Hollywood. Most of the girls behind the counters are
really beautiful, but beauty alone means nothing in this city
of beautiful faces. There is something rather tragic in the case
of thousands who flock to Hollywood for fame or fortunes –
and remain to serve in a menial capacity the very stars they
hoped to emulate.

Two Minutes Silence finally had its official premiere at the Civic
Theatre in Haymarket in February 1934. That week, however,
it also was competing with a range of Hollywood releases that
starred such famous actors as Irene Dunne, Charles Laughton,
and Barbara Stanwyck. Neville Macken remembered that the
Council of Churches had invested some money into the film, and
that several nuns from the council had been invited to attend the
opening night. But when they viewed the scenes of the French
governess holding her illegitimate baby, a consequence of being
raped by a German soldier, the nuns were so scandalised by the
subject matter that they began walking out.

Unsurprisingly, some of the first reviews of the film noted the
depressing subject matter and the static nature of the action. One
even complained about the lack of Australian subject matter in
the film, unfairly comparing the sisters' expertise as filmmakers
to those of the 'big men in the business', Frank Thring and Ken
Hall. But the journalist musters some patronising faint praise by
calling 'the girls' and their team 'sensible'.

Despite the inclusion of wartime newsreel footage interpolated between the dramatic scenes, other critics remarked that it was like merely watching a filmed version of a stage play: 'There are no changes in angle, and very few changes in distance, to give variety. In these circumstances even the best play would become a little soporific'.

This was because the cameraman had to shoot the scenes from an unmoveable box positioned in front of the set, with close-ups and middle shots the only visual variety available under such confining conditions. In her first full-length talkie, even Isabel came in for some criticism: 'Mr Campbell Copelin and Miss Marie Lorraine both show the same weakness – a colourless, monotonous method of delivering their lines'. After viewing the rushes during the shooting of the film, it's possible that Isabel had also come to the same conclusion, that she herself did not possess the vocal technique to transition into a successful 'talkie' film actor. Sons Alan and Charles confirm that she was, retrospectively, unhappy with her performance.

But their old friend, poet and journalist Kenneth Slessor, adored the production. After all, his first published poem, 'Goin'', which had appeared in the *Bulletin* sixteen years previously, was based on a similar theme. The poem is narrated by a dying digger in Europe during the First World War, who reminisces about Sydney and its many famous landmarks. In his review in *Smith's Weekly*, Slessor gave the film the highest possible rating from the *Bulletin*, an 'AA':

> A powerful and convincing story, intelligently directed and capable of challenging comparison with world standards ...
> The whole effect ... is one of beauty and strength. There is nothing cheap about the theme, nothing rubbed or shopsoiled; and the treatment is surprisingly free from banality.

Unfortunately, Slessor's rave review was not enough to ensure either critical or commercial success. Still, the film did find an audience in Britain, as part of the empire quota system.

During the 1970s, in a rare moment of regret, Paulette admitted to Joan Long and Graham Shirley that, 'We were fools to have made *Two Minutes Silence*. The whole world would have eaten out of our hand if we'd made another romantic film. *Two Minutes Silence* was too true. It was too true for a lot of people'.

16

INSIDE THE OUTBACK

(1934–1936)

After the birth of her first child, Isabel was keenly aware that she'd never met her husband's parents and siblings, and so, following the christening, they moved to Charles' home of Perthshire in Scotland. Initially, they lived with Charles' older brother in a flat above the brother's hardware shop in Birnam and Dunkeld, as Isabel missed being around extended family. Later, they moved in with another older brother, into a flat above the brother's bank in Oban, a picturesque coastal town close to Loch Linnhe.

Isabel got on well with her in-laws, except for one of Charles' sisters, who was jealous of Isabel stealing away her cherished younger brother. This rivalry suggests that the clannish Stewart family were almost as enmeshed as the close-knit McDonaghs, which is probably why Charles understood and accepted the deep attachment the younger McDonaghs felt for Isabel. While living there, he spent much of his spare time engaged in his favourite pastime, fishing, mostly on the River Tay.

⇥◉⇤

While living in the Darling Point house, the remaining siblings began throwing parties and inviting all the leading actors and actresses after the theatres had closed for the night. Sometimes, the parties would last for days. One friend remembers turning up at their home one morning to find three days' worth of delivered bread and milk sitting on the porch, while inside, Paulette and Phyllis, still dressed in evening gowns, were surrounded by rambunctious guests.

It was during this time that Paulette, Phyllis, and Paula decided to assume responsibility for Gordon Collingridge's love life, and the target of their scheme was an eighteen-year-old woman named Sheila whose older sister had previously attended Kincoppal Sacred Heart School with the youngest McDonagh.

The sisters organised yet another party and invited Sheila, secure in the knowledge that Gordon Collingridge would be in attendance too. They had already briefed Gordon about Sheila's suitability as a bride, and he took his summons to the party seriously. When Sheila arrived, the sisters took her by the hand and ushered her upstairs to a bedroom. A few moments later, they introduced her to the dreamy yet vulnerable Collingridge.

The teenager was immediately smitten with the much older actor, who was over twice her age. She found him handsome, gifted with a great sense of humour and, ironically for a silent film actor, a beautiful speaking voice. But most of all, she would go on to be impressed by his apparent lack of vanity, despite all the fan mail he still received from admiring young women from around the country. Collingridge was also instantly smitten with Sheila but was well aware of the age gap between them. Later, he suggested that they wait twelve months before he formally proposed, which would give Sheila more time to mature and weigh up her options.

While the sisters were busy matchmaking, Grant, now twenty-five, earned his claim of being a writer when he began publishing eloquent articles in newspapers about the need for New South Wales to establish a film quota system. He also delivered impressive speeches on the same subject at various events, including one at the Talking Picture Producers' Association.

During the early 1930s, Grant was not only developing as a journalist but also as a fiction writer, working hard on a novel, *Love Among Thieves,* inspired by the thrilling mixture of crime and romance that had featured in *The Cheaters.* The plot revolves around an international crook, Julian Marsh, whose drug-smuggling network resides in a grand mansion, Castlecrag. It was built by convicts and stands on the banks of a wide river. Adding extra colour is Marsh's faithful servant, who happens to be a dwarf, and a criminal who is also a hypnotist (no doubt inspired by the McDonaghs' former friend, Rahman Bey).

The setting of the mansion is a fictional version of the McDonaghs' beloved former home, Drummoyne House. The criminals, comprising five men and three women, make use of the tunnels beneath the house to transport their booty to and from riverboats. And, like the daughter in *The Cheaters,* the mastermind criminal's daughter, Elizabeth, is at the centre of a love story.

The novel, written under the pseudonym of Leon Brock, was accepted for publication by local publishers Jackson & O'Sullivan in early 1934.

Grant obviously possessed his sisters' gift for publicity and self-promotion. In May 1935, when the novel was released, he published an article in *The Labor Daily* under the guise of his nom-de-plume, bemoaning the state of Australian fiction in general and of Australian publishing in particular. Just as his sisters had mocked Australian cinema's preoccupation with the outback and the bush, with corny 'Hayseed' storylines, so too did 'Leon Brock' make fun of the prevailing subject matter of Australian novels: 'Local publishers in the past either published very few books or very dull ones, with a flock of sheep on page 1, a herd of cattle on page 2, and rabbits – mostly human rabbits – running right through them'.

The author goes on to declare that the time has finally arrived for more sophisticated and varied publishing ventures and lists nine local publishers who seem to be more 'broadminded' than those of the past. In a breakout of bold type in the newspaper column, Grant shamelessly praises his own literary ability:

> To refer to one of the most enterprising [publishers], Jackson and O'Sullivan Ltd have published over 30 books in the last two years, and in 'Love Among Thieves', 'Cameos in Crime' and 'The Mad Doctor' they have three first-class pieces of dramatic fiction.

Despite Grant's confidence in his literary talent, reviews of the novel were mixed:

> '... a work of a most powerful nature, adding all the qualities of a first-class thriller to one of the strangest love stories ever told.'

> 'Unfortunately, the author has been more ambitious than successful.'

> 'A book of no particular merit.'

Even though Grant had published under a pseudonym, one critic noticed the influence of filmmaking on his narrative voice:

> This master crook has, beside the unpleasant habit of disembowelling failures in his gang, the boring habit of making bad epigrams and alliterative wisecracks that savor of those blurbs which come to us from the publicity factories

of the films. There is, indeed, a good deal of such stuff in this otherwise amusing and exciting story. Possibly, the author has worked with an eye on the screen.

It was as if Grant was struggling to disentangle himself from the emotional and creative tentacles of his older sisters and establish his own identity and name.

On the other hand, between 1936 and 1937, the more experienced Phyllis wrote sketches and short stories that were accepted by newspapers and magazines, including *Smith's Weekly*, the *Sydney Morning Herald*, the *Sydney Mail*, and *Woman*. The sketches were invariably about the beauty of the natural world, from the changing moods of the Parramatta River to the dramatic geography of the Bulli lookout on the New South Wales South Coast. Occasionally hyperbolic, these pieces read like five-fingered exercises for the use, or overuse, of figurative language: 'The sky has changed its azure robe for misty dark draperies and stoops low to catch its leaden reflection in the turbulent water below'. But to be fair, the other sketches published on the same page of the *Herald* are equally faux-poetic, and Phyllis was probably writing to the demands of an editorial brief rather than expressing her own individual prose style, which ran riot seven months later in a playful article about the effect of modernism on Christmas toys: 'A grey submarine lies rammed against a modern liner. White-winged yachts skimming a glassy lake. A silver plane wends its aloof way through space. Close by a pair of futuristic clowns shriek down the spirit of the old Harlequinade'.

Three months later, however, Phyllis adjusted her prose style to her subject matter yet again with the publication of a serious short story, 'The Voice in the Darkness'. It is about a First World War digger dying in hospital, with his wife and son at his bedside. In the crafting of this story, Phyllis no doubt drew on her experiences as the young daughter of a doctor who treated wounded veterans on the top-floor hospital of the family home: 'He was glad they had sent him to the Military Hospital. In some curious fashion it was like coming home. The men who hobbled about, or who sat in the wheelchairs, chatting and smoking in the sun, he belonged to them, and they welcomed him to their brotherhood'.

The experience of producing the film, *Two Minutes Silence,* also seems to have inspired the story. Both narratives employ the use of flashbacks to dangerous war conditions to build tension and momentum: 'A picture suddenly flashed into his brain. A scarred battlefield with ploughed-up earth and twisted wire entanglements, shrill whine of a shell, thunder of artillery'. Unlike the earlier sketches, here the language is direct and compressed, without any extraneous adjectives or flowery language.

But the influence of cinema upon Phyllis's short story writing is no more evident than in 'The Deep', a magic-realist tale set in a London boarding house. Published in *The Daily Mail* in November 1936, it tells the story of a mysterious guest who arrives at the boarding house one day, wishing to rent a room. From the beginning, suspense is established through the distant point of view, narrated years after the event: 'That was, of course, before the fierce light of publicity had singled out No. 14 for its special beneficence. Before the cameras had exhausted every angle of the trim early-Victorian dwelling and the newspapers – the highly sensational and incredible happenings which occurred about that time'.

The new tenant, Mr Blunt, is described as having a pale, greenish, translucent pallor. His eyes were 'humid and protruding, and his mouth was a thin slit that opened and shut mechanically on his somewhat halting speech'. At the dinner table that night, the landlady is unnerved to learn that her new boarder eschews red meat in favour of vegetables. On a subsequent night, a Friday, she is further unsettled when Mr Blunt flees the dinner table after a platter of fish is served. Furthermore, every day the man rises late, and it is not until after lunch that he ventures outside, though he never stays away long, and always returns early to spend his evenings indoors. A suspicious fellow tenant decides to follow him one day and is disappointed to find that Blunt's only transgression is to sit on a seat beside the Thames for an hour, gazing at the currents, before catching the bus back home again. Blunt befriends shrinking violet Miss Daly, also a boarder, and lends her a book about fish, one that contains 'beautifully-coloured plates'. He then upsets the other boarders by spending an inordinate amount of time in the only bathroom. After the landlady knocks on the door to complain, she is confronted by a disconcerting sight: 'His curious protruding eyes looked amazingly alive, and his skin was mottled where the pink flesh struggled to show through its customary pallor. His hair was still wet, and looked dark and oily as it clung tightly to his head – like a seal'.

After one of the other boarders enjoys a big win at the races, he buys a car and drives himself, the landlady, and all the other tenants to the coast. As the rest of the group purchases bathing suits on the esplanade, Mr Blunt resolutely declares that he does not wish to go swimming. But before the boarders have a chance to change into their suits, they notice an almost-robotic Blunt walking fully clothed into the sea. Rescuers attempt to pull him back but are ultimately unsuccessful:

His head was now just a bobbing darkness against the blue … suddenly it disappeared. A cry went up from the crowd. Someone pointed, and the cry became a clamour. Already the rescuers had seen it and were struggling back to shore. A huge green fish appeared suddenly at the surface of the water. It swam along for a few yards. It seemed to pause a moment, a brilliant iridescence against the blue of ocean and sky – then, turning swiftly, it darted out to sea.

While it is tempting to compare 'The Deep' with Franz Kafka's modernist masterpiece, 'Metamorphosis', there are key differences between the two narratives. While Kafka's can be read as a fable about the alienation of the individual within a harsh and uncaring society, 'The Deep' is a story of ultimate liberation from the routines and rules of civilisation. Mr Blunt figuratively and literally sheds the strictures of 'decent society' as he defies the laws of evolution and devolves from a human into a fish.

It's likely that inspiration for this story partly arose after having spent time with her brother-in-law, avid angler Charles Stewart, and flipping through his many books on deep-sea fishing. But no doubt the most powerful influence was a film that screened in Sydney at the Lyceum Theatre in early December 1935, eleven months before the story was published. *The Passing of the Third Floor Back* narrates an almost identical story of a mysterious foreigner who arrives at a London boarding house. The landlady somewhat reluctantly rents him the small third floor back room, overlooking damp roofs and blackened chimneys. The film contains similar oddball boarders, including a downtrodden maid, and a set of parents determined to sacrifice their pretty daughter's hand in marriage to pay off mounting debts. But while the mysterious new tenant of the film turns out to be a kind of guardian angel whose presence and generosity transforms the lives of those around him, in Phyllis's short story, it is the tenant who is transformed radically by his interactions with the other boarders. In this particular tale, the influence of film on Phyllis's fiction writing is so palpable that it teeters on plagiarism. But as the old literary saying goes, 'Amateurs borrow, professionals steal'.

During the mid-1930s, Phyllis and Paulette were also working on another set of film projects that would not be dependent on the participation of Isabel. On 26 September 1934, it was announced in *Everyone's* magazine that the formation of Centralian Film Productions was to take over from MCD Productions, which planned to produce two features and six featurettes. The company was composed of a syndicate that included John McDonagh, Neville Macken, and the Hon. NB O'Connor. The films were to be subtitled into numerous foreign languages and marketed internationally.

Two months before the formation of Centralian, the sisters announced to the press what they intended as subjects for their featurettes and shorts:

> These will show the tribal life of the aborigines, work on
> a big cattle station, and the highlights of the fauna, flora
> and scenery of the centre. By translating the talking part
> of the film into foreign languages, it is hoped to secure a
> market and to make Australia known in Europe as well
> as in English-speaking countries. Arrangements are being
> made for captions and 'talkies' in Chinese, Japanese, Czech,
> Greek, and other tongues.

The shorts had been planned to capitalise on overseas curiosity about the Australian outback and its Indigenous people. In a matter of eight years, the sisters had swerved away from determinedly urban subject matter in a non-specific setting, to embracing themes and stories that were specifically Australian.

Centralian had been formed to produce the film *Flynn of the Inland*, a fictional adaptation of Ion Idriess' 1932 biography of Reverend John Flynn. In 1902, Flynn had joined the Home Missions staff of the Presbyterian Church, and later founded the Aerial Medical Service (Flying Doctor Service) to treat patients in the remote areas of the Northern Territory and beyond. Paulette spent six months, unpaid, writing the scenario, a romance set in Sydney and the outback that centred around a love triangle, with

Flynn and his best friend vying for the affections of a nurse they'd met at Sydney University. The character of the nurse was based on a real-life woman whom Paulette had known. The rivalry between the two men increases when the three are transferred to Central Australia and the nurse is appointed matron of a bush hospital. A thundering cattle stampede was to have featured in the climax of the film.

Paulette mostly used books to conduct her background research, but the invention of the Flynn/best friend/matron romantic storyline was entirely her own. It was to be financed by the Presbyterian Church, to which Flynn had been deeply devoted, but no contracts between the parties had yet been signed. The featurette shorts were to be filmed while on location in the outback, before and after *Flynn* had been shot. In July 1934, the *Sydney Morning Herald* announced the highly ambitious plans of Centralian:

> A fully-equipped expedition will leave Sydney about the end of August. Three cameramen, three technicians, three actors, three actresses, a director, an art director, and a supervisor will comprise the company. It is anticipated that the expedition will be 'on location' for about six weeks and that the production of the film will occupy three months.

Apparently, Centralian had already secured the services of the Inland Mission, a patrol padre, and both the eminent Flying Doctor and his famous aeroplane.

The publicity blitz did not stop there. A week later, the *Sun* reported that Mrs Charles Stewart (Isabel) was expected to return to Sydney at the end of the year to take up production again, with her sisters 'now busily organising an expedition to Central Australia – something of an historic trip for women'. It's highly unlikely, however, that Isabel ever agreed to these plans. Just a few months later, director Alexander Korda, who'd seen her in one or two McDonagh productions when they'd screened in London, would approach Isabel and offer to make her as famous as he had made Merle Oberon. But Isabel replied, 'No, I've got a son. I want to be a married woman and not work anymore'. More likely, Paulette concocted Isabel's fabled return to acting to attract more anticipation, publicity, and finance for her comeback as a director after the disappointments of her previous two films.

The McDonaghs had a habit of publicly announcing their future projects with confidence, bravado, and exaggeration. Little did they realise that while they were freely circulating their ideas in the press, unguarded and without any copyright attached, less talented filmmakers, with more financial, technical, and infrastructural support, could steal their idea and proceed with a rival production.

In contrast to Centralian's extravagant press releases about *Flynn of the Inland*, the reality of the reconnaissance trip to Central Australia was more prosaic. In early 1935, John, now thirty-three, and with only a single cameraman, drove from Sydney to Alice Springs in an old Packard to survey the areas in which they intended to film. The outback contained few sealed roads and, when the car became stuck in sand, they'd have to lay down matting so the tyres could gain traction. In Alice Springs, the cameraman photographed landscapes and the harsh conditions in which the Indigenous peoples were forced to live. John found the outback inhabitants friendly and obliging. They took direction well and appeared to be natural in front of a camera. The cameraman shot a lot of footage to later edit into short documentaries.

Upon his return, however, John was pessimistic about Centralian's ability to produce the feature film, because most vehicles would be unable to traverse the harsh desert landscape without becoming bogged or lost. Still, in June 1935, the intrepid Paulette and Phyllis soldiered on, appearing at a meeting of the

Feminist Club in Sydney to give a talk on Central Australia, and the story behind their upcoming feature.

The quota system that the McDonaghs had been fighting to establish for years was finally approved in New South Wales in September 1935, which recommended a five-year quota for Australian pictures in all programs, with theatre managers obliged to screen twenty Australian films a year for the first five years, rising to sixty films thereafter. It also urged that the new rules become uniform in all other states. The legislation came into effect on 1 January 1936, but it was too little, too late for the McDonagh sisters, who'd been struggling for almost a decade against the chokehold of American film combines.

Only a few months later, National Productions, which had built a cavernous and well-equipped studio in Pagewood in anticipation of the quota legislation passing, announced plans to shoot their own version of the flying doctor story, also featuring a love triangle, with support from the Gaumont-British Picture Company. It would star Hollywood heartthrob Charles Farrell in the lead and be directed by the British actor Miles Mander. The Gaumont company, based in England, had for a long time wanted to shoot a film in Australia, and so it provided technical and financial assistance to National Productions. The British unit arrived in November 1935 and production began at the Pagewood studios in 1936.

In January of that year, Kenneth Slessor reported on the films that were currently in production in New South Wales, all as a consequence of the newly introduced Australian quota legislation. *The Burgomeister*, produced by Harry Southwell, had already been completed and was awaiting release. *Thoroughbred*, featuring Hollywood star Helen Twelvetrees and produced by Cinesound, was in production, as was National Film's flying doctor film at

Pagewood. Slessor also noted that 'simultaneously, the last touches are being added to another "Flying Doctor" film by the McDonagh Company. The McDonaghs were first in the field with this Central Australian theme, but it is not expected that the two productions will clash'. The truth, however, was much more complicated: by early 1936, Centralian Films had yet to shoot a single frame.

Paulette always maintained that the reason the film didn't go into production was because the Presbyterian Church had decided to withdraw its funding. But perhaps the withdrawal was because Gaumont-British had already released a flying doctor film that also included a love triangle. '... it would have been the greatest tribute the Presbyterian Church ever had', Paulette lamented. 'They mightn't have known it then, but they would now.'

What would have galled the wronged director even more was the tepid critical reaction to the high-budget feature:

> the story is weak in the extreme. Instead of selecting and
> developing some definite dramatic subject, it sprawls and
> rambles all over the place, and the real conflict does not
> develop until five minutes before the end. Even then, it is over-
> sentimental and unconvincing.

Most reviews complained that the film seems to have been shot with the eye of a tourist from overseas wanting to record images of his Australian holiday, or a director whose priority is securing multiple international markets, evidenced by the inclusion of Australian attractions and scenes that had absolutely no bearing on the plot, such as cricketer Don Bradman, and shots of the Sydney Harbour Bridge and Bondi Beach. Paulette probably read the following review with a mixture of frustration and schadenfreude:

> The direction of 'The Flying Doctor' is, to put it bluntly, a bit
> muddled ... there are several unnecessary sequences which

interrupt the story, several unexplained actions which disturb the onlooker, several unexpected events which are confusingly illogical, and several other evidences that the film as a picture must have been vague in the director's mind.

Yet again, Paulette had been thwarted by dominant international companies run by powerful men, even though, as an independent, she knew she was far better at making films. But she had neither the Hollywood contacts nor the international distribution resources to compete with National Productions. And without the collaborative contribution of her leading lady, Isabel, she lost the will to continue. The multiple struggles to develop and produce *Flynn of the Inland* had finally broken her. 'Isn't it funny', she said, 'from that moment on I didn't try. I didn't want to, I suppose'.

Sadly, Paulette's final surrender to the dominance of film corporations was probably a wise decision. The following year, Britain reduced its quota act entitlements for Australian films, greatly diminishing the chances of an Australian production securing a UK distribution deal. Moreover, in Sydney, National Productions folded after releasing only one film, and its partner company, National Studios, met the same fate after co-producing an Australian western, *Rangle River*, with Columbia Pictures. The change in the NSW film quota system, which had been legislated to attract overseas production companies to invest in Australian films, had made no significant impact. In three years, war would be declared in Europe, and shortages of manpower and film stock played a role in the plummeting number of Australian features produced. Post-war, the Greater Union Cinema chain altered its policies, withdrawing investment from local productions. Between the late 1940s and the late '60s, the Australian film industry languished from a lack of infrastructure and a dearth of government support. Independent Paulette would not have stood a chance.

Two Minutes Silence would be the last feature film directed by an Australian woman to receive a commercial release for the next forty-six years, until the premiere of Gillian Armstrong's *My Brilliant Career* (1979).

17

DESPERATELY SEEKING SISTERS

(1936–1946)

By 1936, Isabel found herself suffering from post-natal depression and missing her siblings desperately. A concerned and ever-accommodating Charles finally agreed to emigrate to Australia and settle there. After returning to London, the Stewarts set sail for Sydney, with stops in Paris, India, Ceylon, and Fiji.

Paula once observed that Isabel's marriage to Charles was the best thing that ever happened to her. But she also added that it probably wasn't the best thing for him. The reason, again, was the clannish closeness of the three McDonagh sisters, who would always prioritise each other's needs – and, in Isabel's case, those of her children – over a husband or paramour. Paula admitted that she was the same: blood relatives such as her siblings and children would always come first over the needs of her husband.

Upon their arrival in Sydney, Isabel, Charles, and the baby moved into the Belvedere Hotel in Kings Cross, a gracious, white-painted, former colonial mansion. It had a sweeping driveway, a fountain, and an acre of lush gardens brimming with Moreton Bay figs, palms, fragrant magnolias, and camphor laurels. Classical white marble statues gazed down as guests strolled around the

Arcadian paradise. The balconies were wreathed in wisteria, and music could often be heard drifting through the open windows.

Not long after arriving, in late February, Charles joined a fishing expedition led by novelist Zane Grey at Batemans Bay, a half day's drive south of Sydney, which included a documentary film crew. One day, after many attempts, Charles managed to catch a large swordfish, and 'appeared to be mute in his delight'. When the expedition moved on to Watsons Bay in Sydney, Grey often consulted his associate, Dr David Stead, a marine scientist and father to future novelist Christina Stead. The doctor and his family lived on the edge of the bay and he was an expert on the local sea life.

Isabel did not enjoy housework or cooking, so it was fortunate that the hotel had impeccable hospitality and a five-star French restaurant. Inside, Persian rugs lined the floors and crystal chandeliers gleamed from the ceilings. Photographer Rennie Ellis remembered the atmosphere of the Belvedere as 'New Orleans belle epoque' and that 'the famous and the celebrated stayed there', such as violinist Yehudi Menuhin, actor Maurice Chevalier, ballerina Margot Fonteyn, and future designer of the Sydney Opera House, Jørn Utzon.

While Isabel was settling into well-upholstered luxury, younger sister Anita was still pining away in Molong. To relieve the monotonous routine of small-town living, she and Gregory joined the Cumnock Amateur Dramatic Company, which mostly performed in church halls. The fact that her staid husband received glowing reviews for his performances, while hers were never mentioned, must have riled the aspiring actress. In 1936, she secured the female lead in the comedy *Aren't We All?*, which played for two nights, mid-week, in the local School of Arts. Anita was so thrilled by this minor achievement that for years to come her children would never hear the end of it. Unfortunately, the production didn't attract a single review, so we don't know how her performance was received.

By the time the Stewart family arrived in Sydney, the McDonagh siblings had moved out of the Darling Point house and into the Hampton Court Hotel on Bayswater Road in Kings Cross. It was only a two-minute stroll from the Belvedere, so it was almost like they were all living together again. Even though the siblings had retreated from producing films, the McDonagh Census forms for that year list John and Phyllis's occupations as 'Film Producers', while Grant lists himself as a 'Writer'. Only Paula felt beholden to tell the unvarnished truth and listed 'Home Duties' as her source of work. A disconsolate Paulette didn't even bother to fill out the form.

But she was no doubt thrilled to have her older sister back within her orbit, and an equally passionate collaboration would soon begin to grow between the former actress and the former director. But instead of discussing close-ups beneath the heat of klieg lights or rewriting dialogue together, Paulette would devote herself to helping Isabel raise her child. Isabel was still suffering from the effects of post-natal depression and did not have the energy to mother full-time. Paulette would arrive at the hotel early in the mornings and feed the toddler, who was now two, take him for walks, tell him stories, sing him songs, and change his nappies daily. Paulette would not leave the Belvedere until the child was fast asleep at night.

For her part, Isabel became reclusive, refusing invitations and shunning social outings. The rare times she would venture from her home was to accompany her husband and child on fishing expeditions in Australia and New Zealand. Paulette accompanied them on one such trip, and an ever-patient Charles taught her how to catch marlin.

The youngest McDonagh, Paula, was now studying nursing. During her first year, however, she caught a bad case of diphtheria from a patient. While bedridden and feeling sorry for herself, she began to rethink her future. Despite warnings from stern Aunt Mary, Paula realised that, unlike her mother, Aunt Nellie, and her sister Anita, she was not temperamentally suited to nursing. After she recovered, she withdrew from her studies and, in an act of independence rare for a McDonagh, moved on her own to Queensland. There, she found a job selling advertising space in a business directory.

Also in 1936, forty-year-old Gordon Collingridge finally married his young girlfriend, Sheila, who by then had turned twenty-one, and the matchmaking McDonagh sisters were naturally elated. The newlyweds moved to a house in Ryde and would always remain close friends with the sisters, particularly Paulette. Over the years, whenever Sheila fell ill, Paulette would take public transport to the distant northern suburb to visit the patient and fuss over the sickbed.

The following year, Aunt Mary died at the grand age of eighty. At the time, she'd been renting a home in Rose Bay. After the funeral, Paulette, Phyllis, John, Grant, and Paula briefly moved into the home that was still under lease to their aunt. As usual, the siblings had an open-door policy and friends would sleep over for various lengths of time.

By now, John had found a temporary menial job to help put food on the table. While at work he made a friend, Leo O'Brien, nicknamed 'OB', who was apparently down on his luck. One night, John returned home and declared to the others, 'Oh, there's this lovely bloke from New Zealand, and he-- the soles are out of his shoes and he's got nothing'. The siblings empathised with his plight and agreed that John should invite him to stay with them for a while. 'Next thing we knew', said Paula, 'OB was back and he-- he stayed. Never left. He was just one of many'.

Whenever the growing commune ran out of money for food, John and OB would take a net and go prawning on the harbour at night. They'd return in the morning and feed their family and friends, a routine that would continue until someone eventually brought home a pay cheque.

After the lease of Aunt Mary's house expired, Paulette, John, Grant, and Phyllis moved back into the Hampton Court Hotel. John's friend, OB, moved with them. By this time, he and Phyllis had begun a relationship, and Phyllis had found a job in a camera shop. The hotel provided room service from its in-house restaurant and Grant began training as a chef in the hotel's kitchen.

On 30 June 1938, a second son, Charles, was born to Isabel and Charles Senior. The very first memory of older brother, Alan, was his beautiful mother arriving home from hospital, pausing in the fragrant garden of the Belvedere with the newborn in her arms. The family continued to live at the hotel, enjoying the room service, the restaurant, the vibrant company, and the extensive gardens, where children could play safely for hours under Paulette's watchful eye. She adored inventing scary bedtime stories for the children that were filled with exotic monsters and demons. The boys nicknamed their beloved second mother, 'Paw-paw', and to this day still refer to her as such.

Just before war was declared in Europe, OB yearned to return to his home in New Zealand, where he'd been offered a job as a proofreader for a local newspaper. One of Phyllis's close friends, nicknamed Ginge, had connections with newspapers there and promised Phyllis a job as a journalist if she ever wished to make the move across the Tasman. So, Phyllis was persuaded to join OB on his trip back to Wellington. They settled into an apartment and Phyllis immediately began looking for work, eventually securing a position as editor of the New Zealand edition of *Truth*. 'I was called on immediately to organise a Women's War Page – and was fortunate in having success on my hands. Later I was called on to do interviews with visiting celebrities – and to cover theatre and film reviews.'

Of the three older sisters, Phyllis was the least co-dependent. As a young woman, she'd had enough courage to break away from the others to perform as a singer in theatres. She studied art and had been writing and publishing articles and short stories since her teenage years. At the age of thirty-two, she had the courage to enter a rollerskating competition, against much younger competitors, and not only claim first prize as 'Miss Palladium, Queen of the Harbour', but also, in press interviews after her crowning, promote the sisters' upcoming film, *Two Minutes Silence*. Moreover, once their filmmaking careers had come to an end, Phyllis, as a writer, still had a creative outlet, which did not require the presence or input of the other two.

It was also Phyllis who became concerned about the amount of time and energy Paulette was devoting to Isabel and the children, and how she was sacrificing important career opportunities in the film industry for the sake of being a part of Isabel's family, which she expressed in letters to Paulette and the others. But her pleas had little or no effect.

While living and working in New Zealand, Phyllis also extended her matchmaking skills by performing a Cyrano de Bergerac–type act for her single female friend, Ginge, who was keen on a widower named Kidd. Phyllis would write long, effusive letters to the widower on behalf of Ginge, who would have to copy them out in her own hand before posting them. Ginge would complain that the letters were so lengthy that her hand would cramp from rewriting them.

Even so, Phyllis's romantic lyricism created the desired effect: Kidd fell in love with the letters so much that he soon proposed to Ginge and they were promptly married. In later years, a sentimental Kidd would pull out the letters and read them aloud, quoting passages that still affected him deeply. An embarrassed Ginge would sit nearby, poker-faced, never having the courage to admit that she wasn't the true author of the epistolary passion.

Approaching middle age, however, the matchmaker herself remained unwedded, and in 1942, her boyfriend, OB, was drafted into the New Zealand army. By that time, the Second World War had been raging in Europe for three years, and OB and Phyllis were only too aware that there was a good chance that OB would not return alive. Phyllis finally relinquished her independence and they decided to formalise their union, marrying in a simple ceremony. To alert her siblings of the news, Phyllis sent Paulette a telegram.

John had already joined the armed forces in May 1941. Three years later, he was on overseas duty in the medical corps in New Guinea for nine months, and for six months in 1945, mainly in Bougainville. Grant signed up in January 1943, and the following year also served in New Guinea in the medical corps. While there, he composed songs in his spare time and collaborated with celebrated Australian Imperial Force (AIF) bandleader, Jim Davidson. When either John or Grant wrote home, they would invariably send the letters to Paulette, who would then share the news with the rest of the family. Similarly, whenever a sibling had to make a challenging decision, he or she would always discuss it first with Paulette. On a return trip to Sydney on a rest and recreation furlough, Grant stayed with Paulette where, on 7 June 1944, he wrote in her autograph book: 'To Paulette; Here's to our 5 year pact!!! We'll live to laugh at it – both of us – "Memories live longer than dreams!"'.

Grant had good reason to make a pact with his sister to 'live to laugh' for the next five years. Throughout 1943 and early 1944, while in the jungles of New Guinea, he suffered from several serious illnesses, including malaria, bullous impetigo, tonsillitis, and a near-fatal spider bite. In the middle of one particularly hot and steamy night, an alarm sounded, and Grant jumped out of bed, pulled on his shorts, and was suddenly seized by what felt like a red-hot needle piercing his buttocks. He would be bedridden for three months and would later contract a life-threatening case of amoebic dysentery, causing his weight to drop to a dangerous eight stone (fifty kilograms).

Grant's mates managed to capture the offending spider and later stored it in a jar of formaldehyde. He named the spider 'Ethel', and for many years after the war, the arachnid would be proudly displayed on a mantelpiece in his home. In March 1945, following his leave, Grant was assigned to the Indonesian island of Morotai, which had been earlier invaded by the Imperial Japanese Forces. There, he met Australian army nurse Estelle Dyer, who shared his love of literature and music and, as the war in the Pacific began winding down, their interest in one another began gearing up.

Following D-Day, Grant was obliged to remain in Morotai for several months while Estelle was transferred back to Sydney. In early February 1946, she signed her name in Paulette's autograph book, confirming the growing closeness between herself and Grant. When Grant finally returned, he was still gravely ill from the effects of malaria and was admitted immediately to Concord Hospital where Estelle happened to be working and could nurse him personally. And, in a curious repetition of his parents' romance, Grant found himself falling even deeper in love with this young, attractive woman who was gently coaxing him back to health.

During his recuperation, he was keenly aware that Estelle had been engaged twice before to a man in Melbourne. When she was summoned to that city to visit her stepmother on her deathbed, Grant was terrified that she would either not return or become reinvolved with her former fiancé. Before she left for the railway station to travel south indefinitely, he abruptly proposed, and they married that very same afternoon. However, the stepmother's death was not a sprint but a marathon, and the marriage wasn't consummated until Estelle's return to Sydney six months later.

In the early 1940s, while the war continued to rage in Europe, the Middle East, and the Pacific, the McDonaghs' former home and film set, Drummoyne House, was sold yet again. Sadly, the property was divided into nine separate flats and left to deteriorate.

By this time, Paula, in her early thirties, had married and conceived her first child. She met her husband, Bob Dornan, just as the Second World War was breaking out. After leaving the advertising business in 1938, she'd set up her own mobile photography company, with financial assistance from Isabel's husband.

The work involved travelling around the country in a car and selling portrait coupons to people in small towns. The following day, the photographer, Donald Capon, would arrive in the same town and set up a studio in the local town hall where scores of mothers and children would line up to redeem their coupons and pose for pictures, which would be developed within hours. One day, Capon and Paula were working near an army base in Caloundra, Queensland, when some local soldiers arrived to have their photos taken. One of the soldiers, Bob Dornan, later appeared that night at the pub where Paula was staying and invited her to have a drink with him. 'And that was the undoing', said Paula, laughing.

Now expecting her first child, she did not want to give birth in Queensland, so far away from her family, and so she persuaded Bob to move to Sydney and rent a flat in Kings Cross, close to her various siblings and the Elizabeth Bay Private Hospital where she intended to give birth.

Paulette was still living in the Hampton Court Hotel and, when the Dornans found a ground-floor, two-bedroom flat across the lane from the hotel, in a building named Kaindi, Paulette decided that she would move in too. At that time, Kaindi was part of the Hampton Court Hotel, connected by an overhead bridge that straddled the roofs and, whenever the Dornans or Paulette didn't feel like cooking, one of them would simply pick up the telephone and order room service.

After she gave up writing and directing motion pictures in the 1930s, Paulette chose not to look for a job or pursue any other kind of occupation. Perhaps it was the disappointment of her stalled film career, or her devotion to Isabel and the children, or both, but she never attempted to work again – in the film industry or in any other capacity. The descendants of the McDonaghs do not know how she supported herself for the next forty years. Paula maintained that all her brothers and sisters regularly chipped in to help her with rent, bills, and other expenses. Paula's eldest son, however, remembers his mother only giving money to Paulette in the event of an emergency. The most likely scenario, however, is that wealthy Isabel and Charles paid Paulette a permanent stipend, partly in compensation for her voluntary years of childcare and housework, and because they were so intensely close. There may also have been some guilt motivating Isabel's quiet and enduring generosity as her withdrawal from MCD Productions and her subsequent marriage had triggered the end of Paulette's career as a director.

It was also during the early 1940s that the sisters settled into the class system that each of them most preferred, and within which they would stay for the rest of their lives: Isabel into the privileged upper class, Phyllis into the steady middle class, and Paulette into what would be considered the 'working class' or, more precisely, the raffish underbelly of Australian bohemia. In fact, as Sheila Collingridge observed, 'Paulette was the most bohemian of all!'

A good example of Paulette's non-conformity can be gleaned from her taste in men, who were invariably domineering, intelligent, and socially rebellious. In the late 1930s, she fell in love with a defrocked Anglican priest named John Verner Cunningham-Browne, eight years her senior, who was nicknamed 'Bish'. Cunningham-Browne's father had also been a doctor, working as a medic for the Royal Australian Navy. In 1919, at the age of twenty-six, Cunningham-Browne became a clerk of the Holy Orders and married Jessie Russell Ross, who was fifteen years older. The following year she gave birth to their first and only child, a boy.

The reverend's in-laws were rich and powerful. They owned a luxurious country home, Kincraig, in Yarra Glen, where Jessie had grown up, and where the young family frequently visited and stayed over. During one such visit in 1928, Cunningham-Browne, by now a heavy drinker, managed to seduce one of the maids and ran off with the young woman, never to be seen by the family again. In one fell swoop, the anarchic priest had managed to scandalise his parents, the Russell Ross family, and the Anglican Church – from which he was promptly dismissed.

But the renegade reverend was not yet done with besmirching the values with which he'd been raised and educated. He fled to Sydney and, in December of the same year, converted to Catholicism. The Catholic priests of St Joseph's in Woollahra were so chuffed about welcoming a former Anglican clergyman into their flock that they sent out a press release announcing the conversion.

The affair with the maid did not last. For years, the former reverend drifted around Sydney's eastern suburbs, working as a freelance journalist and a private tutor. Paulette met him at the start of the war and loved drinking and discussing literature and history with him. The descendants of the McDonagh sisters all agree that Bish was highly intelligent and well read, but dissolute in his dress and habits. He might have been a married, alcoholic, defrocked priest, but, as one relative remarked, 'it wasn't the kind of family that would have been bothered by this ...' One afternoon, when Paulette's young nephews Alan and Charles were visiting, Bish knocked on the door. She opened it and spoke briefly with him but wouldn't let him into her flat while the children were there.

18

SPLICED TOGETHER AGAIN

(1941-1956)

On 8 May 1941, Isabel gave birth to her third child, a daughter named Sandra, at Elizabeth Bay Private Hospital. The growing family continued to live in the Belvedere for another year until the war in the Pacific suddenly drew dangerously close. On the night of 31 May 1942, three midget submarines, part of the Imperial Japanese Navy, entered Sydney Harbour and attempted to sink Allied warships. While the crew of one submarine scuttled their vessel, and another was successfully attacked and sunk, the third submarine tried to torpedo the heavy cruiser, USS *Chicago*, but mistakenly sank the converted ferry, HMAS *Kuttabul*, killing twenty-one sailors.

Most residents of Kings Cross were terrified by the sound of the bombing and hid in basements and under beds. However, once Paulette heard the nearby shelling, she did not shrink or hide away. Instead, she ran to the Belvedere to be with Isabel and the children. Nephew Charles distinctly remembers that 'she wanted to die with us'.

After the attack, most residents of the neighbourhood were terrified and began swiftly moving to safer areas: the Blue Mountains, and further west into rural New South Wales. Charles

Stewart was determined to protect Isabel and his young children and purchased a house on Marion Street in Strathfield, three blocks away from Rookwood Cemetery and almost ten miles west of the city. Charles was so concerned about another invasion that, in the event of a subsequent attack, he'd arranged for the use of a ship that would spirit his family away from Sydney to the shores of the safer United States. Paulette remained in the Kings Cross flat, but from then on, she caught the train to Strathfield every morning to spend the day with Isabel and the children, continuing her role as unofficial nanny, housekeeper, and devoted companion.

The home on Marion Street sat on a corner quarter-acre block, where Charles Senior developed a lush and tranquil garden of flowers, herbs, and vegetables. Alan and Charles Junior remember their childhood as being idyllic, even though they didn't enjoy school, preferring to be at home in the company of their parents and indulgent aunt.

'None of us really liked school', said Charles. 'We couldn't wait to get back to our garden. The garden of Eden, I suppose.' Unsurprisingly, the only subject that Charles was interested in was drama. At the age of ten, he tried to persuade his teachers to stage a production of *Hamlet* because he was convinced that he was now ready to play the lead.

The discipline that Isabel had imposed on her younger sisters and brothers while they were in her care during the 1920s did not extend to her own children. When the family went out to a restaurant, they were permitted, like the adults, to quaff wine or champagne with their meals. If they came home and declared that they didn't like a particular school, Isabel would remove them immediately and unofficially home-school them until the authorities intervened and compelled her to send them to yet another school. By this time, a formal education was not as vital as the examples and lessons to be learned from life and literature. Perhaps she was also aware that her children would inherit the family fortune and would never have to work for a living.

At the age of fifteen, Charles first read the collected works of Percy Bysshe Shelley and began writing poetry in imitation of him. He then moved on to Milton and Yeats, the latter of whom he still admires today.

The youngest child, Sandra, inherited the McDonagh yearning for risk-taking and adventure. 'She was a remarkable person because anyone who met her was very affected by her', observed Charles. Eight years younger than Alan, and three years younger than Charles, she was a proud tomboy, wilder and braver than her brothers. They fondly remember her performing hair-raising stunts on her bicycle, such as lying flat on the handlebars as she flew down a steep hill.

Following the Japanese submarine attack on Sydney Harbour, there was another resident connected with the family who was keen to escape the eastern suburbs. Her name was Mrs Levins, and she owned a house at 20 Towns Road in Vaucluse. By this time, Anita's husband, Gregory Blackall, and his brother had spent eight years in Molong competing with an already-established pharmacy, before they finally gave up and closed the business. To make matters worse, daughter Ann's asthma had barely improved during their long tenure there. Anita and Gregory moved back to Sydney where Mrs Levins, keen to move to a safer area, gave them the keys to her home on Towns Road, allowing them to live in the house while they gradually paid it off. Even though Anita was probably the most rebellious McDonagh sister, she decorated the home with a plethora of Catholic icons and reproductions.

As a couple, Anita and Gregory were opposites. Gregory was quiet and reserved; Anita was gregarious and exuberant. He had a strong work ethic; she liked to socialise. He was a conservative man with sober tastes; she still longed to become a famous actress.

Throughout his marriage, Gregory did not take his wife out for dinner, or accompany her to any social events. If he disapproved of the way his wife or one of his children behaved, he simply withdrew and stopped talking to the offending party for several days. Youngest daughter, Moya, suffered for almost a week under his silent treatment for the offence of merely cutting off her braids. In contrast, Anita was a warm, affectionate, and loving mother.

The children remember Gregory and Anita frequently arguing. Unlike the rambunctious McDonaghs, their father rarely drank. He also did not appreciate the attention his wife attracted from admiring men and often had jealous outbursts. But decades later, when he was dying in hospital, he admitted to his youngest daughter, Moya, 'I loved her so much'.

Anita enrolled her daughters as boarders at Kincoppal. Occasionally, she would collect Moya from school and walk up the hill from Elizabeth Bay to visit Paulette in her flat. Whenever Isabel was visiting at the same time with her own daughter, Moya noticed that for the duration of the visit, Isabel and Sandra did not let go of one another, that they sat side by side, constantly holding hands.

During the middle of the war, on 12 October 1942, Stella's husband, Willie, died at the age of fifty-six. A bereft Stella had no living relatives or children of her own and had been married to Willie for twenty-four years. Not long after Willie's death, empathic Paula began scanning Lonely Hearts newspaper columns in an attempt, like her father a quarter of a century earlier, to find Stella a suitable companion and husband. She eventually hit upon a listing by a travelling salesman, Francis (Frank) Leo Hitchens, forty-eight. Through romantic epistolary exchanges, Paula answered the listing in Stella's voice and name. Frank replied to her letter with enthusiasm. The two soon met, love blossomed, and they were married only twelve months after the death of Willie Waddock. Frank gave up his work as a travelling salesman, moved into Stella's home in Vaucluse, and settled down to a job as a storeman.

The following year, during a respite from the war and a brief return to Sydney, John McDonagh also married. His bride was forty-three-year-old Elsie Lillian Ross, a clothes designer and dressmaker who was two years his senior. However, John would remain in the army until June 1946. When he was finally discharged from the services and reunited with his bride, he was forty-four to her forty-six. In his discharge papers, he describes his once-fair hair as being grey.

Once settled into civilian life, the couple moved into an apartment at 442 New South Head Road, Double Bay. John became a journalist and manager of *Newsweek*, heading up their Australian bureau. By all accounts, Elsie was a lovely woman, but she gradually developed an addiction to alcohol, just like her parents and two brothers and sisters. Her siblings had overcome their addictions by joining Alcoholics Anonymous; Elsie, however, refused to accept help or attempt reform. While John was travelling interstate on business for *Newsweek*, he'd be desperately worried about his always-inebriated wife, and would often rush home, wracked with anxiety. The stress was so great that he eventually resigned from the publication to take care of her.

Paula's sons occasionally stayed over at John and Elsie's home when they were visiting Sydney. Nephew John remembers his uncle, nicknamed 'Bill', as a nice man whose favourite drink was brandy, while recalling that Elsie was usually in bed, her addiction often reducing her to the condition of invalid. Uncle John did all the shopping, cooking, and household chores, and he soon developed a way to earn a living while remaining at home and caring for his wife. The apartment they rented was spacious and contained many rooms, so he converted part of it into a commercial gym, with barbells, medicine balls, and punching bags. He even installed a full sauna where clients such as jockeys and boxers could relax after workouts.

As the years passed, however, John developed a reliance on alcohol too – so much so that he also became an alcoholic. All the McDonagh siblings enjoyed drinking and partying with one another, but not to the extent of John and Elsie. 'John's wife finished him', said an irate Paula, who would occasionally lose her temper with her brother. Later, Paula would regret treating him harshly over his addiction and remained torn about the rift for the rest of her life.

Still, John's later-life alcoholism may have had a hereditary aspect: after all, his grandfather had died of cancer of the liver and cirrhosis of the liver; and his father of an accidental cocaine overdose.

The Kaindi flat was becoming too small for Paula and Bob's growing family, so they returned to Queensland to live and work on the farm owned by Bob Dornan's parents. But it was not long before Grant and Estelle took advantage of the vacated bedroom in Paulette's flat. The couple moved in and would live with her for several years.

At night, the feral cats that prowled the laneway would fight and fornicate, filling the apartment with shrieks and howls. If a window that faced the lane was opened, the ammoniac stench of feline piss would permeate the room.

Paulette's relationship with Bish continued unabated, and she enjoyed verbally sparring with the articulate and well-read man. Once, during an argument, he grew so exasperated with her that he shouted, 'You should be hung up by the heels, like Mussolini!'

Bish had not kept in contact with his relatives in Victoria, and for their part, the scandalous former reverend was 'wiped', never to be mentioned in polite company. One day, however, a curious teenage niece tracked him down in Sydney but later regretted it, recoiling from his drunkenness and louche lifestyle. From the age of eight, his son, John, had been raised solely by his mother and grandparents. Years later, when John was conducting business in Sydney, he accidentally found himself face to face with the father who'd deserted him decades earlier. We don't know what transpired during the unplanned reunion, but after it ended, John never again met up with his father.

In 1947, Grant opened his own café, The Song and Star, on the corner of Pennys Lane and Kings Cross Road, just a few steps away from Kaindi. Just as his father had collected signed memorabilia and photographs from his famous patients, Grant collected signatures of actors and celebrity customers in an autograph book he kept in the café. He installed an upright piano on the premises and exercised his creative side by composing songs and engaging leading jazz pianists to play them, with one composition being broadcast on ABC radio. With typical McDonagh bravado, he boasted, 'it's harder to make one omelette than to compose an operetta'.

Grant and Estelle's first child, Susan, was born in 1951 while they were living at Kaindi. Paulette was nominated as the child's godmother, which was a blessing for the doting aunt because, three weeks after the birth, her beloved Bish died of cirrhosis of the liver at the age of fifty-six. By this time, Bish had been estranged from his family for over twenty years and Paulette did not know how to contact them. Still, according to his wishes, she organised a funeral for him at the Sacred Heart Catholic Church in Darlinghurst that included a Requiem Mass, and he was buried in an unmarked grave in the Catholic cemetery of Rookwood. Paulette gratefully inherited Bish's library, which included works by Rabelais, St Augustine, and Laurence Sterne.

Despite running a successful café, Grant's 1949 Census form still listed his occupation as 'Writer'. This was because he'd also begun editing and publishing a regular tourist booklet, *This Month in Sydney* – a forerunner to *Time Out* – which listed information on current and forthcoming entertainment events, including theatre, film, concerts, exhibitions, and dance. He often added his own poetry, reviews, show business gossip, and short articles on Sydney's most famous landmarks: Manly Beach, the Sydney Harbour Bridge, and Sydney's red-light district, Kings Cross.

However, his article failed to mention how dangerous Kings Cross could be after the sun went down, when it was flooded with standover men, prostitutes, drug dealers, and gang members. Late one night in 1951, his waitress, eighteen-year-old Mrs Quintal, who was pregnant, left the café and began walking down the dimly lit Pennys Lane. Grant kept a protective eye on her as she passed a group of seven hooligans, who started to harass the waitress. Grant, well built and over six feet tall, immediately came to her defence and they reluctantly backed off. After he saw the waitress off safely in a taxi, Grant naively returned along the same route, where the hooligans lay in wait. They jumped him and bashed him mercilessly, breaking his nose, fracturing his jaw and cheekbones, and inflicting so much damage that blood began pooling in his lungs and he collapsed. He was found unconscious and rushed to hospital. Upon attempting to set his nose and cheekbones, he experienced a bad reaction to the anaesthetic and his heart stopped beating three times on the operating table. His survival was a miracle, but the bones in his nose never properly reset.

After the bashing, Grant and Estelle moved into the Hampton Court Hotel so she could nurse him back to health while Paulette babysat her niece, Susan. Later, she took the toddler on picnics at nearby parks, to Redleaf Pool for paddling, and read her classics such as Oscar Wilde's *The Happy Prince* and Robert Louis Stevenson's *Treasure Island*. Susan remembers that Paulette collected ceramic animal figurines, some wearing bow ties, others wearing hats. Whenever the toddler refused to eat, Paulette would create a game by assembling all the miniature animals on a table, pretending to spoon food into each of their mouths. She would then offer a spoonful to the amused child, who invariably accepted it.

Susan rarely slept in a cot because Paulette would insist on holding her goddaughter in her arms, and when relatives visited, they treasured the child so much that they merely passed the dozing toddler around from lap to lap. Some years later, cousins Alan, Charles, and Sandra even constructed an elaborate dollhouse for her. When Estelle fell pregnant for a second time, however, she and Grant decided they would have to move to a bigger home. Estelle also realised that if she and Grant remained living with Paulette, their children would grow up being utterly spoiled. 'We couldn't stay a minute longer', Estelle admitted to daughter Susan years later, 'because you would have been ruined'.

Three years after the attack in Pennys Lane, Grant closed the café and he and Estelle moved their family to the more salubrious suburb of Manly, only a block from the beach, on Whistler Street. During this time, Estelle secured a position as a nurse at a private hospital in Manly, eventually rising to the position of matron. In a prescient role reversal, Grant remained at home to develop a business venture in athletic shoes and help raise what would turn out to be four children. Naturally, they and the other siblings tried to persuade Paulette to move out of Kings Cross, but she staunchly refused all suggestions and offers. She adored the district's demi-monde atmosphere of artists, writers, gangsters, prostitutes, actors, runaways, post-war European immigrants, and misfits. For example, her neighbour James, who lived upstairs with his wife, Patsy, enjoyed dressing in women's clothes before stepping out alone to stroll the neon-lit streets. And though Paulette didn't know it at the time, Russian spy Fedor Nosov, who represented Soviet news agency TASS in Australia, also resided in Kaindi during the early 1950s. And directly above Nosov's flat lived a married couple, Joan and Dudley Doherty, who were ASIO agents. The Dohertys drilled a hole in the living room floor so that they could spy on and record the secrets Nosov was passing on to Moscow.

It was a complex and colourful community simmering with danger, secrets, and mystery, and Paulette was in her bohemian element. She loved to stroll the streets of the Cross, helping herself to flowers from gardens and over fences. With its delicatessens, espresso coffee, continental restaurants, bookstores, and galleries, Kings Cross was the most cosmopolitan area in Australia and, as a deliberately unmarried middle-aged woman with a love of art, literature, and cinema, it was the one place in Sydney that could accept and even embrace her stubborn non-conformity.

During the 1950s, Paulette began a relationship with an artist named Douglas Drew. After learning of Paulette's love of clowns, he painted a large harlequin for her. The framed painting would hang on her living room wall until her death two decades later. She also developed a close friendship with a married man, Vic Whibley, who moved into the building on an upper floor, and who would visit her daily and enjoy drinks with her.

Isabel's eldest son, Alan, also developed an interest in art and studied oil painting for two years before he began his national service in 1953. He attended classes with well-known artist Jean Bellette and Hungarian painter Desiderius Orban, who'd immigrated to Australia in 1939. In 1906, Orban had moved to Paris to study art and became friends with Picasso, Modigliani, Braque, and Matisse.

⇥⟨○⟩⇤

Grant loved living by the beach but missed Paulette so much that he would call her from a phone box every evening. He insisted that daughter Susan dial the number and speak to her godmother, before taking the receiver to speak to her himself. 'It was like a boy talking to his mother', she recalls. 'Paw-paw was his surrogate Mum.' But the conversations were not always congenial, and sometimes the two would argue. He not only missed Paulette but also Kings Cross. Roughly every second weekend, he would take the entire family on a ferry ride from Manly to Circular Quay. They would then take a taxi to St Mary's Cathedral, where Grant would pray and light candles with Susan, while Estelle and the younger children would play in Hyde Park. Throughout his life-threatening illnesses and injuries, Grant's faith in Christianity never wavered. Another taxi would then deliver them to either Paulette's building or John and Elsie's flat in Double Bay.

The latter's home was known as 'the party house' and was almost always filled with visitors. Regular revellers included actors Gordon Collingridge and *The Cheaters'* male lead, Josef Bambach. The adults drank spirits, but there were always bottles of cold Coca-Cola in the fridge for the children, who were encouraged to perform for the adults by standing up and singing in the middle of the living room. The apartment smelled richly of wood and was furnished with antique furniture and artwork – relics of Dr McDonagh's collection, including the tiger tapestry that had appeared in *The Cheaters*, and the portrait of Dr McDonagh by Tom Roberts. The children loved playing with the gym equipment, especially the medicine balls.

As a parent, Grant was unusually overprotective, forbidding his children to play on the road or go swimming unsupervised. Perhaps the early loss of his parents, coupled with his own near-death experiences, had made him crucially aware of how dangerous and unpredictable life could be. Whenever Susan stayed in Potts

Point with close family friends, Grant made Paulette promise to take his daughter to mass on Sunday morning. Paulette would always keep her promise, but only to a certain extent: she would walk the little girl down the hill to St Canice's Catholic Church, deliver her through the doors and into a pew, and wait outside on the steps, smoking, until the service was finally over.

While Phyllis enjoyed her marriage and the career opportunities available in New Zealand, she was homesick for Sydney and the reassuring company of her siblings, especially Paulette and Isabel. OB sensed her loneliness, and her restlessness, and agreed to move back to the place of her birth.

In September 1954, Grant published a tongue-in-cheek article in *Truth* newspaper about the return of Phyllis and OB from New Zealand after an absence of sixteen years. It poked fun at all the changes that had taken place in Sydney since their departure in 1938, such as the removal of tram lines on King Street, the wartime covers still blocking the clocks of the General Post Office in Martin Place, the disturbing murders in Sydney via thallium poisoning, and the recent visit by the newly crowned monarch of the Commonwealth, Queen Elizabeth II.

After such a long separation, the siblings' devotion to one another was stronger than ever. Grant begins his article thus: 'Dear Phyllis, Welcome home! We're proud of your achievements as an editress and authoress, but not in the least bit surprised by them. For to us, your family, you were always a top-drawer goddess'.

Susan remembers her mother tying ribbons into her hair in preparation to meet the ship from New Zealand that was transporting Phyllis and OB home. After an emotional wharf-side family reunion, the couple moved in with Paulette and began looking for a home to buy.

Phyllis enjoyed a well-earned break of twelve months and then returned to journalism, becoming the wise, calm voice behind a regular Agony Aunt column in the *Daily Mirror*, 'Dear Lynne'. She and OB eventually purchased a new apartment on the second-highest floor of a tall modern building in Randwick, which allowed them to watch the horse races for free from their living room. Now settled, Phyllis and OB began nurturing close relationships with the next generation of the McDonagh family, and every Christmas, they would take sister-in-law Estelle and her four children to see a Christmas pantomime at Her Majesty's Theatre.

In late 1959, a colleague named Ian Smith offered Phyllis the position of social editor at Murdoch's new flagship publication, the *North Shore Times*. At the age of sixty, when most people are lured by the promise of retirement, Phyllis jumped at the chance to increase her responsibilities and workload. She resumed her nocturnal routine and began writing at 6 pm and did not finish until the early hours of the morning. 'When the first issue came out on the streets I had a whole front-page story with pictures, two feature news articles and one page of women's news ...' The new position kept her so busy that she had to relinquish her Agony Aunt column.

Compared to her formulaic and sometimes overwritten short stories, Phyllis's non-fiction writing was taut and original, devoid of cliches and overblown language. Her name and phone number appeared at the top of every *North Shore Times* column she published, which over the years connected her to scores of readers and admirers who would become close friends. She relied heavily on the telephone to keep her connected with the wider community and came to be on a first-name basis with leading political, cultural, and social figures. For the next eighteen years, she would mirror the behaviour of her social butterfly father, attending theatre performances and cultural events several times a week, her energy and enthusiasm seemingly inexhaustible.

Paula and Bob Dornan had been living with Bob's parents on the Dornan family farm in southwest Queensland, raising their young children, but Paula found her mother-in-law judgmental, critical, and overly demanding. After one spectacular argument, Paula collected the children and stormed out, calling over her shoulder, 'Bob, are you coming?'

Bob didn't dare defy his wife in favour of his mother and obediently followed. The family jumped into their car and began driving back to Sydney. Upon their arrival, they bought a caravan and parked it in the yard of a friend while they looked for a place to buy.

Eventually, they found a huge citrus and dairy farm at Ourimbah on the Central Coast that they liked but didn't have the money to purchase. And so, just as Dr McDonagh, and later Paula, had come to Stella's rescue in times of need, Stella and Frank rose to the occasion. They loaned the couple enough money for the deposit, and it would take years for the Dornans to pay them back. During this time, in the early 1950s, Stella and Frank were keen to retire and live life at a more leisurely pace. A few years after the loan was made, they sold their home and moved to Ourimbah with the Dornans, who built an extension onto their farmhouse for the ageing couple. Stella took pleasure in helping to raise another generation of McDonagh children, often babysitting, feeding, and playing with them, until her death in 1969 at the age of eighty-three. Following her passing, second husband Frank lived on the farm for another thirteen years before he died at the age of ninety.

As adults, the McDonagh siblings did not always get along, and Isabel was the only one determined to remain on good terms with all of them. Anita was now estranged from most of the McDonaghs, and Paula and Paulette were not speaking with John. On Christmas Day, Isabel, Charles, and the three children would pile into their Bentley to visit the siblings individually. They'd drop in on Grant and his family in Manly, then motor over the bridge to the eastern suburbs, visiting Anita and her family in Rose Bay, and then on to John and Elsie at their Double Bay flat. Lastly, they would drive up Bayswater Road to Paulette's apartment in Kings Cross, where they'd celebrate with her, Phyllis, and OB and eat Christmas dinner together. The farm at Ourimbah, where the Dornans lived, was too far away to fit in for a festive drink.

Paulette still loved throwing parties, even in the close quarters of her Kings Cross flat. Paula's eldest son, John, remembers raucous celebrations enjoyed by the McDonagh siblings, most of whom would drink, smoke, and tell stories throughout the night. Her bathroom always smelled of scented face powder, which she'd puff onto her complexion before guests arrived. He also remembers that Paulette's dark apartment would be so wreathed in tobacco smoke that often he could barely see across the room. The lack of visibility was exacerbated by the fact that no natural light could penetrate the home because the windows were always covered by heavy drapes. But one thing he and his brothers loved to do was take the elevator to the roof of the building, where the towering neon DUNLOP TYRES sign flashed over the red-light district, and where they'd play for hours.

By this time, the Dornans drove to Sydney regularly to sell crates of oranges. Paula would steer the truck straight to Kings Cross, park outside Paulette's building, and dash into her sister's flat for a drink and a catch-up while the boys returned to the rooftop. But unlike their wayward aunties forty years before, they refrained from throwing pitchers of water – or indeed anything else – onto the innocent pedestrians passing below.

Even as children, Paula's sons recognised the intense closeness of the sisters. Paula never enjoyed the company of her female neighbours in the country and politely declined most social invitations (though she would always put on lipstick before she walked to the dairy or into the yard to hang out the washing). In the presence of a sister, however, she became animated and ebullient, as if she'd suddenly been connected to a vital source of energy. Similarly, they noticed an even deeper attachment between Isabel and her three children, who by the 1950s seemed to have become fused into a single unit. Whenever Isabel and her brood visited the farm at Ourimbah, they would arrive in Alan's late-model Bentley, a gift from his generous and indulgent father. After greeting each other, Paula would usher the Stewarts into the house. But instead of allowing Isabel to catch up with her sister, her children would sit close beside her and continue talking to their mother as if no one else was in the room. During these visits, Charles Senior always stayed home: he could not compete with the many relatives jostling for his wife's attention.

Isabel began to tire of living in the safe but predictable suburbs. Alan was hardly ever home due to his national service, and the younger children were seventeen and fourteen respectively. Daughter Sandra had taken up the study of ballet. Phyllis was back in Sydney after a sixteen-year absence, living only a short bus ride from Paulette's flat in Kings Cross. So, with both sisters living so close to one another, Isabel longed to be closer too. She and Charles purchased an apartment in posh Darling Point and set about styling and redecorating while preparing to put the Strathfield house on the market.

But before the house was sold, Isabel and the children returned home one afternoon to find that Charles Senior had collapsed on the floor and died of what turned out to be a heart attack. 'We just came up to the house and found him', said son Charles. 'Our mother called us ...' The shock of the sudden death was compounded by the fact that only two weeks before, Charles Senior had had a full physical with his doctor, who'd proclaimed that the sixty-six-year-old possessed 'the heart of a man half his age'.

'It took a long time to get over it', said Charles Junior, '... I think that made us get more together. The three of us and our mother'.

Following the death of Charles, Isabel and the children were so bereft they felt as if they could no longer move into the newly purchased Darling Point apartment. Both the apartment and the Strathfield house were sold, and the grieving Stewarts turned to their next closest relative for help and emotional support – ever-reliable Paulette – who invited them to move in with her. It is interesting to note that the wealthy Stewarts could have afforded to move to any fashionable address in Sydney, but the four opted to stay in Paulette's tiny two-bedroom apartment in dingy Kings Cross, where they could comfort each other and experience the kind of love and reassurance that only a close family member could offer.

From then on, eldest son, Alan, would always drive the family car, with Isabel beside him, and Charles and Sandra in the back seat. He motored with authority, but also with great speed. He even assumed his father's former responsibility of handling the family's cash as Isabel didn't like to touch either bills or small change due to her fear of germs.

Phyllis was back from New Zealand. Paulette was alone and always available. Was there any chance they could revive their creative collaborations?

By this time, however, the sisters were not the bright young things who'd made superlative silent films in the 1920s and '30s. They were now in their mid-fifties and much had changed in the intervening decades. Not only had sound been added to feature films, but also sound effects, colour, and Technicolour. By 1956, cinema audiences were diminishing due to the introduction of yet another technological advance – television – which cut the number of people attending the cinema by half.

Even if the sisters had yearned to return to filmmaking, the odds, as usual, were stacked heavily against them.

19

ISABEL RISING
(1957–1965)

In early 1952, an American production of the Cole Porter musical *Kiss Me Kate* was staged by JC Williamson at His Majesty's Theatre in Melbourne. It starred American actor Hayes Gordon, who played the role of an actor touring opposite his estranged actress wife (Joy Turpin) in a production of Shakespeare's *Taming of the Shrew*. In essence, it was theatre about theatre, a play within a play, a work of art about art. Hayes had been discovered by a scout of Oscar Hammerstein when he'd been working in a theatrical stock company and was soon installed as the understudy for Judd in the first New York production of *Oklahoma*. He'd also played the leads in musicals *Brigadoon* and *Showboat*, among many other roles.

By the time Hayes arrived in Australia, he was thirty-two years old and his career on the American stage was all but over. The year before, his name had been mentioned in the newsletter *Redworks*, which was devoted to the naming of communists and their sympathisers. Consequently, the government requested that Hayes sign a loyalty oath declaring that he was not a communist. Affronted by the demand and its implication for his fellow actors, he refused. For defending his principles, Hayes was virtually blacklisted from the American stage, triggering his subsequent exile in Australia.

A few years after Hayes' Australian debut, Phyllis attended a theatre in Sydney to write a review of the play in which Hayes Gordon was appearing. Afterwards, she went backstage to interview Hayes, and the actor found the former film set designer uncommonly astute about the arts in general and acting in particular: '... she observed things about my character that others hadn't. And I tried to round out the characterisation, and phrase the relationships, and bring out the funny in the dramatic and the serious in the comic, and these are things I think she discussed with me'.

Hayes and Phyllis became fast friends. The American actor and director found her witty and intelligent, and, in the press, the admiring journalist championed his work. 'I think we appreciated the same sorts of things in performing', said Hayes. 'To put it in clichéd terms, we appreciated honesty. We appreciated roundness of character ... She didn't believe in simply entertainment for the sake of entertainment. She always wanted something for the audience to carry away with them.'

After he'd established his residency in Australia, Hayes began tutoring students from the Independent Theatre and later invited these same students to join him when he founded the Ensemble Studio and the Ensemble Theatre in Kirribilli, a cooperative acting school and performance space, which became Australia's first theatre-in-the-round. Hayes is also credited with introducing the Stanislavski method to Australia, which includes accessing memories and experiences from the past to trigger an honest performance in the present.

During this burgeoning friendship, Hayes learned of the films Phyllis and her sisters had made thirty years before and found the legend of the McDonagh sisters fascinating. Similarly, Phyllis shared her experiences of the friendship she'd developed with

Hayes with Isabel and her children. By this time, they had moved out of Paulette's flat and into the Majestic Hotel, which was on the same street, but across the road and two blocks east. There, they would be relieved of domestic duties and could collectively devote themselves to an appreciation of the arts – regularly attending plays, concerts, operas, films, and ballets.

The family was still living off the profits of Charles Stewart's judicious investments and did not need to work to support themselves. The children were now twenty-five, twenty, and seventeen respectively and would live together as a close-knit unit for the rest of their lives. So, if one member of the Stewart clan decided to do something outside of their ordinary routine, the other three would automatically follow, just as the three sisters had done a generation earlier.

When Isabel's son Charles learned about Hayes Gordon's acting ensemble, he grew curious about the company and wanted to sign up. Naturally, the others, including Isabel, also enrolled, though Hayes presumed it had been Isabel herself who had initiated the approach. It's likely that Charles yearned to experience the same *frisson* of creative collaboration that his mother and two aunts had three decades before, and to become part of the fabled McDonagh family mythology. Like his mother, he decided to adopt a 'stage name' and settled upon 'Kyle', though he retained the surname, 'Stewart'. At the time that they signed up for lessons at the studio, Isabel was nearing sixty.

'At first, well, after Phyllis told me the history', said Hayes, 'I wondered what Isabel was doing coming to study acting. And I think the idea that she was trying to find out what it was she was doing all those years that she'd worked in an instinctual era ...' It was true that Isabel had never received any formal training as an actor; in the days of her filmmaking with her sisters, she'd obediently followed Paulette's detailed instructions about expressions, movements, and reactions, which had to be delivered in a single take. In short, she had successfully faked the emotions she'd brought to the screen, but Hayes believed that she now wanted to understand the technical aspects of delivering a convincing performance, and one that also included her voice. 'She was a very avid student', recalled Hayes. 'Very authoritative, very compliant. She was a charm to direct, an absolute charm.'

Hayes remembered the Stewart quartet usually arriving a few minutes late for classes, and he and the other students would wait in anticipation of what they referred to as 'the duck parade': '... it was a very charming thing to see. [Isabel] followed by her oldest son, then her next oldest son, [then] by her daughter. And they would parade, and they would sit in, and they would listen avidly. And then came the time for exercises. They'd get up and do them very conscientiously, almost dutifully'.

By this time, Alan had completed his army service and was a crack rifle shot, and gun enthusiast Hayes kept several firearms on the premises. One night during a play, some hooligans scaled the walls of the theatre and began throwing stones onto the roof, disrupting the performance. Hayes sought out Alan and they both armed themselves. But by the time they managed to climb onto the roof, the hooligans had fled. To provide after-hours security, a paranoid Hayes asked his students and staff members to join a roster and take it in turns to sleep overnight inside the theatre. Over three years, the Stewart family assented to this request several times.

The family enjoyed studying at the Ensemble Studio so much that they purchased an apartment on the harbour in nearby Neutral Bay and promptly moved in, allowing them to walk to the studio and theatre without having to commute across the harbour. For a time, Alan hoped that his education at the Ensemble Studio would lead to a career as a theatre director. A newspaper photograph taken of them at the time reveals two handsome and stylish young men dressed in dark suits, and a slim attractive girl wearing a fashionable dress, standing on the balcony of the theatre. All three are looking directly at their mother, dressed in a leopard-skin caftan, as if awaiting important instructions from her.

Over three or so years of study with Hayes, Isabel appeared in two plays: *Orpheus Descending* by Tennessee Williams and *Time Remembered* by Jean Anouilh.

Hayes recalled that in *Orpheus Descending*, Isabel played a supporting role as a townsperson, but she 'made so much of it that we could have dispensed with most of the others and just let her to represent the entire town ... She was very sensitive, very alive, and fine attack. When anything had to be done, she didn't ease into it'.

Isabel, however, was not the first of the family to appear on stage in the late 1950s; instead, it was her second son, Charles. '[Charles] appeared in the first big success we had, which was *The Man*, actually', said Hayes, adding that it ran for 150 performances. Charles remembers the play clearly, a role which had him delivering groceries in a ten-minute scene opposite Clarissa Kaye, who would later become the last wife of James Mason. In the scene, Kaye's character is being terrorised by a maniac, who is at that time hiding nearby, and Charles's character is too ignorant to realise that she's secretly trying to tell him of the maniac's proximity.

Like his Aunt Paulette and Uncle Grant, Charles had a slight stutter early on in life, but surprisingly it would always vanish when he appeared on stage. '... he flung himself into things more courageously than the others', said Hayes. 'But you can still see that out of the corner of his eye, he's watching to see whether he was receiving approval or not, and I suppose his mother's approval'.

At the time, teenage Sandra was shy, quiet, and intensely watchful. 'For a little while, we didn't think she could talk', recalled

Hayes. He also remembered firstborn son, Alan, appearing in *The Drunkard,* and his performance being 'very good'. He continued, '... they were all good, but they weren't as assertive as she was. It was almost as if they were living in the shadow of Isabel'.

As Isabel's star rose in the world of theatre, Paulette's appreciation of good acting never wavered. In April 1962, she attended the Palace Theatre to see the French farce *Nina,* by André Roussin. It starred American character actor Edward Everett Horton, best known for his appearances in Astaire/Rogers films such as *The Gay Divorcee* and *Top Hat.* According to reviews of the play, Horton was hysterically funny as an avenging husband: 'His timing is a joy to observe and every nuance of his facial expressions is a lesson in the art of comedy'. Paulette agreed with the critics. In fact, she was so impressed by Horton's performance that after the final bows were taken, she raced backstage, burst through the door of Horton's dressing room, and gave him a big, smacking kiss on the lips, leaving the homosexual actor blushing deeply.

Paulette continued to enjoy her status as a popular neighbourhood character who could banter and joke with the best of them. Many people in the area knew of her former career as a film director and respected her as an artist as well as a fellow misfit, which is why she chose to remain in rambunctious Kings Cross. From this time on, most of Paulette's socialising would be conducted over the phone, especially on Saturday afternoons, when she and Phyllis would share tips for the day's horse races before Paulette walked down to the TAB to place her bets. With their love of a flutter, both Phyllis and Paulette were repeating the compulsions of their father, who loved nothing more than to lay a wager on boxing matches.

⋆⟶◉☷⋆

In 1959, Paula's eldest son, John, graduated from high school with excellent marks in English and professed his intention to become a journalist, just like his Aunt Phyllis and uncles John and Grant. Paula was alarmed by John's starry-eyed plans and quickly arranged an intervention. Both Phyllis and husband, OB, sat John down one day and explained the challenges that faced the professional newspaperman. The hours were long and unpredictable. But what was worse, they added, was the hard drinking, and the blokey culture of journalism, where you're expected to spend all your free time in smoky pubs, trading yarns and news leads.

Paula had noticed how comfortable life had been for Anita and her pharmacist husband, Gregory. They still owned a beautiful home in Vaucluse, financed by two successful chemist shops, one in Darlington and another in Edgecliff. And so, Paula decided that the best path for her son was to become a pharmacist too. She made some sort of arrangement with sister Anita for him to take up an apprenticeship in Gregory's shop while John studied at Sydney University. But when young John turned up for his first day, Gregory made it clear that he already had an apprentice working under him and had no desire to take on another. A confused John retreated but eventually secured a position with a Soul Pattinson franchise on Crown Street in Surry Hills.

By this time, Anita had long given up on her dream of becoming an actress and had settled into a restless middle age. She began attending card parties with friends, including a woman named Monty Miller, where all the players drank heavily. She gradually became an alcoholic and the addiction began to affect her marriage. Hardworking husband, Gregory, suspected she was having an affair and hired a private detective to follow her. Anita was eventually discovered in the back seat of a car with another man and photographed in a compromising position. This indiscretion further alienated her from her younger sister, Paula.

After her separation from Gregory, Anita moved into a flat in Double Bay and, like her brother John, turned it into a health studio, which also contained a dedicated steam room. The great irony was that these two siblings, who made a living out of promoting healthy habits, were both chronic alcoholics. To supplement her income, Anita also worked as a children's nurse for wealthy families in the eastern suburbs. As her alcoholism deepened, she became 'a bad drunk' and was argumentative and defensive.

Brother John, on the other hand, was apparently a 'good drunk', with alcohol stimulating his warm and affable nature. When he checked into a sanatorium in Burwood to dry out, Anita and daughter Moya walked into the main ward during a visit and glimpsed John sitting up in bed, holding court before the other patients. He was amusing them with a hilarious anecdote, as if he were not at all sick and suffering from withdrawals, but merely entertaining guests. Naturally, mother-hen Paw-paw put her feud with him aside and visited him religiously.

In the late 1950s, a rare copy of *The Cheaters* surfaced in the library of an avid Australian film collector, while another of *The Far Paradise* was discovered in a film hire package. Later, in the early 1960s, two children who lived near Gordon and Sheila Collingridge were playing in the garage with a spool of film and laughing. Gordon rushed in and said, 'How dare you!' Exasperated, he explained to the startled children that on that film was 'the greatest actress Australia had ever produced!' He sent it on to one of the sisters, most probably Paulette. It turned out to be *The Far Paradise*.

Fortunately, the NFSA has since acquired and made copies of both films. In 1962, Isabel's children viewed them for the first time in Canberra and realised the extent of their mother's and aunts' achievements. After the screening, Isabel, accompanied by her children, celebrated at a nearby restaurant by dining on expensive steak and quaffing Côtes du Rhône red wine. During the meal, Charles raised a glass and toasted his mother with, 'I think this is the best day I've ever had in my life'. Isabel smiled enigmatically and replied: 'That's the nicest compliment anyone has ever paid me'.

The two films were also presented at a private event organised by the sisters at the State Theatre in the mid-1960s, and it was the first time that the silent version of *The Cheaters* was screened publicly. Besuited Alan and Charles Stewart acted as ushers. The McDonagh siblings and their descendants attended en-masse. Before the screening, Isabel's daughter, Sandra, was sitting beside Isabel in the front row when her Aunt Anita appeared. Sandra moved to another seat to let the McDonagh sisters view the film together, saying, 'I have Mum with me all the time, so you should sit next to her'. An appreciative Anita turned to her and said, 'You know that you have the most beautiful mother in the world?' It would be the last time Isabel and Anita would see one another.

However, amid all the warmth and affection, Isabel, Phyllis, and Paulette were annoyed with Grant, who adored publicity and arranged for a press photographer to take their picture. Paulette frostily responded, 'This is a private event. We don't need publicity. We've already made history'. Still, the sisters were photographed outside the theatre, being feted with bouquets of flowers.

The trailblazing McDonaghs, however, would have to wait a further fifteen years to receive due recognition for their pioneering contributions to Australian film.

⭑⭆◉◗⭅⭑

While footage was being discovered, at least one of Paulette's scenarios was inadvertently being destroyed. After the last of the many relatives who'd lived with Paulette moved out, her spare room became an unofficial storage unit, filled with junk and possessions for which she no longer had any use. It had been sealed for several years, with mould growing in a toxic sludge over the walls and contents, when Paula thought she'd do Paulette a favour and clean it out. Frequently gagging at the stench of mildew, she bagged most of the contents of the room and arranged to have them burnt. It was only after the last of the bags were taken away that Paulette realised that her original scenario for *The Far Paradise* had been mistakenly incinerated with the discarded items. 'Paulette was very angry with me for that', she admitted.

Also accidentally discarded was the scenario of the unmade film of *Flynn of the Outback*. '... and it was the whole script', complained Paulette, 'the whole flipping thing went. Exactly as I [wrote it], every movement, every scene, the whole thing. That to me is the greatest tragedy. 'Cause that could have been one of the greatest films, if it was made today'.

Phyllis was more than content with her work as an editor and journalist and rarely talked about their former lives as filmmakers, but whenever she visited Paulette, her sister would bring out the scrapbooks she'd kept and once more they'd go through the press clippings and fondly discuss the old days. Nephews Alan and Charles witnessed this ritual many times.

Grant was still living with his wife and four children in Manly, where he'd spent years inventing and modifying a shoe attachment that he hoped would revolutionise the mobility of the disabled and the flexibility of the abled. In October 1962, speculation about his invention had reached Canada and the United States, with articles appearing in *Brandon Sun* in Manitoba and the *Nevada State Journal* through the Consolidated Press news wire. The original article was probably written by Phyllis and published via her various media contacts.

The invention was a shoe heel made of rubber embedded with steel springs. The articles that appeared were redolent of the usual McDonagh bravado, with Grant claiming he could walk 'fifty miles a day with little effort with the heel'. He adds breezily, 'You can idle along at three miles an hour, cruise in comfort at four or five miles an hour, accelerate at six miles an hour and, if you're really in a hurry, reach a top speed of eight miles an hour – and keep it going'. There are no details about how the heel attached to a shoe, but apparently, a pair could be purchased for $2.50. Nephew John remembers that Grant installed the springs in men's classic black leather shoes, which were used briefly by the police force and sold in pharmacies. No doubt Grant hoped to cash in on his fanciful accessory, but according to sister Paula, he made little money from it.

While Grant was springing like a pogo stick all over Manly, Paula continued to enjoy a happy marriage. In her mid-forties, however, she was shocked to find herself pregnant, this time, after the birth of five boys, with a much-anticipated girl. In honour of her older sister, Paula decided to name the child Phyllis. When she told her sisters of the unexpected news, they were all overjoyed at the prospect of this new and unexpected arrival in the family. But the collective joy was only short-lived: the daughter was born suffering from a heart defect and died a short time later. The loss left Paula utterly bereft. Suffering from deep grief and chronic depression, she remained in hospital for three months.

Once she had sufficiently recovered, Paula was offered a two-week job as a real estate receptionist in Gosford, while the regular receptionist was on holidays. At first reluctant, she eventually accepted the position and found she enjoyed it so much that she decided to stay on permanently. To add to her credentials, she took a real estate course in Sydney and earned her licence.

She rose to the management position of Goodland's agency on the Central Coast of New South Wales and became successful as an independent agent. Paula eventually bought a block of flats as an investment, and a newsagency which she worked in daily.

Growing up in Sydney, Isabel's eldest son, Alan, had always been keenly aware that he'd been born in London and, in 1965, at the age of thirty-two, he expressed his long-held desire to return to that city. Most of all, however, Alan craved access to the greatest theatres, museums, and galleries in the world.

But the closeness of the family was so intense that no one ever thought he would travel to London alone. If one of them wished to embark on an adventure, all of them would have to agree to do so too. By this time, the four of them had dispensed with the pronoun 'I', just as the sisters had done forty years earlier, and referred to themselves exclusively as 'we'. In restaurants, they would peruse the menu, consult each other on the various offerings and, after much discussion, order four plates of exactly the same dish.

Upon hearing the news that the Stewarts were moving to the United Kingdom indefinitely, Paulette was understandably devastated. She'd devoted many years to raising the Stewart offspring and was still inextricably entwined with Isabel. 'She treated us as her own children', said Charles. 'And she loved the three of us so much. Saying goodbye to her was terrible. Really terrible.'

The night before the Stewarts were booked to fly out of Sydney, Paulette threw a farewell party for them at her place, with Phyllis as the only other guest. This would be the last time they would ever be together, and the sisters and Isabel's children stayed up until 5 am, talking and embracing one another. As dawn was pressing through the streets of Kings Cross, the Stewarts gathered themselves to take their leave. A taxi was waiting to transport them to their hotel, from which they would collect their luggage and proceed to the airport.

Paulette stood out on the street in the cold wind, shivering, her face smeared with tears, and waved the departing taxi goodbye.

20

SECOND COMING
(1966–1975)

In the late 1960s and early '70s, the city and suburbs of Sydney suffered a tsunami of destruction. The Hotel Australia, one of the country's most distinguished landmarks, and where the sisters had shot key scenes for *The Cheaters,* was demolished in record time to erect the MLC Centre, a skyscraper that today still dominates the skyline. The Prince Edward Theatre, dubbed in the 1920s as 'Australia's first cathedral of motion pictures', and where the sisters had successfully premiered their first two films, was also bulldozed. Another to go was the sisters' childhood home, one of the houses that formed Burdekin Terrace on College Street, which was eventually replaced by a high-rise international hotel. In 1969, the Belvedere Hotel, where the Stewarts had lived upon their return to Australia, was flattened to make room for the Kings Cross Tunnel and expressway leading to the eastern suburbs. And in 1971, hallowed Drummoyne House, with its mesmerising mythology of convicts, smugglers, and silent filmmakers, was demolished to make way for a block of modern flats. Today, the only vestiges of the grand colonial mansion are some ornamental sandstone steps and balustrading near the Parramatta River.

Even Paulette's beloved Kings Cross was at the mercy of greedy developers and a corrupt state government. Just a few footsteps away from her apartment, entire blocks were being bulldozed to make way for an underground railway station. While over on Victoria Street, lifelong residents were being evicted from 19th-century homes and terraces that would be replaced with crude, high-rise flats, triggering the green ban movement in Kings Cross and the disappearance of anti-development campaigner and Mark Foy's heiress Juanita Nielsen.

While so many iconic buildings associated with the McDonagh sisters were being destroyed, Australian director, producer, and writer Joan Long began resurrecting the history of Australian silent films in preparation for her documentary *The Passionate Industry*. One of her first plans was to view every fragment of Australian film from the 1920s, from actuality sequences to features, held at the National Library. 'Probably the biggest revelation', she admitted, 'was the work of the McDonagh sisters. Later, when *The Passionate Industry* was shown, theirs were the excerpts that drew the most comments'.

A new generation began admiring the sisters' achievements, but director Ken G Hall was one of the very few in the industry who continued the sexist trend, popular forty years before, of dismissing the McDonaghs as avid amateurs and dilettantes. Hall was one of the many men who ascended into the industry with the introduction of sound. He was able to negotiate the complicated structures of male-dominated film combines, distribution systems, and publicity machines to produce films such as *On Our Selection* and *The Squatter's Daughter*.

In a 1976 interview with Graham Shirley, Hall admitted that he had visited the set of *Two Minutes Silence* in the old showground studio, in 1932, and had stood in the background and observed the action. In the interview, Hall is dismissive of Paulette's framing techniques and mocks her habit of waving a pencil instead of yelling 'Cut' to indicate the end of a scene. (Unlike Hall, Paulette had never enjoyed the luxury of being able to travel to Hollywood to observe the directing techniques of experienced filmmakers.) Moreover, according to Hall, Isabel was 'all right', but 'she was not a great actress'. Even brother John, who was assisting on the set, did not escape Hall's scorn. John might have almost completed a medical degree, but it was Hall's considered opinion that he was 'not terribly bright'.

The director's supercilious attitude towards the McDonaghs was typical of the misogyny that flourished in the Australian arts scene in the earlier part of the 20th century: 'But women ... You know women', he said. 'No one would take much notice of women in *those days*. The last thing anybody thought of is women's lib.' And even though Hall did not know the McDonaghs personally, or their background, he parroted the common misconception, shared by many men in the film industry of the 1920s and '30s, that in the process of producing their films, the sisters had been merely out for a lark: 'They made it more or less a hobby, you see. Three girls together – three girls having fun. That's how it started it, really, I'm sure it did'.

Hall's condescending attitude also begs the following question: if he truly believed that the McDonaghs were such hapless amateurs, why did he bother to turn up at the set of *Two Minutes Silence* to observe them in action? Ironically, back in the 1920s, Paulette had already made a mockery of him. Railing against the artificiality of many silent film sets, she once observed, 'see, with Ken Hall and all those stupid people, they'd make paper things, little stupid things and they think they got away with it. They never did'.

When the Stewarts arrived in London, they moved into the second-floor apartment of an elegant Georgian terrace house in Manchester Square, just behind Selfridges department store. Musician Paul McCartney and his then-girlfriend, Jane Asher, would often visit a friend who lived in the terrace and invariably wave and say hello to the Stewarts whenever they passed them on the landing.

Once settled, the family began absorbing the city's arts and cultural offerings by going to museums, theatres, operas, and galleries. The following year, they shifted to another rented flat in Hampstead, where they would live until 1971. The Stewarts had no plan, and Isabel placed no expectations on her now-adult children. The four simply lived day-to-day, each content to be part of an enthralling whole.

What had been planned as an indefinite trip overseas for the Stewart family gradually became a permanent resettlement. In 1971, they found a way to become even closer as a family and purchased a custom-made motor home with four beds, cooking facilities, and a bathroom, and began travelling around England. At this point, Isabel was seventy-two. Alan did the driving; Sandra did the cooking; and Charles wrote and recited poetry. The quartet travelled around the country for six years, visiting the home counties, Cheltenham, and Gloucestershire.

They spent some nights taking in a concert or a play in any given city, after which they'd repair to a restaurant to enjoy a late dinner. When niece and cousin Susan McDonagh lived in London between 1972 and 1975, the Stewarts would park their motor home on the outskirts of London on Friday nights, send a hire car to pick her up from her place of work, and meet her outside a theatre or concert hall before escorting her into the auditorium. Later, of course, they'd enjoy a sumptuous supper.

One night, after a long dinner at a five-star restaurant, the Stewarts decided they wanted to toast Phyllis's birthday with pink champagne, her preferred beverage. So they dragged Susan into a taxi, which drove them around London until they finally found a bottle of the rare, rouged bubbly.

During one of these evenings, Isabel made an observation to Susan about how difficult it must be to be separated from her parents, who were still in Sydney. When Susan shrugged off the inquiry, Isabel took her thirty-two-year-old daughter's hand and remarked airily, 'Sandra has never spent a night without me'.

In 1973, while the Stewarts were still travelling around England in their motor home, Isabel began experiencing chest pains. She first wrote to actor Peter Sellers for advice, via his agent, as it was public knowledge that he too suffered from a heart condition. While waiting for his reply, she also wrote to well-known journalist James Cameron, who replied immediately and recommended his famous London specialist, Edward Lawson McDonald. After her first consultation, he sent her to the London Hospital in Whitechapel for a week of tests and took her on as a patient. A panicking Alan, Charles, and Sandra were almost welded to her bedside, so much so that the nursing staff would have to ask them to leave at the end of the day. In the meantime, Peter Sellers responded to Isabel's request with a delightful and kind letter, recommending his own doctor. But by this time, she was in good hands with McDonald, who prescribed a range of medications for her condition. After being discharged from the hospital, Isabel returned to the motor home and hit the road with her children again.

After the departure of the Stewarts, Paulette remained in the non-conformist world she'd curated for herself in Kings Cross. As Paula reminisced:

She would walk out at night. She knew every Prostitute ...
She knew everybody. They all loved her. They adored her.
The homosexuals used to all come to her door because she
had such a tolerant, magnificent outlook, and her advice was
there. She became a sort of little queen in a ... in a damn
broken-down, old-fashioned flat ... So she didn't actually lose
herself, she found a new identity as the queen of that little
particular area. They knew she'd been a famous person, as a
woman director. They paid homage to her, and somehow her
ego must've had some satisfaction from that.

In true bohemian style, now that Paulette was unable to create a
work of art, she could, at least, become one. She probably viewed
her unconventional lifestyle as one of her greatest creations.

Moreover, Paulette had always thought of herself as 'a man's
woman' and did not embrace the rise of second-wave feminism
in the 1970s. In fact, in 1977, she went so far as to state, 'I hate
women. Most of them have nothing on top ...' Of course, this
wasn't entirely true, as she adored her intelligent and talented
sisters, and valued her friendships with Sheila Collingridge,
whom she'd matchmade with Gordon Collingridge, and the non-
conformist women around Kings Cross, including prostitutes and
gangsters' wives. Perhaps a more accurate assertion would be that
she hated women who uncritically adopted traditional roles.

But she could not have failed to notice that second-wave
feminists such as *Caddie* screenwriter Joan Long were now
jostling to enter the second wave of Australian film, which by this
time was being handsomely funded by the Whitlam government,
a resource that Paulette was never able to enjoy. These second
waves gained further momentum by the creation of the nation's
first film school, AFTRS.

By this time, younger sister Paula had sold her newsagency business and block of flats, and decided to spend the rest of her money, and her days, on travelling. Concurrently, she realised how much Paulette missed Isabel and the children and offered to fly her to London. After much discussion, Paulette was still ambivalent about accepting Paula's generosity and the thought of travelling overseas. Paula assumed that her older sister was merely being modest and proceeded to book two airline tickets to London. But Paulette still baulked at leaving Sydney, refusing to abandon her collection of stray cats living in the lane adjacent to her apartment, which she fed every day. By now, she'd also adopted a white cat, whom she named 'Bill', which was also the nickname of her brother, John. Whenever she wrote birthday and Christmas cards to her many great-nieces and great-nephews, she always signed it 'Paw-paw and Naughty Cat'. Perhaps, by the age of seventy-three, she was set in her ways and did not want to disrupt her cosy routine, which still included betting on horses with Phyllis. Ever independent, Paulette thanked her younger sister for her kind gesture but ultimately chose to remain at home.

Paula had to apply for an Australian passport for her first overseas trip, which meant she had to source her original birth certificate. Once she received the certificate, she was shocked to discover that her official Christian and middle names were different from the ones she'd been raised with: 'It was P-a-o-l-a instead of P-a-u-l-a', she said. 'Paola Marie. No Ernestina. Or Leonora!' Their mother must have chosen the Spanish spelling of the Christian name and invented the middle names of Ernestina and Leonora, to secure the good favour of her generous Chilean uncle.

In 1972, John's wife, Elsie, died of cirrhosis of the liver. A devastated John had a breakdown, drinking himself daily into oblivion.

By this time, Grant and Estelle had moved from Manly to a house in Narrabeen, and a concerned Grant converted the basement into a self-contained flat and moved John into it, where he was able to keep a caring eye on him. John lived there for two years before he too passed away in 1974, the first of the siblings to die. His legacy, however, would later be recognised through his pioneering film production work with his three older sisters.

Paulette rarely bothered to throw anything out, including the daily newspapers that she read voraciously. Now that the small spare room had been cleared and cleaned by Paula, she began storing the newspapers in there. One day, a visitor discovered a copy of the film, *Two Minutes Silence*, sitting beneath a window seat. The visitor exclaimed, 'Oh, that's the most dangerous thing you can have in a flat, Paulette! It can explode'. The visitor quickly dispensed with the reel and what was left of the film was lost forever.

Up until 1951, film stock was composed of cellulose nitrate or 'celluloid', which was highly flammable and decomposed over time. Kept under the right conditions, nitrate film could last up to 100 years, but more often, the prints were not valued and, once they failed to attract necessary profits, were discarded by exhibitors or sold to travelling picture show men. Over time, celluloid could warp, shrink, harden, or grow mould. The picture show men would exhibit these films until they became so scratched and warped that they could no longer be threaded into the sprockets of a projector. Many were simply thrown away or sold to factories as raw material for the manufacture of paint or boot polish. The films that survived this process had a better chance at longevity, but if not stored in congenial conditions, the celluloid would become bubbled and gluey, and eventually deteriorate into a treacle-like mass, which then dehydrates into a coarse brown dust.

Due to the high cost of 35 mm film stock in the 1920s and '30s, theatrical prints of Australian feature films were only made in small numbers, possibly as few as four or five copies, which reduced the possibility of one of them surviving. By the time film archives began to be established from the mid-1930s, most of the precious films from the silent era, such as those of the McDonagh sisters, were either lost, destroyed, or neglected so much that they would have been impossible to save or restore. For example, only several excerpts of *Those Who Love* survive, including one that features actress Sylvia Newland dancing the Charleston on Tamarama Beach, and a close-up of Marie Lorraine's face, imbued with sadness and longing, her wide expressive eyes pleading to be liberated from the rough wharf-side bar in which she is trapped.

In the 1960s, the Film Division of the National Library of Australia had copied the silent version of *The Cheaters* from a 35 mm nitrate print held by Melbourne collector Harry Davidson. But it wouldn't be until the 1980s that the NFSA would gain access to the original nitrate print of the silent version from Davidson's estate. In 1986, part of the first reel of the sound-on-film version of *The Cheaters* would be discovered in a Sydney laneway, and two years later, more footage of the same version would mysteriously surface. In the 1990s, yet another copy would be created from all available prints and sequences, with a music track by Ron West added to the film.

After *The Far Paradise* and *The Cheaters* were added to the collection of the NFSA, Paulette and Phyllis began to receive admiring letters from students. A section of *The Far Paradise* was included in Joan Long's documentary on Australian film, *The Passionate Industry*, and was hailed as one of the most distinguished of the feature. Further, *The Cheaters* began to be screened at film festivals around Australia.

Later, in 2017, *The Cheaters* would undergo a restoration through a collaboration between the NFSA and Haghefilm Digitaal, which would be screened at the 2018 Melbourne International Film Festival, the 2019 Sydney Film Festival, the 2020 London Film Festival, the 2021 Seoul International Women's Film Festival, and a program at the Museum of the Moving Image in New York City, 'Pioneering Women in Australian Cinema', in July 2022.

It is only in retrospect that *The Cheaters* has gained the international acclaim that it was denied in 1929 when the film's nuanced dramatic qualities were overshadowed by the introduction of talkies. Australian critics Andrew Pike and Ross Cooper, for example, praised the sisters for their 'unusual sensitivity to the expressive range of the camera and their awareness of careful scenario construction as a key to emotionally powerful cinema'. Film historian Graham Shirley admired 'the care and dramatic unity' of the silent version but noted how these qualities were compromised by the added sound sequences. Film historian Hartney Arthur judged the surviving McDonagh production as among the best silent movies ever made.

In the 1970s, two scenes from *Those Who Love* were discovered to be in the possession of collector and Channel 7 employee Roger McKenzie. When Paulette heard about this, she became incensed: '... nobody's got a right to have anything of *Those Who Love*, we should have them, they should be in the National Gallery'. Filmmaker Joan Long contacted McKenzie to organise a loan and a viewing of the film, but McKenzie refused to cooperate. (After Paulette's death several years later, however, McKenzie would donate the nitrate reel to the NFSA collection.)

McKenzie also owned a copy of the documentary on Phar Lap, which was donated to the National Library. In the 1970s, Neville Macken had a print of the documentary too, which he loaned to the ABC. But the ABC misplaced the print and it ended up in the Channel 7 building. Without establishing copyright or seeking permission, the network began broadcasting it every Melbourne Cup Day, which infuriated Paulette all over again. Phyllis eventually contacted Channel 7 and proved to be a shrewd negotiator for not only credit but also payment.

In 1971, twenty-three-year-old filmmaker Graham Shirley interviewed retired producer Neville Macken about the making of the three versions of *The Cheaters*. Shirley had already viewed the silent version and been astonished by the sophisticated storytelling, clever plot, restrained acting, and the assurance of the direction. Over time, he grew more and more curious about these three fascinating sisters. Initially, Shirley contacted Phyllis by phone, but she was always too busy to talk, let alone meet. During a rushed conversation, she suggested that he talk with Paulette instead, and gave him her phone number. After being contacted, Paulette invited him over to visit.

When Shirley entered her building, he had to walk down a long hallway on the ground floor. As he neared the end of it, he was confronted by the distorted reflection of himself in a flawed, life-size mirror. Amused by this, he recoiled from the image, knocked on the door, and was greeted by an older woman dressed in fashionable brown culottes with a matching top. Her hair was dyed black, and when she smiled, he noticed that she had one or two front teeth missing. Beside her stood a short-haired white cat, tail undulating. 'You can come in', said Paulette. 'The cat's accepted you'. As she ushered him into the flat, she added, 'If the cat had bolted, I wouldn't have let you in'.

The apartment was furnished with an eclectic mix of McDonagh antiques and heirlooms and contemporary 1970s furniture, including a television. Her father's treasured silk tapestry of a growling tiger hung on the wall, as did the framed watercolour of a harlequin, by former lover Douglas Drew. The dining table was set with Jatz crackers, along with cheese, tomato, and olives skewered with toothpicks. Immediately, the sherry came out and Shirley, a non-drinker, obediently imbibed.

'Look, we had all the publicity we could have dreamed of in our day', she remarked. 'We don't want any more now.' Restless, and with rapid speech, she would rarely sit down and conversed with Shirley while pacing the room.

As they chatted, she thumbed through the sisters' scrapbook and many film stills and vintage photographs. She kept insisting that she didn't want to talk about the past, but in fact, couldn't keep herself from telling absorbing stories from forty and fifty years before. Now and then she'd pause and, like a doting grandmother, proclaim to Shirley, who sat on a wooden chair at a table, 'You're not eating!'

Because of his naturally blond hair, she nicknamed Shirley 'The golden boy'. She would occasionally tease him about his tresses and playfully accuse him of having dyed them. And in testament to her unconventional past, she hinted at the many male friends she'd enjoyed throughout her life but had resolved to never marry. So many, in fact, that in the 1970s, her sisters still teased her about her 'stable of stallions'.

Paulette also refused to acknowledge her age.

'Well, you always think young', she said. 'Never think old. And I think if you think young, you always stay the same age.' An example of her 'thinking young' can be found in her affection for the Hare Krishnas, who arrived in Kings Cross in the 1970s, and who wore pale orange robes as they chanted and danced with finger bells about the streets. However, it was not the religion of the Hare Krishnas that captivated Paulette, but their unabashed theatricality.

She also maintained a fabulous sense of humour, kept up with current events, and adored animals, still feeding birds and stray cats daily in the back lane adjacent to her apartment. Shirley also remembered:

... once you had entered her world, had been summed up and invited again, whole life experiences were conjured in grand gestures of the anecdote. She lived with great determination in the present. Thinking of her career, her main wish was to be young again, and have the chance to direct with actors and equipment now available.

Paulette forbade Shirley to take notes during his visit, and he had to memorise the most important information, run to his parked car, jump in, and jot the material down before he forgot it. Paulette also forbade him to photograph her.

Paulette's friend Brian Seamark remembers her as one of the 'characters who made the Cross so colourful', calling her 'highly intelligent and a fun person from the day I met her'. Another young film historian, Andrew Pike, arranged to visit her while conducting research for his book with co-writer Ross Cooper, *Australian Cinema: 1900–1977*. After he knocked on her door mid-morning, he was bemused to find seventy-three-year-old Paulette greeting him while sipping from a sherry gin cocktail mixed in a flat champagne glass. She offered Pike a cocktail, but the young researcher politely declined.

Paulette was intrepid and brave but not completely fearless. She also nursed private vulnerabilities. Like the female lead, Lola, in *Those Who Love*, Paulette had always been terrified of thunderstorms. Whenever they descended, she would hang towels and drapes over the mirrors of her home. In the mid-1970s, one such storm began lashing Kings Cross – with lightning scissoring the sky, cracking thunder, and pounding rain. Panicking, she phoned the home of Graham Shirley for comfort, but Shirley's father answered the phone and told her that Graham wasn't at home. The father sensed her distress and stayed on the phone with her for twenty minutes, talking to her gently until the storm passed and Paulette calmed down.

⊶⇌◉⇌⊷

In August 1974, Paulette agreed with Graham Shirley's suggestion to be introduced to filmmaker Joan Long, whose work she greatly admired, and the three soon gathered at her Kings Cross flat. While the two women chatted, Long boldly pulled a battery-operated tape recorder from her bag and placed it on a shelf behind Paulette, deliberately defying Paulette's ban on recorded interviews. Out of respect for Joan, Paulette didn't object to or even acknowledge Joan's daring move.

Throughout the conversation, the two drank sherry. Occasionally. Paulette expertly rolled tobacco into cigarettes for herself and Joan. Her self-deprecating humour was still obviously strong, especially whenever any praise came her way. The interviewers told her of a man named Hartley Arthur, a former theatre producer and now a university lecturer in Australian film at Fairmont University in the United States. Joan explained that Arthur had recently visited Australia and viewed all the silent films available at NSFA in Canberra:

> JOAN LONG: ... the films that he picked out as the most outstanding of any in that era were yours. And his words to me, he said, these three girls must be revealed to the world! (Pause)

> PAULETTE: That was no achievement ... because the others were so rotten!

Throughout the 1970s, when the filmmaking community of Australia began taking an interest in the former careers of the McDonagh sisters, Phyllis began mythologising their past in newspaper articles and interviews. The habit began in 1971 when she was interviewed for an article called, 'When Three Dashing

Sisters Made a Movie'. In it, Phyllis compares new feature film release *Love Story*, starring Ryan O'Neal, with the first film by the McDonagh sisters, *Those Who Love*, noting similarities between the plotlines of the two pictures. The seventy-one-year-old is affectionately described by the journalist as 'a dashing figure in [a] purple pantsuit ... with a jolly face and unchagrined personality'. During the interview, Phyllis cheekily knocked ten years off their ages and stated that they'd begun making films shortly after they'd left high school, when their father, who believed in their talent and ambition, bequeathed them 1000 pounds in his will to make their first feature. This myth is often repeated in articles and essays about the McDonagh sisters up until the present day.

The truth, as we now know, was rather different: the sisters were actually in their mid-to-late twenties when they began making films; their Uncle Ernesto, a foreigner whom they'd never met, and who'd had no idea about their interest in cinema, had conveniently died and left them a sizable amount of money in his will at a time when they were itching to make *Those Who Love*.

The reason for Phyllis's mythologising was not personal sensitivity about her age or her past. The truth is that she adored her job at the *North Shore Times*, but News Corp had a strict policy of forced retirement at the age of sixty-five. Phyllis simply had to reduce her age, and those of her sisters, to maintain her position at the newspaper. '... she had to do a bit of juggling of history', said Paula, 'which was a great source of humour to us all'.

In 1971, history wasn't juggled as much as it was tragically repeated: one morning, Phyllis left her apartment to post a letter, when she crossed a street and was hit by a car. Both her legs were broken, and the injuries eventually left her with one leg shorter than the other. Just like her father, she would walk with a limp for the rest of her life, but she still stubbornly continued to work as social editor and journalist for the *North Shore Times*.

Graham Shirley never met London-based Isabel, and only met Phyllis a couple of times. The first time was in the foyer of the Sydney Opera House in 1975, before the beginning of *Hedda Gabler*, starring Linda Jackson. While most attendees were flitting around, sipping champagne and air-kissing, he noticed a woman standing in a corner with an older gentleman, away from the others, quietly leaning on her walking stick and observing the room. Now in her mid-seventies, she had dyed her hair blonde and styled it into a fashionable pageboy cut.

Just by her presence and appearance, Shirley intuited immediately that this woman would have to be the storied Phyllis McDonagh. He introduced himself to her and her husband, OB. He found OB an affable individual, who was very much his own man, confident and masculine. Phyllis was delightfully charming yet shy. Though he would soon learn that beneath Phyllis's veil of bashfulness lay a steely resolve.

In 1976, Shirley approached her on ABC television's behalf to seek permission to use excerpts from *The Far Paradise* in a documentary on early Australian films, *Sunshine and Shadows*. But he found pretty, demure Phyllis a tough and unrelenting negotiator. During discussions, she freely acknowledged the fee being offered by the ABC, but would calmly reassert the actual rate that she and her sisters charged, which was almost double what the ABC was offering. Since the era of silent films and early talkies, she had obviously matured business-wise. The production company finally acquiesced, and Phyllis secured the fee that she had originally requested.

The year 1975 was a significant one for the McDonagh sisters as interest in both feminism and Australia's silent film era intersected and peaked. *The Cheaters* was featured in a series of screenings organised as part of International Women's Year. Also in 1975, the Sydney Film Festival presented the first-ever retrospective of Australian films in a week-long program at the State Theatre. Film critic David Stratton remembers being a part of the committee that organised the program. Not only would there be screenings of 'vintage' films, but also presentations and Q&A sessions with anyone associated with the process of making them. Some of the films included *Smithy* (with director Ken Hall) and *Sons of Matthew* (with actor Michael Pate), and also *Back of Beyond, For the Term of His Natural Life, A Son is Born* and *The Power and the Glory* – which were accompanied by either a director, writer, producer, or actor involved with the making of them.

Stratton remembers programming the silent version of *The Cheaters* for Monday 9 June 1975. The committee informed Paulette and Phyllis of the screening and invited them both to a Q&A session on stage afterwards. However, the festival board never heard back from them and assumed that they were not interested in participating in the event. Stratton believed *The Cheaters* was a fascinating production for its time and 'a very good film'.

But Phyllis and Paulette, now in their mid-seventies, did attend the event together – anonymously – along with Graham Shirley, who sat between them. Also in attendance were Paula Dornan and some of their younger relatives. The theatre seated 2000 people and the event attracted a full house. Both sisters were nervous about the reception of the film – over forty-five years since they'd produced it – which is probably why they turned up to the screening incognito. The process of making *The Cheaters* had been brutal; the initial reviews of the sound version that had appeared in 1930 had been devastating, and they no doubt worried how an old silent film would be received by an audience in the sophisticated 1970s. Instead of quietly watching their work, however, they constantly whispered throughout the screening, explaining to Shirley who contributed what to the film and when, to the extent that audience members had to shush the excited sisters. Typically, Paulette ignored them and continued chattering throughout the movie.

Paulette and Phyllis needn't have worried about the reception of *The Cheaters*; at the end of the screening, the theatre erupted with extended applause. A thrilled and relieved Paulette congratulated Ron West on his organ accompaniment, and thanked David Stratton for his introduction, cheekily adding that the thirty-six-year-old critic would look better without a beard.

The sisters left the theatre in a state of euphoria.

21

CURTAIN CALL

(1976–1982)

In May 1976, two members of the feminist collective that published *Lip* magazine arrived at Phyllis's home in Randwick to interview her for an article they were planning to write on the McDonagh sisters. Phyllis was prepared for the interview with full make-up and her hair neatly styled, but when she opened the door, she seemed to be taken aback by one of the interviewers, Sue Johnston, who had short, cropped hair, no make-up and was wearing men's clothing.

During the conversation, Phyllis was polite and professional but, as Spunner has shared in a 2021 interview, she did not warm to her guests and did not elaborate on what Spunner felt were rehearsed answers. The apartment itself was dark and heavily cluttered with antique furniture and elephant ornaments, which Phyllis had collected throughout her life. Spunner and Johnston were not allowed to photograph her, nor were they permitted to remove the McDonagh scrapbooks from the flat to make copies for the magazine.

In the printed interview, the first statements made by Phyllis are ones that she had mythologised previously, as if she wanted to take control of the conversation and establish the fictional version of their film careers before the interviewers had a chance to think otherwise: that they were only teenagers when they began making films, that their father had always believed in their talent as budding filmmakers, and that he'd left them 1000 pounds in his will so they could finance their first film, *Those Who Love*. At the time, the interviewers took her at face value, recording her answers on a cassette tape and printing the statements word for word.

When asked if she received favours from powerful men because she was a woman, you can almost hear Phyllis bristling: 'I cannot agree', she replied frostily, 'it was the enterprise that counted'. One interviewer noted that the female leads in their first three films were working class and that they always seemed to express a stronger moral backbone than the male characters. 'Yes, I agree, looking back. But I don't think it was anything intentional.' When asked if their films ever meant to contain a message, Phyllis again baulked: 'No, no message at all. Nothing'.

The following year, Phyllis contributed an article to her old high school's newsletter, again repeating the myth that 'our father, who had complete faith in our capabilities, put up one Thousand Pounds behind us to form our own Company (McDonagh Productions) [sic]'. Phyllis was an experienced writer and journalist and the grammatical and spelling mistakes, plus her confusion over the true name of their production company, suggests that, in the year before her death, she was struggling with pain and illness. In the same article, she states their father and mother had died within a year of each other, when in fact four years had separated their deaths. She also explains that their careers as filmmakers ended due to the arrival of talkies 'in 1936', and that it was 'some two years before the full talkie equipment reached Australia'. As we now know, talkies arrived in Australia in 1929, and the first full Australian talkie feature to both enter production and receive a release, *Showgirl's Luck*, premiered in 1931.

In April 1977, perhaps also sensing her life was beginning to ebb, Paulette granted a rare interview to journalist Barbara Muhvich, who was writing a profile on her life. During the conversation, Paulette was uncharacteristically philosophical, as if reconciled to all the challenges and defeats of her past, and yet proud of her accomplishments and unconventional choices. Muhvich was obviously surprised by the humble circumstances in which Paulette, now seventy-six, chose to live, describing her home as a 'modest flat in a crumbling old building'. The article reads as if Paulette sensed the journalist's bewilderment and addressed it immediately. 'I grew up in the lap of luxury and now I have nothing. Money isn't important – even a millionaire leaves the world as naked as the day he was born. We spent every penny we made. We had no business sense and lived a wild, carefree life, throwing parties and entertaining friends. But I've got my peace now and it's wonderful. I have no regrets'.

The one sister who did harbour regrets was family misfit Anita. By her early seventies, she'd moved back into the family home with daughter Ann as husband, Gregory, had moved out. In her later years, she was bored, very lonely, and once again, due to her alcoholism, estranged from her sisters. Her envy had soured into bitterness, and she often complained to her children that she never got to inherit any of the McDonagh family heirlooms.

After six years of being on the road, and when Isabel was seventy-eight, the Stewarts sold their motor home and moved into a rented flat in Chelsea. Alan found work as a security guard at the British Museum, where he would remain for eleven years. When he could, he joined Isabel and his siblings as they attended the latest art gallery openings, West End theatre premieres, and concerts.

They all had the pleasure of viewing multiple performances by Laurence Olivier, John Gielgud, Ralph Richardson, and Joan Sutherland, and were in the audience during Maria Callas's bitter-sweet final concert. As avid fans of German-born Otto Klemperer, an orchestral conductor and composer who was hailed as 'the last of the few really great conductors of his generation', the Stewarts were in raptures every time they saw him perform, which was no less than twenty times.

Charles and Sandra remained at home, cocooned in creative endeavours. Both were writing fiction and sharing their efforts with their mother. It was also in the Chelsea apartment that Charles began to read aloud the collected works of Henry James – all twenty-three novels and 113 short stories – which turned into an ongoing, cosy literary soirée for three. Isabel's favourites were the novels *The Tragic Muse*, *What Maisie Knew*, and *The Ambassadors*.

When they went to plays and concerts, Sandra and Isabel would always sit in the middle. 'I think she was quite shy in public', said Charles of his sister. 'But I can tell you she wasn't quiet at home. She had very strong opinions. When a moderator suggested [at a film festival] that DW Griffith was too melodramatic, she stood up in the audience and declared, "Don't you think to attack Griffiths that way is like breaking a butterfly on a wheel?"'

'She had the best taste of anyone I've known', continued Charles. Like her mother, she could 'see through anything that was false – in acting, in cinema. I'd often like a film, and she didn't. But she'd be able to convince me I was wrong [with regard to] music, cinema, and books'. Older brother, Alan, compared her to Jane Austen, balancing home duties with her love of creative writing: 'She was a wonderful chef'. Charles added, 'And then she had her writing on the side'.

Paula confirms that Sandra had inherited much from Isabel, both physically and emotionally. Like her mother, she was quiet in public but enjoyed authority within the home. Isabel once told Paula, 'She rules us all like a rod of iron ... the boys do exactly what she tells them to do ... So do I!'

When Paulette was diagnosed with bowel cancer in 1978, Paula left her home on the Central Coast to move in with her. By this time, Paula was often on-call whenever the ageing Phyllis or Paulette needed help, and they grew increasingly dependent on her. Paula was only too willing to oblige, as she felt deep gratitude for her older sisters who had raised her with such patience, love, and protection. During the four months she lived at Kaindi, she noticed that Paulette was responding well to chemotherapy and that she had a good chance of recovery.

While Paulette was receiving treatment at Sydney Hospital, recognition at last came in the form of the nation's highest screen accolade, the Raymond Longford Award from the Australian Film Institute (AFI). First presented in 1968, the Award celebrates a person or team who has demonstrated an unwavering commitment to excellence in film and contributed substantially to the enrichment of Australian screen culture. The award was to be presented in Perth at a gala ceremony and televised live nationally. Paulette was too ill to travel to the event, so she and Paula talked Phyllis into flying over and accepting the award on her and Isabel's behalf, even though Phyllis was also ill. 'I'm only doing this for you and Paulette', a reluctant Phyllis told Paula on the phone.

By then, Phyllis was suffering from severe, unexplained stomach pains, but she stubbornly refused to consult a doctor. She summoned the will and energy to fly to Perth, with OB accompanying her.

Meanwhile, Paulette, still receiving treatment at Sydney Hospital, exercised her own stubborn streak by refusing to watch the live broadcast from a television installed in the ward. Determined to have her own way, she tried to sweet-talk the doctors into allowing her to return home for the night to be able to watch the award ceremony from the comfort of her own living room. Even though Paulette's immune system had been depleted due to the chemotherapy, the hospital staff finally relented. A shocked Paula received a phone call from one of the nurses, asking her to come down to the hospital, collect Paulette, and accompany her home.

By the time Paula arrived, it was around 5 pm. It was late August and bitterly cold, with northerly winds blading up from the harbour. Paulette was discharged and Paula rang a taxi to take them back to Kings Cross. The sisters waited outside on a bench in freezing weather. Paula tried to persuade Paulette to return to Intensive Care, but the intractable former film director would not hear of it.

The taxi did not turn up. Paula returned to the payphone inside and urged the company to hurry. The traffic was thick with after-work vehicles jammed along Macquarie Street. The sun had set, and they were now waiting in darkness and plummeting temperatures. Still, the taxi didn't arrive. Paula made a third call, pleading with the company. Finally, after an hour, a cab pulled up and beeped its horn.

Once safely home, a frail Paulette got on the phone and called all her friends and associates, including the family solicitor, her doctor, and her surgeon, urging them to watch the live television broadcast. Finally, after half a century, she and her sisters were receiving the accolades and credit that they so richly deserved – even if they were late in coming.

At the ceremony, politician Barry Jones announced the winner of the Raymond Longford Award. The room burst into applause and Phyllis joined him to accept the honour, making a short, appreciative speech. Later at the table, however, Phyllis's stomach pains intensified, and she whispered to OB, 'We'll have to go'.

He bundled her into a taxi to take them back to their hotel. Phyllis was in so much pain that they both forgot the coveted AFI award statue and left it in the back of the cab.

By the time Phyllis and OB had returned to Sydney, Paulette had been readmitted to hospital. While she didn't know it at the time, watching her sister on television that night, accepting the AFI's highest honour, would be the last time she would see her. During the gruelling wait for the taxi outside the hospital, Paulette had contracted pneumonia, and by the time she returned to the hospital, there was little that the staff could do for her. She died on 30 August 1978, never having held the award statue that had meant so much to her.

After Isabel and her children heard of the devastating news, nephew Charles was moved to write a poetic eulogy for his cherished aunt, who'd raised and cared for him as much as any doting mother:

FOR PAW-PAW
when we heard that you were dead
all the clocks in the world stopped at once
seeing you that last time
your topcoat wrapped around you in the dark
the cold wind making your eyes water
smiling and waving in the early morning street
accustomed as we were to the separation of geography
we were not prepared for these eternities
the clocks have started up again now
at least most of them have
in the last note you wrote to us you said:
Darlings – the only thing I'm living for now

is the thought of seeing you all again –
that's the one dream I have left.

Phyllis, growing more ill herself, was ravaged with grief. Still, she persevered with writing for and editing the North Shore Times, grateful for any distraction from her overwhelming loss. But on 17 October, while sitting at her desk and writing copy for the magazine, she too collapsed and suddenly died. A mere seventeen months separated the births of Phyllis and Paulette, but there was only a six-week interval between their deaths.

The autopsy concluded that she'd died of a bowel stoppage, which had been the source of all those stomach upsets. At once, floral tributes began pouring into her home from hundreds of friends and colleagues. On 25 October, a full-page obituary appeared in the North Shore Times, celebrating the recent AFI Award, and her achievements as a writer, journalist, humanitarian, and arts enthusiast. The proprietor of the Music Hall Theatre Restaurant in Neutral Bay, George Miller, opined, 'She lived the theatre. Phyllis was a great supporter of the arts. She was the Music Hall's mascot'.

When Paula learned of the loss of the AFI statue in the back of the Perth taxi, she was so disappointed she contacted Paulette's friend, director Joan Long, who then contacted the AFI and arranged for another award to be manufactured. Sadly, Paula would never get to see the award either. Paula's daughter-in-law, Yvonne, collected the second award and passed it on to OB. Unbeknownst to the rest of the family, OB gave it to Grant's daughter, Mandy, who was also his goddaughter and studying acting at the time. After the deaths of Paulette and Phyllis, in an escalating family feud, Mandy refused to relinquish it. Today, it is still in her possession, but according to her sister Susan, it is now broken in two.

The tug of war over the award statue caused a rift in the family. At the time, Paula was gathering material for the McDonagh files at the NFSA and wanted to add the award to the acquisitions. 'We loathe disloyalty', said Paula of the incident. 'We were so loyal to each other that, to me, that was like treachery, you know?' Due to her dogged collecting of McDonagh memorabilia, OB nicknamed Paula 'the bowerbird'.

Brother Grant did not cope well with the sudden losses. Paw-paw had been a beloved mother figure to him throughout his life, and he'd worshipped Phyllis. Temperamentally, he was more like his older sisters than John, Anita, and Paula. He was creative, inventive, independent, curious, adaptable, and a consummate dreamer. Only fourteen weeks after Phyllis died, he too passed away at the age of seventy.

After the deaths of her two sisters and brother, Paula travelled to London to visit Isabel, Alan, Charles, and Sandra. By then, Sandra had learned shorthand and typing to help Charles with the writing of his novels. During the visit, Isabel persuaded Charles to read some of his poems aloud, and Paula was genuinely impressed by their depth and lyricism. But even by McDonagh standards, she found her relatives delightfully eccentric. Her son John and granddaughter Catherine recall Charles as being gregarious and effusive, while Alan and Sandra were quieter and more composed. But they were all superb raconteurs, and whenever relatives visited London, the Stewarts would insist on taking them to the finest restaurants. One night, over a sumptuous meal accompanied by the best wines, Sandra joked, 'Do you know how hard it is for an anarchist [Sandra], a socialist [Charles], and a fascist [Alan] to live together?'

After the deaths of her two sisters, Isabel and her children did not go out as much. In 1981, they gave up their rented flat in Chelsea and purchased one in Bloomsbury for 19 000 pounds. Together, they enjoyed renovating and redecorating the new home. By now, Charles was about halfway through his reading of Henry James's collected works, and it would take him another year to complete it. 'One of the most satisfying things I have done in my life', he later remarked. During that year, the National Film Theatre (now called the BFI Southbank) screened *The Cheaters* twice at the Barbican Arts Centre, where Isabel, aged eighty-two, grandly appeared on stage and introduced them. She and her children attended both sessions. Sadly, the second viewing would be the last time Isabel would ever see the film.

On the morning of 5 March 1982, only a week after Charles had finished reading the final James volume, Isabel rose from her bed and, feeling particularly unwell, calmly announced to her children, 'I think I'm going to die today'. An ambulance was immediately summoned to spirit her to hospital. By the time the Stewart children arrived at the emergency room, only a five-minute walk from their home, Isabel had already passed away from a heart attack.

After their mother's death, Sandra took over the household and essentially became a surrogate mother to her shattered brothers, attending to them and providing comfort – just as her own mother had done for the McDonagh siblings in 1924. Charles found succour in his ritual of writing. He also found the time to translate the collected works of Paul Valéry. Whenever his parents or siblings had a birthday, he would always write and gift them a commemorative poem.

The Stewart children believed that there was no need for a traditional grave and headstone, or indeed any marker, to identify the place where their mother's remains were buried. When cousin Susan asked to visit Isabel's grave, they replied that they would give her instructions on how to locate the site, but they would not be accompanying her. They explained in their own inimitable way that they felt no connection with the corpse lying six feet under the surface of the earth, and that the spirit of their mother was with them all the time – not a bus ride away in a damp cemetery. They took great comfort in the Gospel According to Luke: 'Why seek ye the living among the dead? He is not here, but is risen'.

The three siblings grieved together for five years. Once they recovered, they set out on adventures, travelling around Europe. 'We went to Paris about thirty times', said Charles. 'Spain. Vienna. Rome many times'. Their travelling continued, on and off, for the next twenty years, until Sandra developed colon cancer. According to brother Charles, she did not fret about her illness, and was calm and reconciled to her fate. During the last week of her life, Alan and Charles placed mattresses on either side of her hospital bed, physically and emotionally bracketing their adored little sister. Sandra died on 13 July 2012. At the time of her death, she'd been researching a play about Rasputin.

'We've had one trip to Paris since then', said Charles, 'but it's not the same, as you can imagine. You need a female influence, I think'. At the time of publication, Alan and Charles, eighty-nine and eighty-four respectively, still live together in the same family apartment and, in honour of what they believe to be their Spanish ancestry, they dine at midnight every night.

*

Late in her life, perhaps anticipating her own death, Paulette decided to go to confession, most probably at St Canice's in Rushcutters Bay, a two-minute walk from where she lived. She'd been born and raised a Catholic but hadn't practised her faith in decades.

Once she entered the confessional box, she announced to the priest, 'Listen, Father. Don't let us waste time. There's not a sin on the calendar that I haven't committed'.

The bewildered priest advised her, as penance, to say fifty Hail Marys. But Paulette was in one of her feisty moods. 'Forget the Hail Marys', she announced, shaking her head and laughing. 'I enjoyed every bit of it!'

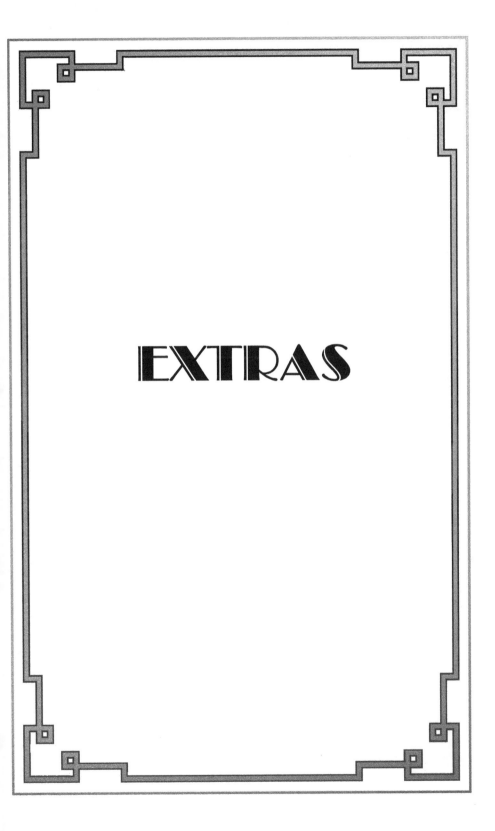

EXTRAS

Minutes from the House of Representative, 19 October 1978. Delivered by Barry Jones, Labor Minister for Lalor.

I want to draw the attention of the House to the deaths of two of the most remarkable women in the history of Australian cinema, Paulette and Phyllis McDonagh. Their achievement has been undeservedly forgotten, and I want it to be recorded for the national parliament. There were three McDonagh sisters, all born in the first decade of this century [sic], the daughters of a Sydney doctor. They grew up under the influence of Hollywood films, spent many hours watching and analysing them and finally decided, with fiercely independent spirit, to take on the United States industry and produce their own films. The eldest sister – Isabel McDonagh, Mrs Charles Stewart – was an actress who performed under the name Marie Lorraine. She is still living in England. Paulette was director and principal writer and died on 29 August 1978 ... Phyllis McDonagh was the business manager, publicist, and art director. She died two days ago, on 17 October. They produced four feature films – Those Who Love *made in 1926;* The Far Paradise *made in 1928;* The Cheaters *made in 1930; and* Two Minutes Silence, *made in 1933. The first and last of these films are now lost – a mournful indication of the poor archival holdings of our important films.*

Apart from their four feature films, the sisters also produced documentaries. Their films were amazingly inexpensive. They often made effective use of the interiors of their own home, Drummoyne House. Their films secured release in England. Their last two features were talkies. Their style was naturalistic and they stressed the importance of the low-key cinema style of acting in contrast to the more flamboyant stage acting. I invite [the] honourable members to consider the audacity of these young women and the enormous odds they overcame. All their films were box office successes and critical successes as well ... For 40 years they were ignored. They never received any official recognition; no OBEs or AMs were pushed in their direction. However, on 19 August 1978, in Perth, at the Australian Film Awards presented by the Australian Film Institute, Phyllis McDonagh – Mrs Leo O'Brien – accepted the Raymond Longford Award on behalf of the three sisters in recognition of their pioneering work in Australian film production.

... Sad to say, even the Raymond Longford Award this year did not generate any interest in the remarkable achievements of the McDonagh sisters, and their deaths were ignored by the media. They deserve far better recognition than that. I think that we ought to be ashamed, as a nation, of the neglect that we often hand out to our pioneers.

Filmography

FEATURE FILMS

Those Who Love

Director: Paulette McDonagh, PJ Ramster

Writer: Paulette McDonagh

Art director and production manager: Phyllis McDonagh

Cinematographer: Jack Fletcher

Production company: MCD Productions

Distributor: JC Williamson Films

Release dates: 22 November 1926 (premiere); 11 December 1926 (cinema release)

Running time: 89 minutes (6000 feet)

Country: Australia

Languages: English intertitles

Budget: 1000 pounds

CAST

Marie Lorraine as Lola Quayle

William Carter as Barry Manton

Robert Purdie as Sir James Manton

Sylvia Newland as Bébe Dorée

George Dean as Parker

Kate Trefle as Lady Manton

Big Bill Wilson as Ace Skinner

Charles Beetham as Austin Mann

Reginald Reeves as Sir Furneaux Reeves

Jackie Williamson as Peter
Nellie Ferguson as nurse
Howard Harris as doctor
Edith Hodgson
Herbert Walton

The Far Paradise
Director: Paulette McDonagh
Writer: Paulette McDonagh
Art director and production manager: Phyllis McDonagh
Cinematography: Jack Fletcher
Production company: MCD Productions
Distributors: British Dominion Films (Aust); Universal Pictures (UK)
Release dates: 14 July 1928 (Aust); May 1930 (UK)
Running time: 85 minutes (7000 feet)
Country: Australia
Language: English intertitles
Budget: 2000 pounds
CAST
Marie Lorraine as Cherry Carson
Gaston Mervale as James Carson
Arthur McLaglen as Karl Rossi
John Faulkner as Howard Lawton
Paul Longuet as Peter Lawton
Arthur Clarke as Lee Farrar
Harry Halley as Brock

The Cheaters (silent version, 1929; sound-on-disc version with Vocalion, 1930; sound-on-film version with Standardtone, 1931)
Director: Paulette McDonagh
Writer: Paulette McDonagh
Art director and production manager: Phyllis McDonagh
Cinematography: Jack Fletcher

FILMOGRAPHY

Production company: MCD Productions
Release date: 1 June 1930 (preview, sound-on-disc version)
Running time: 94 minutes
Country: Australia
Language: English

CAST

Marie Lorraine as Paula Marsh
Arthur Greenaway as Bill Marsh
John Faulkner as John Travers
Leal Douglas as the Lady
Josef Bambach as Lee Travers
Nellie McNiven as Mrs Hugh Nash
Elaine de Chair as Louise Nash
Frank Hawthorne as Keith Manion
Reg Quartly as Jan
Stanley Court as Jules Severie

Two Minutes Silence

Director: Paulette McDonagh
Writer: Leslie Haylen, based on a play by Leslie Haylen
Art and production design: Phyllis McDonagh
Cinematography: James Grant
Sound recordist: Jack Bruce
Production company: MCD Productions
Distributor: Universal
Release dates: 18 October 1933 (Canberra premiere); 10 February
    1934 (Sydney premiere)
Running time: 75 minutes
Country: Australia
Language: English
Budget: 1500 pounds

CAST

Frank Bradley as General Gresham

Campbell Copelin as Pierre

Marie Lorraine as Denise

Frank Leighton as Captain Lessups

Leo Franklyn as Private Simpson

Ethel Gabriel as Mrs Trott

Victor Gouriet as Corporal Smith

Leonard Stephens as James

Eva Moss as Miss Tremlitt

Peggy Pryde as Mrs Breen

Arthur Greenaway as curé

Frank Hawthorne as Reverend Thomas

Bert Barton as Toby

Katie Towers as nun

Fred Kerry as flower seller

Hope Suttor

Dorothy Dunckley

ACTUALITY FILMS (DOCUMENTARIES)

Australia in the Swim
Director: Paulette McDonagh
Production company: Neville Macken Productions
Release Date: 1932

How I Play Cricket
Director: Paulette McDonagh
Production Company: Neville Macken Productions
Release Date: 1932

FILMOGRAPHY

The Mighty Conqueror
Director: Paulette McDonagh
Producer: Neville Macken Productions
Release Date: 1932

The Trail of the 'Roo
Director: Paulette McDonagh
Production company: Neville Macken Productions
Release Date: 1932

Billy Bluegum
Director: Paulette McDonagh
Production company: Neville Macken Productions
Release Date: 1932

BIBLIOGRAPHY

Ansara, Martha, *The Shadowcatchers: A History of Cinematography in Australia*, Australian Cinematography Society, North Sydney, 2012.

Campbell-Bone, E, *Knock Around the Cross*, Sydney City Library, Sydney, 1995.

Deacon, Desley, *Judith Anderson: Australian Star, First Lady of the American Stage*, Kerr Publishing, Melbourne, 2019.

Edmondson, Ray and Andrew Pike, *Australia's Lost Films: The Loss and Rescue of Australia's Silent Cinema*, National Library of Australia, Canberra, 1982.

Ellis, Rennie and Wesley Stacey, *Kings Cross*, Thomas Nelson, Melbourne, 1971.

Fitzpatrick, Peter, *The Two Frank Things*, Monash University Publishing, Clayton, 2012.

Grey, Zane, *An American Angler in Australia*, Derrydale Press, New York, 2002.

Hall, Ken G, *Australian Film: The Inside Story*, Summit Books, Sydney, 1980.

Hall, Ken G, *Directed by Ken G Hall: Autobiography of an Australian Filmmaker*, Lansdowne Press, Melbourne, 1977.

Haylen, Leslie, *Two Minutes Silence: A Play*, Macquarie Head Press, Sydney, 1933.

Hickman, Lorraine, 'When Three Dashing Sisters Made a Movie', *The Australian Women's Weekly*, 21 April 1971.

Hogan, Sandra, *With My Little Eye*, Allen & Unwin, Crows Nest, 2021.

Humphries, Barry, Andrew Sayers and Sarah Engledow, *The World of Thea Proctor*, Craftsman House, Fisherman's Bend, 2005.

Hurley, Neil, *Soul in Suspense: Hitchcock's Fright and Delight*, Metuchen, New Jersey, 1993.

Johnston, Susan and Suzanne Spunner, 'Interview: Phyllis McDonagh', *Lip*, no. 2, 1977.

Kirkpatrick, Peter John, *The Sea Coast of Bohemia: Literary Life in Sydney's Roaring Twenties*, University of Queensland Press, St Lucia, 1992.

Lant, Antonia and Ingrid Periz (eds), *Red Velvet Seat: Women's Writings on the First Fifty Years of Cinema*, Verso, London, 2006.

Long, Joan and Martin Long, *The Pictures that Moved: A Picture History of the Australian Cinema 1896–1929*, Hutchinson of Australia, Richmond, 1982.

Matthews, Jill Julius, *Dance Hall & Picture Palace: Sydney's Romance with Modernity*, Currency Press, Sydney, 2005.

McDonagh, Phyllis, 'Sisters Behind the Klieg Lights', *North Shore Times*, 2 April 1975.

Muhvich, Barbara, 'She Helped to Put Us on the Film Map', *Sun Herald*, 24 April 1977.

Murray, Robert, *The Confident Years: Australia in the 1920s*, Australian Scholarly Publishing, Melbourne, 2020.

Naher, Gaby, *The Truth About My Fathers: A Memoir*, Random House Australia, Milsons Point, 2002.

Nowra, Louis, *Kings Cross: A Biography*, NewSouth Press, Sydney, 2013.

O'Connell, Deirdre, *Harlem Nights: The Secret History of Australia's Jazz Age*, MUP, Carlton, 2021.

O'Hara, Helen, *Women vs Hollywood: The Fall and Rise of Women in Film*, Robinson, London, 2021.

Petrie, Graham, *Hollywood Destinies: European Directors in America, 1922–1931*, Routledge & Kegan Paul, London, 1985.

Pike, Andrew and Ross Cooper, *Australian Cinema Film: 1900–1977*, Oxford University Press, Melbourne, 1980.

Porter, Hal, *Stars of Australian Stage and Screen*, Rigby, Sydney, 1965.

Reade, Eric, *Australian Silent Films: A Pictorial History 1896–1929*, Lansdowne Press, Melbourne, 1970.

Roberts, Kenneth, *Captain of the Push: When a Larrikin Chief Ruled the Rocks*, Lansdowne Press, Melbourne, 1963.

Russell, Eric, *Drummoyne: A Western Suburbs' History from 1794*, Municipality of Drummoyne, 2nd edition, 1982.

Savos, Sandy, 'Tributes in Sad Farewell to Beloved Writer', *North Shore Times*, 25 October 1978.

Sayer, Mandy and Louis Nowra (eds), *In the Gutter, Looking at the Stars: A Literary Adventure Through Kings Cross*, Random House, Milsons Point, 2000.

Shirley, Graham, 'The Coming of Sound: Standardtone versus Cinesound', *History: Magazine of the Royal Australian Historical Society*, no. 137, September 2018.

Shirley, Graham, 'McDonaghs of Australian cinema', *Filmnews*, vol. 8, no. 12, December 1978.

Shirley, Graham and Brian Adams, *Australian Cinema: The First Eighty Years*, Angus & Robertson and Currency Press, Sydney, 1983.

Stewart, Meg, *Autobiography of My Mother*, Random House, Milsons Point, 2007.

Thorne, Ross, *Picture Palace Architecture in Australia*, Sun Books, South Melbourne, 1976.

Tulloch, John, *Legends of the Screen: The Australian Narrative Cinema: 1919–1929*, Currency Press, Sydney, 1981.

Wilson, Victoria, *A Life of Barbara Stanwyck: Steel-True 1907–1940*, Simon & Schuster, New York, 2013.

Wright, Andrée, *Brilliant Careers: Women in Australian Cinema*, Pan Books, Sydney, 1986.

NOTES

To avoid repetition, I list details of relevant interviews only once at the beginning of each chapter.

1   Upstairs, Downstairs (1816–1897)
Paula Dornan interview with Graham Shirley [transcript], 1988, Title No. #1530844, National Film and Sound Archive.
Alan and Charles Stewart interviews with Mandy Sayer, 2021–22.
Ancestry.com

4   'John's father studied medicine in Dublin, graduating as a doctor and surgeon.' <oa.anu.edu.au/obituary/mcdonagh-patrick-27632>.
4   'John Grant was also born in Kilkenny, in 1816, and had immigrated alone to Australia as a nineteen-year-old Catholic missionary.' *Empire*, 1 March 1864, p. 2.
4   'Four years after his arrival in Sydney, Grant received his sub-deaconship and his deaconship on the same day ...' *Empire*, 1 March 1864, p. 2.
5   'He was appointed Dean of Bathurst upon his return ...' *Empire*, 1 March 1864, p. 2.
5   'On 3 December 1863, as part of his duties as Dean ...' *The Mercury*, 5 December 1863, p. 3.
5   'After Patrick McDonagh completed his medical training in Dublin, and when son John was about two years old, the family left Ireland and settled for a time in Cape Town, South Africa.' *Australian Town & Country Journal* (Sydney, NSW), 29 June 1889, p. 10.
5   'In 1857, the foundation stone of Bathurst's St Michael and St John's Cathedral was blessed by the first Catholic Archbishop of Sydney, Dr John Polding, and it finally opened for services in April 1861.' <www.cathedralparish.org.au>.
6   'There, he immersed himself in charitable work ...' *Freeman's Journal*, 16 June 1866, p. 383.
6   'On 12 May 1867, his wife, Isabella, gave birth to a daughter ...' *Sydney Morning Herald*, 23 May 1867, p. 8.
6   'He first attended Lyndhurst College in Glebe ...' <peopleaustralia.anu.edu.au/biography/mcdonagh-john-michael-27630>.
6   'After his tenure at Lyndhurst, John completed his secondary education at St Patrick's College, Melbourne. He then gained admission ...' <peopleaustralia.anu.edu.au/biography/mcdonagh-john-michael-27630>.
6–7 'He then gained admission to the University of Sydney ... after a three-year absence.' *Government Gazette of the State of NSW*, 'Register of Medical Practitioners for 1916', Sydney, 21 January 1916, p. 360.
7   'In 1889, his adored father died prematurely of cirrhosis of the liver, coupled with cancer of the liver ...' *The Daily Telegraph*, 29 June 1889 p. 1.

7 'In 1890, Williamson seized control of the company from his other two business partners and began to run it on his own ...' *Australian Dictionary of Biography*, <adb.anu.edu.au/biography/williamson-james-cassius-4859/text8117>.

7–8 '... those in the upper echelons of society would still consider playhouses as "Synagogues of Sin"' Hal Porter, *Stars of Australian Stage and Screen*, Rigby, Sydney, 1965, p. 86.

8 'In 1893, the doctor himself appeared on stage at the Lyceum Theatre ...' *Referee*, 3 May 1893, p. 7.

8 '... expressing his "earnest and deepest wishes for the future happiness of Mr Goodman and his future lady"' *The Referee*, 3 May 1893, p. 7.

9 'One such soirée was reported in the social pages of May 1894 ...' *Australian Town and Country Journal*, 12 May 1894, p. 35.

10 'Jane Annie (Anita) Amora [who] was born ...' *Sydney Morning Herald*, 25 March 1869, p. 9.

10 'Her father, Joseph Horatio Amora, had been born in Valparaíso ...' <huntershillmuseum.org.au/wp-content/uploads/2015/11/BunkAugust2015.pdf>.

10 'He immigrated to Australia in 1864 ...' *New South Wales, Australia, Gaol Description and Entrance Books, 1818–1830*, p. 432.

10–11 'How he managed to become a founding member of the Sydney Amateur Sailing Club ...' <huntershillmuseum.org.au/wp-content/uploads/2015/11/BunkAugust2015. pdf>.

11 'At the height of his popularity, in 1882, Amora was appointed Honorary Chilean Consul in Sydney.' Charles Potter, *New South Wales Blue Book*, Government Printer, Sydney, 1893.

11 '... and later as Honorary Vice-Consul for the Netherlands, Hawaii, and Nicaragua' *New South Wales, Australia, Government Gazettes*, 1853–59, p. 867; *The Evening News*, 31 October 1896, p. 1; *New South Wales, Australia, Government Gazettes*, July–August 1896, p. 87.

11 'By the mid-1880s, however, he was working as a lowly ferry master for Charles Jeanneret's ...' <huntershillmuseum.org.au/wp-content/uploads/2015/11/ BunkAugust2015.pdf>.

11 'By July 1893, however, there was a reshuffle in the hierarchy, with younger sister, Nell, being appointed to the position.' *National Advocate*, 27 July 1893, p. 2.

12 '... the first public season of moving pictures in Sydney was screened ...' Graham Shirley and Brian Adams, *Australian Cinema: The First Eighty Years*, Angus & Robertson and Currency Press, Sydney, 1983, p. 7.

12 'Less than two weeks later, cinematographer and projectionist Marius Sestier ...' Shirley and Adams, 1983, p. 7.

13 'The press reports of the screening were so enthusiastic that soon a more permanent venue, dubbed 'Salon Lumière' ...' Shirley and Adams, 1983, p. 7.

13 'Because the Salon was not associated with the bawdier vaudeville and variety programs at the Tivoli ...' Shirley and Adams, 1983, p. 7.

13 'Later that year, in Sydney, Sestier again came within Dr McDonagh's orbit when he shot what would turn out to be Australia's oldest surviving first film, entitled *Patineur Grotesque* ...' <https://www.screeningthepast.com/issue-28-first-release/patineur-grotesque-marius-sestier-and-the-lumiere-cinematographe-in-australia-september-november-1896/>

14 '... Joseph Horatio Amora was charged by the Water Police Court in Sydney for stealing 290 pounds.' *The Maitland Daily Mercury*, 10 February 1897, p. 2.

14 'In those days, the average price of a home was just under 100 pounds.' <https://www. macrobusiness.com.au/2013/02/the-history-of-australian-property-values/>

14 '... he also appeared as a character witness for him on 26 February 1897.' *Evening News*, 26 February 1897, p. 5.

15   '... Amora's mental condition had caused much anxiety.' *Evening News*, 26 February 1897, p. 5.

15   '... Amora was sentenced to two years' hard labour in Darlinghurst Prison.' *New South Wales, Australia, Police Gazettes*, 1854–1930, p. 70.

15   'In 1872, he'd been fined five shillings, plus two shillings sixpence costs, for failing to keep his (Glenn St) premises clean.' *Sydney Morning Herald*, 22 August 1872, p. 2.

15   'In August 1882, the Marine Board ruled that the shipwreck of the steam collier, *Llewellyn*, near Wollongong in May of that year had been caused by negligent actions of the master, Amora ...' *Adelaide Observer*, 10 June 1882, p. 13.

15   'Further humiliation came in 1892 when landlord William Lloyd seized all the furniture and belongings of the Amora family home on Moore Park Road, Paddington, for failure to pay the rent ...' *The Australian Star*, 14 September 1892, p. 2.

15   '... in June 1885, the Insolvency Court recorded his assets as twenty-two pounds and ten shillings, while his liabilities added up to a staggering 540 pounds and twelve shillings.' *The Sydney Mail and New South Wales Advertiser*, 20 June 1885, p. 1299.

15   'By the time his daughter Anita married Dr John McDonagh at St Joseph's Catholic Church, Woollahra, on 4 December 1897 ...' *The Sydney Stock and Station Journal*, 21 January 1898, p. 3.

16   'Five years later he died in Leichhardt Hospital at the age of fifty-six ...' *Sydney Morning Herald*, 27 November 1904, p. 4.

2   The urban playground (1898–1909)

Paula Dornan interview with Graham Shirley [transcript], 1988, Title No. #1530844, National Film and Sound Archive.

Alan and Charles Stewart interview with Mandy Sayer, 2021.

18   'In 1900, among Australia's earliest films were those shot and incorporated into a mixed medium performance created by the Salvation Army ...' Ray Edmondson and Andrew Pike, *Australia's Lost Films*, National Library of Australia, Canberra, 1982, p. 13.

19   'The green plaque near the front door of the house proclaims, HORBURY TERRACE, which was originally part of a series of eight identical homes, built in 1847, whose distinguished tenants have included Isaac Nathan, Australia's first classical composer, and colonial politicians Robert Lowe and Edward Broadhurst ...' <dictionaryofsydney.org/building/horbury_house>.

20   '... warrants for his arrest were issued in New South Wales and Victoria, which describe him as "5 foot 9, medium build, fair complexion, fair moustache, with a scar or a stab on the left side of his arm. Dresses respectably".' *New South Wales Police Gazette and Weekly Record of Crime*, 11 June 1930, no. 24, p. 462.

20   'The girls appeared at the church hand in hand, wearing white silk dresses with blue sashes, and bonnets decorated with chiffon, fancy straw, and feathers ...' *Sydney Morning Herald*, 27 February 1904.

21   '... an ivory embossed silk dress prettily insetted with fancy stitching and fans of accordion-pleated chiffon, edged with black velvet ribbon, the bodice made en-suite with Brussels lace.' *Sydney Morning Herald*, 27 February 1904.

21   'In 1877, with his older brother Eugene, he'd purchased 12 000 acres of prime land west of Gulgong, New South Wales.' <dibley-history.blogspot.com/2015/02/patrick-oconnell.html>.

21   'Pat, Eugene, and their mother, Margaret, had been the publicans of the Goodiman Hotel, Gulgong, which they changed to O'Connell's Wine Saloon, and together they ran it for six years until 1889.' <dibley-history.blogspot.com/2015/02/patrick-oconnell.html>.

23   'Nothing that has happened to me since through my adult years has equalled the thrill of that discovery.' Phyllis McDonagh brief autobiography [manuscript], 26 May 1975, Title No. 790864, National Film and Sound Archive.

23   'The success went to my head ...' Phyllis McDonagh brief autobiography [manuscript], 26 May 1975, Title No. 790864, National Film and Sound Archive.

23-24   'In the early part of the century, almost everybody in Australia could read and write, but roughly 90 per cent of Australians received no secondary education.' Robert Murray, *The Confident Years: Australia in the 1920s*, Australian Scholarly Publishing, Melbourne, 2020, p. 16

24   '"We three would sit there", said Phyllis, "quiet as mice, looking and listening to all these fabulous theatricals. We cut our teeth on theatre".' *Australian Women's Weekly*, 21 April 1971, pp. 4–5.

24   'Her Majesty's Theatre had been built for Rignold in 1886, which he'd managed for nine years.' *Sunday Times*, 14 September 1902, p. 2.

24   '... who'd introduced the Queensberry code of boxing into Australia ...' Kenneth Roberts, *Captain of the Push: When a Larrikin Chief Ruled The Rocks*, Lansdowne Press, Melbourne, 1963, p. 78

25   'Foley was keenly aware that those in The Fancy could help him make money ...' Roberts, 1963, p. 37.

26   'In 1911, a cartoon of Dr McDonagh appeared in Sydney's *Truth* ...' *Truth*, 22 October 1911, p. 4.

26   'By the 1890s, almost every suburb in Sydney and Melbourne, as well as many country towns, could boast about having their own rink.' Tony Buckley, *At the Coliseum DeLuxe* (motion picture) 2019, Sydney, PTB Screen.

26   'By the time of the cartoon's publication, the doctor had already become one of the principal controllers of the Coliseum Rink in North Sydney ...' *Town and Country*, 13 February 1920, p. 6.

27   'On 1 May 1912, Dr McDonagh and Larry Foley opened the Imperial Skating Rink, near William Street in the city.' *Truth*, 5 May 1912, p. 2.

27   'In 1909, a man named Mr W Eckard committed to a marathon at the Sydney Skating Rink.' *Orange Leader*, 12 June 1909, p. 5.

27   '... his general physical condition was marvellously good.' *Orange Leader*, 12 June 1909, p. 5.

28   'However, his adventures in theatrical production were stalled when the actor Henry Lee asked the doctor if he could borrow the staggering amount of 150 pounds.' *Evening News*, 20 March 1906, p. 4.

28   'He suddenly broke from character, abused the offending party for their "outrageous conduct", and vowed that he would never appear on stage in Sydney again.' *Punch*, 19 November 1902, p. 31.

28   'He referred Lee to a business associate, Kitching, who, on 6 December 1902, arranged for the cash to be forwarded to the actor and for a promissory note to be drawn up ...' *The Arena*, 15 January 1903, p. 14.

28   'When the case went to court four years later, the doctor's lawyer argued that McDonagh had not received a notice of dishonour and therefore was not guilty of any offence ...' *Evening News*, 20 March 1906, p. 4.

29   'According to a report in the *Bulletin*, "Dr McDonagh's three little girls ... snatched the prize from all competitors"' *Bulletin*, 9 November 1911, p. 22.

29   '... twelve-year-old Phyllis, by now an accomplished skater, stood out as "A Doll in a Box"' *Sunday Times*, 11 August 1912, p. 4.

30   'The quartet came dressed as the "Kismet Eastern Princesses"' *Sunday Times*, 28 July 1912, p. 4.

30   '... handing first prize to the "silvered brilliance of the ancient Eastern costumes" worn

by skaters Miss Dorothy Thomas and Mr Frank Cruikshanks.' *Cumberland Argus and Fruitgrowers Advocate*, 23 May 1914.

3   Those girls are going to do something outstanding one day (1909–1920)
Paula Dornan interview with Graham Shirley [transcript], 1988, Title No. #1530844, National Film and Sound Archive.
Paulette McDonagh interview with Joan Long and Graham Shirley [transcript], c. 2010, Title No. #1062964, National Film and Sound Archive.
Various details about Kincoppal, Isabel's friendship with Kathleen Coen, and her visits to Yass are from Meg Stewart's brilliant work of non-fiction, *Autobiography of My Mother*, Random House, Milsons Point, 2007.

31   'Moving pictures were being exhibited in existing buildings such as halls and former theatres: some eighteen in the city and ninety-six in the suburbs.' Ross Thorne, *Picture Palace Architecture in Australia*, Sun Books, South Melbourne, 1976, p. 17.

31   'In [1909], JD Williams opened Australia's first continuous cinema at the Colonial Theatre in George Street ...' Graham Shirley and Brian Adams, *Australian Cinema: The First Eighty Years*, Angus & Robertson Publishers and Currency Press, Sydney, 1983, p. 23

34   'It was run by French nuns who each wore a black habit with a white frill circling the face. Every time a student passed a nun ... Taronga Zoo.' Meg Stewart, *Autobiography of My Mother*, Random House, Milsons Point, 2007, pp. 86–7.

35   '... a very nice girl, a very kind girl. Dreamy – as her eyes showed.' All subsequent quotes of Estelle McDermott are from an interview with Bud Macken and Estelle McDermott by Graham Shirley.

35   'In years to come, when the sisters began publicising their films, they promoted the myth that they'd written the first draft of their first film, *Those Who Love*, in the recreation room of Kincoppal school' Phyllis McDonagh brief autobiography [manuscript], 26 May 1975, Title No. 790864, National Film and Sound Archive.

36   '... the Williamson company was able to turn the predicament to its advantage. It formed its own film company and started shooting moving picture versions of its theatrical productions ...' Joan Long and Martin Long, *The Pictures that Moved*, Hutchinson of Australia, Richmond, 1982, p. 46.

37   'Between 1911 and 1926, there were approximately 220 features produced in Australia, and 170 of them contained bush settings', Graham Shirley correspondence with Mandy Sayer, February 2022.

37   'In fact, so popular did the bushranging film become ...' Peter Fitzpatrick, *The Two Frank Thrings*, Monash University Press, Clayton, 2012, pp. 69, 121.

41   '"It was not that I had any particular talent for the stage", she reflected, "but I wanted to experience the actual background if I ever decided to write a stage novel"' Phyllis McDonagh brief autobiography [manuscript], 26 May 1975, Title No. 790864, National Film and Sound Archive.

42   'Isabel also regularly assisted her father in his surgery – even during operations.' The Cinema Museum, 'Interview with Charles and Alan Stewart' [video], cinedumonde, YouTube, 31 July 2016.

44   'First, a few cases – diagnosed as influenza. But they all died ...' Melissa Coburn, 'Debs Dance At Peak of Spanish Flu', *The Australian*, 16 May 2020.

45   'For the first time in history, young women such as [the McDonaghs] could walk in pairs or groups ...' Jill Julius Matthews, *Dance Hall & Picture Palace: Sydney's Romance with Modernity*, Currency Press, Sydney, 2005, p. 28.

46   'On Thursday 5 June 1919, the girls made their debut, along with seventy other young socialites, at a Peace Ball held at the Sydney Town Hall ...' *The Daily Telegraph*, 6 June 1919, p. 5.

46 'Seven years later, Paulette would register for copyright an early film scenario ... "crowning day of her young life".' Paulette McDonagh, 'A Greater Love' [film scenario], 1926, Title No. #202331, National Archives of Australia.

46–47 'In preparation for the event, volunteers spent months crafting tinted paper flowers ... "a sort of mad tango".' *Sun*, 15 June 1919, p. 6.

47 'Some young female attendees had already had their hair cut and styled into the modern, fashionable bob that would go on to define the style of the 1920s jazz age, but not the McDonagh sisters ...' *Sydney Mail*, 11 June 1919, p. 10.

4   The mansion by the river (1920–1924)
Paula Dornan interview with Graham Shirley [transcript], 1988, Title No. #1530844, National Film and Sound Archive.
Paulette McDonagh interview with Joan Long and Graham Shirley [transcript], c. 2010, Title No. #1062964, National Film and Sound Archive.

49 'On the following Saturday at 9.45 am, a cortège left 14 College Street ...' *Sydney Morning Herald*, 30 January 1920, p. 5.

49 '... the referee and participants in the main event wore black crepe armbands.' *The Referee*, 4 February 1920, p. 10.

51 '"Wyong" is an Indigenous word meaning either "edible yam" or "place of running water"' <en.wikipedia.org/wiki/Wyong,_New_South_Wales>.

51 'an extension of the town of Wyong, embracing fine river frontage blocks and interior lots in a go-ahead town on the Northern line, within easy distance of Tuggerah Lakes, the great boating and fishing resort.' *The Times, Wyong, Gosford, Woy Woy*, 24 February 1921, p. 11.

52 '... three months later advertised another two lots on the Wyong River for 110 pounds each.' *Sydney Morning Herald*, 11 May 1921, p. 11.

52 '... Aunt Mary's retired husband, Pat O'Connell, stepped up and bought the mansion himself ...' Private correspondence with Councils Local Studies Librarian at Five Dock Library, John Johnson, 2021.

52–53 'The forty-room stone property had been built by convicts in the mid-1850s from plans submitted by the owner of the land, Captain Wright ... discovered years later, in which to store valuables.' Eric Russell, *Drummoyne: A Western Suburbs' History from 1794*, The Municipality of Drummoyne, 2nd edition, 1982, pp. 92–94.

53 'In the mid-1900s, it was purchased by Elizabeth Hordern ...' Eric Russell, pp. 92–94.

53 'One day he found one of the family dogs playing with a human brain in the backyard, using it as a ball.' The Cinema Museum, 'Interview with Charles and Alan Stewart' [video], cinedumonde, YouTube, 31 July 2016.

55 'Paula was thrilled to see her name in the Sunday papers as the first-prize winner of a Beauty and the Beast drawing competition.' *Sunday Times*, 6 May 1923, p. 7.

55 'Fourth daughter, Anita, won a writing competition with a sophisticated Christmas story ...' *Sun*, 30 December 1923, p. 3.

57 'All were dressed fashionably, with Isabel wearing a gown of "white satin and tulle with flowers", Phyllis in pink "mousseline de soie", and Paulette in "unrelieved white"' *The Catholic Press*, 20 April 1922, p. 10.

5   Orphans (1924–1925)
60 'Later, Phyllis teamed up with JC Williamson vocalist Betty Vane to appear as a duo at the Lyceum Theatre.' *The Referee*, 16 December 1925, p. 15.

60 'The company opened at the New Palace Theatre in Melbourne with the comedy, *The Man in the Dress Clothes*. After the first performance, it received thirty curtain calls and a bouquet of flowers tossed by Dame Nellie Melba.' *The Telegraph* (Brisbane), 14 June 1927, p. 3.

61   'The farce was nicely produced, the café scene at the close being beautifully arranged and artistically produced.' *The Sun*, 12 February 1924, p. 10.

61–62   'At Kincoppal, the sixteen-year-old made a habit out of teasing the old gardener, Mortice ... "Only a McDonagh could have done it"' Meg Stewart, *Autobiography of My Mother*, Random House, Milsons Point, 2007, p. 94.

62   'Marginalia of the Kincoppal registry at the end of 1924 states that they were "both asked not to return"' Kincoppal archives.

63   '... they thought "it was beneath them", and believed they were destined for greater achievements.' Moya Joyes interview with Mandy Sayer, 2021.

63   'Today, this so-called disease has a name – enmeshment ...' <www.overcoming enmeshment.com>.

64   'The clannish trio speak of "we" that and "we" this, and all-for-one and one-for-all idea, that fits their chumminess admirably.' *Sunday Times*, 22 July 1928, p. 23.

66   'Phyllis combined her interest in cinema with her desire to make money as a freelance writer by researching and writing an article for the *Sunday Times* ...' *Sunday Times*, 22 March 1925, p. 5.

66   'In June 1925, the estate of the deceased Pat O'Connell, no doubt executed by Aunt Mary, sold Drummoyne House to two men, Richard Lonergan and John O'Brien.' Private Correspondence with Councils Local Studies Librarian at Five Dock Library, John Johnson, 2021.

6   Living and breathing as one (1924–1926)

Paula Dornan interview with Graham Shirley [transcript], 1988, Title No. #1530844, National Film and Sound Archive.

Paulette McDonagh interview with Joan Long and Graham Shirley [transcript], c. 2010, Title No. #1062964, National Film and Sound Archive.

Sheila Collingridge interview with Graham Shirley [sound recording], 1977, Title No. #376624, National Film and Sound Archive.

Alan and Charles Stewart interviews with Mandy Sayer, 2021.

The Cinema Museum, 'Interview with Charles and Alan Stewart' [video], cinedumonde, YouTube, 31 July 2016.

Paulette McDonagh, 'The Greater Love' [film scenario], Title No. #202331, 1926, National Archives of Australia.

Paulette McDonagh, 'Those Who Love' [film scenario], Title No. #202329, 1926, National Archives of Australia.

70   '... we'd just stare at her for ages and think: "Is she our sister?" We were so proud of her.' *Australian Women's Weekly*, 21 April 1971, pp. 4–5.

78   'The local incarnation of the league was a product of the better films movement, based in New York, which had declared that its mission would be "a conscious effort to encourage the production and exhibition of a high type of film by discriminating patronage at best"' Wilton A Barrett, 'Better Films Movement in 1923', *Film Year Book*, New York, 1924, p. 499.

78   'a movement for encouraging better cinema films and the use of educational films, and also for giving women more influence in the censorship of films.' Report of the Standing Committee on Education', Biennial Reports 1921–22, National Council of Women of NSW, p. 23.

79   'Reviews of the film were generally positive, with the *Bulletin* claiming that it was "a faithful reflection of the spirit of the pioneers, who battle in the open spaces, with a broad vein of humour running through it"' *Bulletin*, 28 August 1924.

79   'Statistics collected later in the decade confirmed the sisters' conclusions: of the 721 motion pictures screened in Australia throughout 1925, 676 had been produced

in Hollywood.' *Parliament of the Commonwealth of Australia: Report of the Royal Commission on the Moving Picture Industry in Australia*, Canberra: Government Printer, 1928, p. 3.

79 'Attendance at Australian cinemas was among the highest in the world – roughly eighteen films for every resident; two-thirds of the attendees, however, were young, independent women.' Cinema Industry Trends, Admissions and Key Events, 1901–1932', *Screen Australia*, 47.

81 'We felt that we could improve upon all previous Australian efforts ...' 'The Tigress', *The Herald*, 14 July 1927, p. 8.

81 'The kinema [sic] must please the women or die', Antonia Lant and Ingrid Periz, *Red Velvet Seat: Women's Writing on the First Fifty Years of Cinema*, Verso, London, 2006.

81 '"The three of us talked and talked", said Phyllis ...' *Australian Women's Weekly*, 21 April 1971, pp. 4–5.

82 '... it created more sympathy for the woman in the picture.' Susan Johnston and Suzanne Spunner, 'Interview: Phyllis McDonagh', *Lip*, no. 2, 1976.

82 '... was usually crafted from silk crepe de Chine, and the most popular colours were the monochromatic creams, greys, blues, and whites.' Robert Murray, *The Confident Years*, Australian Scholarly Publishing, North Melbourne, 2020, p. 10.

83 '"scoffed at the idea of girls succeeding where others had failed: The sisters gritted their teeth and decided to proceed on their own".' Joan Long, 'Australian Women Filmmakers, Part 1', *Cinema Papers*, June–July 1976, p. 38.

83 'We practically lived and breathed as one.' *Australian Women's Weekly*, 21 April 1971, p. 4–5.

7   Camera rolling (1925–1926)
Paula Dornan interview with Graham Shirley [transcript], 1988, Title No. #1530844, National Film and Sound Archive.

85 'a scenario writer of exceptional ability and it is by her that the story of *Those Who Love* was written.' *Bathurst National Advocate*, November 30, 1927, p. 3.

86 'In the difficult process of writing a scenario, every character becomes alive ...' *Truth*, 18 February 1934, p. 27.

88 'In 1971, Phyllis admitted that the plot was a bit corny, "but it had a human element that people wanted"' *Australian Women's Weekly*, 21 April 1971, p. 4–5.

89 'In fact, two years before, when Raymond Longford and Lottie Lyell planned to produce the mystery/thriller *Fisher's Ghost* for the same amount ...' Joan Long, 'The Passionate Industry' [Episode 2], *History of Australian Cinema Series* (motion picture), National Film and Sound Archive, Canberra, 1973.

89 '"There was nothing haphazard in our approach to film production", wrote Phyllis, "we had one fixed rule – only to use the best".' *Kincoppal-Rose Bay Newsletter*, 1977.

90 '"We were utterly determined and took every mishap in our stride", said Phyllis. "At the outset the three of us agreed to abolish the word *No* from our vocabularies".' *Australian Women's Weekly*, 21 April 1971, pp. 4–5.

90 'Fletcher's father encouraged his son's keen interest in filmmaking ...' Martha Ansara, *The Shadowcatchers: A History of Cinematography in Australia*, Australian Cinematography Society, North Sydney, 2012, p. 127.

90 'Most cameras exposed eight frames per turn of the handle ...' Ansara 2012, p. 24.

92 'As the master of suspense proclaimed, "... the best screen actor is the man who can do nothing extremely well".' Alfred Hitchcock, *Hitchcock on Hitchcock, Vol. 1 Selected Writings and Interviews*, University of California Press, Oakland, 2014.

92 'After a day of shooting your eyes were raw and watery and you couldn't see much at all ...' *Australian Women's Weekly*, 21 April 1971, pp. 4–5.

93   'The poor man was in a terrible way ... shivering and sweating ...' *Australian Women's Weekly*, 21 April 1971, pp. 4–5.

94   '... who "danced and made merry to the strains of a three-piece slapstick orchestra"' *Sunday Times*, 11 July 1926, p. 24.

94   '"At first it is something of a strain", she admitted. "The nervous tension and responsibility are tremendous"' *Truth*, 18 February 1934, p. 27.

95   'The processing of film in the 1920s involved "the rack and tank" method ... in the sunshine on large revolving drums.' Ansara, 2012, p. 21.

96   'For example, an older millionaire once approached him ... unceremoniously dumped him back in Sydney.' Jack Bruce interview with Joan Long [sound recording], Title No. # 367399, 21 August 1971, National Film and Sound Archives.

96   'In June 1926, an article appeared in the *Daily Telegraph* to promote the upcoming release of *Those Who Love*, describing Paulette as an experienced Hollywood screenwriter: "Paulette has written four scenarios which have been accepted in America".' *Daily Telegraph*, 8 June 1926, p. 5.

96   'Furthermore, in August 1926, the sisters began creating a romantic mythology around the film's inspiration: "The scenario is founded upon the story contained in some old documents found when clearing out a cellar at Drummoyne House"' *Sun*, 21 August 1926, p. 6.

97   '... and the title of the finished film was publicised in the Society column of the Sydney *Sun*.' *Sun*, 5 September 1926, p. 30.

97   'We sat in the dress circle, side by side, so nervous we couldn't breathe ...' *Australian Women's Weekly*, 21 April 1971, p. 4–5.

98   'When the governor, Sir Dudley de Chair was leaving the theatre, he assured the sisters ...' Susan Johnston and Suzanne Spunner, 'Interview: Phyllis McDonagh', *Lip*, no. 2, 1977.

98–99   'At the time, "Australian Film" was still considered by many as an oxymoron, and one critic even addressed the reluctance to pay money to watch one by stating, "Certainly Australia has never approached the standard this film has set". ... "Search as you will, you cannot find even a shadow of a Hayseed, a suntanned young squatter, or a Man They Could Not Hang".' *Smith's Weekly*, 18 December 1926, p. 10.

99   'When they tried to secure a distributor, they were met with bemusement and told, "Go home, little girls".' Ross Cooper, 'The McDonagh Sisters', *Cinema Papers*, July 1974, p. 261.

99   '... claiming that the picture "had received the best public reaction of any picture he could recollect in the past fifteen years".' *Everyone's*, 6 February 1927.

99   'Marie Lorraine is a Sydney girl whose histrionic ability is remarkable ...' *Everyone's*, 27 October 1926.

101   'We are prepared to find the money for them to do as many more pictures as they like on the same standard.' John Tulloch, *Legends of the Screen: The Australian Narrative Cinema: 1919–1929*, Currency Press, Sydney, 1981, p. 293.

8   Wild and carefree (1926–1927)

103   'We ... lived a wild, carefree life, throwing parties and entertaining friends.' Barbara Muhvich, 'She Helped to Put Us on the Film Map', *Sun Herald*, 24 April 1977.

103   'It was a time when Sydney was an industrious port city ...' Jill Julius Matthews, *Dance Hall & Picture Palace: Sydney's Romance with Modernity*, Currency Press, Sydney, 2005, p. 8

104   'Quite recently a criticism from a foreign quarter was made about Australians ...' Beatrice Tildesley, 'The Cinema in Australia', *Australian Quarterly*, 15 December 1930, pp. 89–90.

105   'He determined to put into his theatre every conceivable idea of showmanship ...'

'Story of a Brilliant Showmanship Achievement', *Everyone's*, 30 June 1937, p. 30.

109 '... the ladies of the chorus glitter in costly costumes in the palace ballroom.' *Truth*, 17 July 1927, p. 11.

109 'In an interview with the *Daily Telegraph*, she bemoaned the restrictions of her own youth ... "of the black and mysterious things that are said about her".' *Daily Telegraph News Pictorial*, 21 July 1927, p. 29.

9   The sisters should always get what they want (1927–1928)

111 'In the great rambling home at Drummoyne the girls had long dreamed of the time when they could prove the ability of their sex in the making of films.' *The Sydney Mail*, 6 June 1928 p. 22.

112 'Posters, stunts, tie-ins, fan and romance magazines, product sponsorship, radio programs and a vast array of other star publicity developed in Sydney people the movie habit.' Jill Julius Matthews, *Dance Hall & Picture Palace: Sydney's Romance with Modernity*, Currency Press, Sydney, 2005, p. 133.

112 'Records reveal that during the silent era, the population of six million people in Australia attended the cinema a staggering 110 000 000 times annually.' Royal Commission into the Moving Picture Industry in Australia, Report, Parliamentary Papers, General Session, 1926–28, Vol. 4, Government Printer, Canberra, 1928, CI. 63–4.

112 'On the other side of the camera, in the year following the release of *Those Who Love*, the Australian film industry provided employment for approximately 20 000 people.' Royal Commission into the Moving Picture Industry, Minutes of Evidence, Government Printer, Canberra, 1928. Evidence of Stuart Doyle.

113 'As one manager complained, "it is not so much a matter of choosing programmes as taking what we are given". 'Cinema in Australia', *Australian Variety and Show World*, July 1920.

118 'Though the newspapers made a big play of the novelty of three sisters going into the movie business, it never occurred to us that we were doing anything remarkable ...' *North Shore Times*, 2 April 1975, p. 23.

119 'So many mushroom film companies, self-watered with their own glowing prospectuses, have sprung up and shrivelled lately that it is good to record the persistence of the McDonagh sisters.' *Bulletin*, 9 May 1928, p. 34.

121 'We have been asked to state that Mr Ramster had no connection whatsoever with the production of "Those Who Love" or "The Far Paradise"' *Sunday Times*, 15 July 1928, p. 5.

121 '"For the picture", said Phyllis, "we turned our old home into a studio; but we were very much more settled in Bondi Junction"' *The Sydney Mail*, 26 June 1928, p. 22.

122 'He'd sheltered alone in a hut there for five weeks after having been accidentally shot by a pea gun.' *Sydney Morning Herald*, 27 January 1927 p. 9.

124 'With their unusual personalities the McDonagh girls should always get what they want.' *The Sydney Mail*, 6 June 1928, p. 22.

124 'When Beaumont Smith tried to book the Sydney Town Hall ... In general, filmmakers of the silent era "received little co-operation and much bureaucratic obstruction from authorities in New South Wales".' Joan Long and Martin Long, *The Pictures that Moved*, Hutchinson of Australia, Richmond, 1982, p. 78.

124 'a striking use of shadows, depth of focus and backlighting.' Graham Shirley, 'McDonaghs of Australian Cinema', *Filmnews*, vol. 8, no. 12, 1978, pp. 15–18.

124 '... adroitly conveyed by a shot of her overworked hands dissolving to the same hands toying with a rose during the ball.' Graham Shirley and Brian Adams, *Australian Cinema: The First Eighty Years*, Angus & Robertson and Currency Press, Sydney, 1983, p. 84.

10 Two decent proposals (1928)

126 'Isabel accepted and the engagement was announced in the press on 9 February.' *The Sun*, 9 February 1928, p. 21.

128 'In early 1928, an article about Drummoyne House … ' *Labor Daily*, 23 January 1928, p. 4.

129 '… the *Sun* declared that the McDonaghs had produced "a thoroughly convincing and really entertaining screen play"' *The Sun*, 19 June 1928, p. 19.

129 'It will burn its appeal into hearts and rouse the slumbering emotions as no other drama in screen history.' *The Labor Call*, 25 October 1928, p. 9.

130 '… an ongoing war between Hoyts and Union probably contributed to the staggered releases of the film around Australia.' John Tulloch, *Legends on the Screen: The Australian Narrative Cinema: 1919-1929*, Currency Press, Sydney, 1981, p. 304.

131 'The scenes showing the deteriorating relationship between father and daughter …' Graham Shirley, 'McDonaghs of Australian cinema', *Filmnews*, vol. 8, no. 12, 1978, pp. 15–18.

131 'Her pink pompadour frock against the black stage and the blue and gold curtains make for an admirable setting for her Dresden china beauty.' *Sunday Times*, 22 July 1928, p. 23.

132 '… at the start we should confine our production to simple stories. The more ambitious productions will come later … Australian audiences would soon get tired of the ordinary bush story.' Royal Commission into the Moving Picture Industry of the 1940s, Minutes of Evidence, 1928. Evidence of Isabel McDonagh, p. 927.

132 'It would not be a bad idea for the Government to advance money to producers to be paid back later.' Joan Long and Martin Long, *The Pictures that Moved*, Hutchinson of Australia, Richmond, 1982, p. 121.

132–33 'Despite impassioned pleas from hundreds of individuals for more strategies to support Australian cinema, the commission determined that "there is no American combine in existence in Australia exercising a stranglehold over the motion picture industry". It recommended, instead, a quota system such as the British had implemented, but failed to pass the legislation that would have implemented the recommendation.' Graham Shirley and Brian Adams, *Australian Cinema: The First Eighty Years*, Angus & Robertson and Currency Press, Sydney, 1983, p. 97.

133 '… had a reputation for relishing "the wheeling and dealing, and the startling amounts of money that it could generate".' Peter Fitzpatrick, *The Two Frank Things*, Monash University Press, Clayton, 2012, p. 121.

133–34 '… send them to Hollywood and sit them on golden thrones.' Graham Shirley, 'McDonaghs of Australian cinema', *Filmnews*, vol. 8, no. 12, 1978, pp. 15–18.

134 'Over the years, Paulette, perhaps trying to justify her intervention against Isabel's wedding to Graham, would often say, "I'm so glad you never married Frank Graham. If you had, you wouldn't have had your three kids"' Charles Stewart interview with Mandy Sayer, January 2022.

135 'We would like to say that Miss Lorraine has a screen future here …' *Everyone's*, 20 June 1928, p. 5.

135 'In April 1928, the sisters told a Melbourne journalist …' *Table Talk*, 26 April 1928, p. 6.

135 'Women were allowed to flourish to a certain point and no further', Helen O'Hara, *Women vs Hollywood: The Fall and Rise of Women in Film*, Robinson, London, 2021, p. 29.

136 'To pay off their growing debts, in August 1928 the sisters proceeded with the sale of Drummoyne House to Walter John Simpson …' Private correspondence with Councils Local Studies Librarian at Five Dock Library, John Johnson.

Notes

11   Magic and miracles (1929)

Paula Dornan interview with Graham Shirley [transcript], 1988, Title No. #1530844, National Film and Sound Archive.

Neville Macken interview with Graham Shirley [sound recording], 1971, Title No. #227531, National Film and Sound Archive.

Alan and Charles Stewart interviews with Mandy Sayer, 2021–22.

140 'As Cam Bone recalls in her memoir *Knock Around the Cross*, "rents were low and one could starve much slower in the Cross than anywhere else in Sydney".' E Campbell-Bone, *Knock Around the Cross*, Sydney City Library, Sydney, 1995.

140 'While there, he secured a job as a labourer ...' Electoral Rolls, Australia, 1930.

141 'There was Selena who made junk jewellery from glass beads and copper fuse wire, Nancy who ...' Louis Nowra, *Kings Cross: A Biography*, NewSouth Press, Sydney, 2013.

143 'One of the best publicity stunts round town is being staged by Bruno Valetty [sic], who now again brings his Egyptian, Rahman Bey, to Romano's ...' *Truth*, 28 October 1928, p. 11.

144 'Rahman Bey first appeared in public in London in 1926 ...' *Newcastle Morning Herald and Miners' Advocate*, 19 June 1926, p. 14.

144 '... though in another article he admits to eating meat and other Egyptian dishes ...' *Cairns Post*, 1 September 1926, p. 3.

149 '... "the religious and educational atmosphere of St Ignatius College (London) prior to World War One", which was "heavily baroque and was congruent with the new wave of Expressionism".' Neil Hurley, *Soul in Suspense: Hitchcock's Fright and Delight*, Metuchen, New Jersey, 1993, p. 81.

149 '... in April 1928, the Commonwealth had finally acted upon two of the nineteen recommendations from the Royal Commission ...' Graham Shirley and Brian Adams, *Australian Cinema: The First Eighty Years*, Angus & Robertson and Currency Press, Sydney, 1983, p. 98.

149 'In 1927, the federal government received 140 000 pounds a year from duty on imported films and a further 37 000 pounds a year from an entertainment tax.' Royal Commission into the Moving Picture Industry of the 1940s, Minutes of Evidence, 1928. Evidence of Miss Mildred Maude Tildesley.

150 'In March 1927 he sold his "Mani" sheep station ... far too young to put his feet up and retire.' Neville Macken interview with Graham Shirley [sound recording], 1971, Title No. #227531, National Film and Sound Archive.

150 '"Paulette was the brains behind the whole thing", Macken once remarked. "She was an extraordinary girl".' Neville Macken interview with Graham Shirley [sound recording], 1971, Title No. #227531, National Film and Sound Archive.

12   Trouble with talkies (1929)

Paula Dornan interview with Graham Shirley [transcript], 1988, Title No. #1530844, National Film and Sound Archive.

Neville Macken interview with Graham Shirley [sound recording], 1971, Title No. #227531, National Film and Sound Archive.

Neville Macken interview with Graham Shirley [transcript], c. 2011, Title No. #1076826, National Film and Sound Archive.

Susan Fryer interviews with Mandy Sayer, 2021.

Graham Shirley interview with Mandy Sayer, 2021.

Moya Joyes interview with Mandy Sayer, 2021.

153 'My man at the top in this instance was the Commissioner of Police ...' Susan Johnston and Suzanne Spunner, 'Interview: Phyllis McDonagh', *Lip*, no. 2, 1977.

154 'When I told the secretary I wanted to see the director on important business ...' Johnston and Spunner 1977.

157 'On calling here to see Miss McDonagh, we found her looking very pretty and efficient ...' *Sunday Times*, 9 June 1929, p. 33.

157 'It offered a sense of keen and cool delight to the visitor ascending from the grime of the city streets ...' Barry Humphries, Andrew Sayers & Sarah Engledow, *The World of Thea Proctor*, Craftsman House, Fisherman's Bend, 2005, p. 7.

158 'In the same month, a creditor's petition from Kenmore Ltd, directed at Isabel, appeared in the press ...' *Sydney Morning Herald*, 19 October 1929, p. 14.

158 'On 2 November, another bankruptcy notice appeared, this time in relation to unpaid taxes.' *Sydney Morning Herald*, 2 November 1929, p. 14.

158 'Three days later, yet another petition appeared from Kenmore Ltd.' *Sydney Morning Herald*, 5 November 1929, p. 6.

158 'Then, on 3 December 1929, Mr A G de L Arnold appeared for the petitioning creditors, but it was adjourned again, with a view to a settlement ...' *Sydney Morning Herald*, 3 December 1929, p. 10.

158–59 'But the matter wasn't resolved until February the following year when leave was given by the court to withdraw the petition ...' *Sydney Morning Herald*, 18 February 1930, p. 8.

160 '"Now, are you ready?" came her cry at last; "We're really going to take it this time"' *The Sun*, 26 November 1929, p. 23.

13　The crash (1929–1930)

162 'The president of RKO, for example, announced that unless radical changes were made, "the industry would be bankrupt within three months"' Victoria Wilson, *A Life of Barbara Stanwyck, Steel-True, 1907–1940*, Simon & Schuster, New York, 2013, p. 279.

162–63 'By the end of the 1920s, the distributor Australasian Films ...' Martha Ansara, *The Shadowcatchers: A History of Cinematography in Australia*, Australian Cinematography Society, North Sydney, 2012, p. 51.

164 'When we explained to Mr Trevelyan that we would be employing Australian musicians ...' *The Herald*, 12 March 1930, p. 3.

164 'Two years before, the Sydney office of the Musicians' Union had staged a war against a thirty-piece Italian orchestra ...' Deirdre O'Connell, *Harlem Nights: The Secret History of Australia's Jazz Age*, MUP, Carlton, 2021, pp. 145–6.

164–65 'When it came to jazz music, Clause (q) of Section 4 of the union's rule book stated their vehement opposition to "colored musicians" ... "principle".' O'Connell 2021, p. 150.

165 'Ironically, Trevelyan was one of the most unprincipled men in show business ...' O'Connell, 2021, pp. 153–4.

165 'Any member of the Musicians' Union who plays for or in any way assists in the making of mechanical music for films will be expelled immediately.' *The Herald*, 12 March 1930, p. 12.

165 '"We have had so many applicants", they stated to a journalist ...' *The Register News Pictorial*, 18 March 1930, p. 3.

165–66 'A disgruntled Trevelyan put the word out that members of the union ...' *The Register News Pictorial*, 18 March 1930, p. 3.

166 'According to veteran projectionist Albert Wright ...' Ina Bertrand, *The Cheaters*, Metro Magazine #206, 2020, p. 116.

166 'The judges were members of the Commonwealth Film Censorship Appeal Board ...' *Sunday Times*, 25 May 1930, p. 9.

168 'The Cheaters, frankly, is not a good film ...' *Sydney Mail*, 11 June 1930, p. 27.

Notes

168 'This didn't stop budding journalist Grant McDonagh from publishing an article ...'
Labor Daily, 1 December 1930, p. 4.

169 '"'The Cheaters' was at first a bitter experience", Paulette admitted in 1934.' *Truth*,
18 February 1934, p. 27.

170 'She absorbed the whole milieu of the criminal underworld from Fritz Lang.' The
Cinema Museum, 'Interview with Charles and Alan Stewart' [video], cinedumonde,
YouTube, 31 July 2016.

172 '... and thank God I didn't ... I don't believe in marriage. I always wanted to be my
own woman.' *Sun Herald*, 24 April 1977.

172 'In July 1931, he was listed in the *Los Angeles Times* as co-director of the motion
picture production company Triumphant Films ...' *The Los Angeles Times*, 4 July 1931
p. 14.

172 'In 1934, Bey returned to Sydney for a season at the Tivoli ...' *The Sun*, 22 April 1934,
p. 31.

172 'The following year, he appeared as part of a vaudeville line-up at the Civic Theatre,
Haymarket ...' *Truth*, 8 September 1935, p. 35.

172 'On 6 October of that year, Bey began a series of broadcasts over 2UW in Sydney
entitled, "Mysteries of Egypt"' *The Nowra Leader*, 4 October 1935, p. 8.

172 '... it was reported he'd given up show business to sell silk stockings.' *The Sun*,
28 August 1938, p. 4.

173 '... and did not emerge again publicly until July 1944, when he was listed at the very
bottom of the bill for a show at the Tivoli in Newcastle, New South Wales, and merely
described as a "mystic"' *The Newcastle Sun*, 7 July 1944, p. 5.

14 Always do what you're afraid to do (1930–1934)

Paulette McDonagh interview with Joan Long and Graham Shirley [transcript], c. 2010,
Title No. #1062964, National Film and Sound Archive.

Neville Macken interview with Graham Shirley [sound recording], 1971, Title No. #227531,
National Film and Sound Archive.

Neville Macken interview with Graham Shirley [transcript], c. 2011, Title No. #1076826,
National Film and Sound Archive.

Paula Dornan interview with Judith Kelly [sound recording], 1983, Title No. #330324,
National Film and Sound Archive.

Paula Dornan interview with Judith Kelly [transcript], n.d., Title No. #1530845, National
Film and Sound Archive.

Paula Dornan interview with Graham Shirley [sound recording], 1988, Title No. 188932,
National Film and Sound Archive.

Paula Dornan interview with Graham Shirley [transcript], 1988, Title No. #1530844,
National Film and Sound Archive.

Alan and Charles Stewart interviews with Mandy Sayer, 2021.

John and Kathy Dornan interview with Mandy Sayer, 2021.

178 'Leslie Haylen', *Two Minutes Silence: A Play*, Macquarie Head Press, 1933.

180 'The day before the grand opening of the Sydney Harbour Bridge in March 1932,
Phyllis attended a "monster carnival"' *The Sun*, 21 February 1932, p. 26.

181 'The competition was ostensibly about popularity and charity, but when Phyllis was
later interviewed ...' *Daily Telegraph*, 26 August 1932, p. 5.

181–82 'Some of the sets would need to accommodate battle scenes and dugouts, and
so former actor and singer Josef Bambach ...' *Sydney Smith's Weekly*, 20 August 1932,
p. 10.

182 'We had to build a large asbestos box to enclose the cameraman ...' Susan Johnston
and Suzanne Spunner, 'Phyllis McDonagh', *Lip*, no. 2, 1977.

184 'On the 23rd, another injunction was granted, restraining both parties from using the building or its equipment until Wednesday of the following week ...' *Sydney Morning Herald*, 23 July 1932, p. 10.

184 'According to Macken's brother, Bud, Macken was "practically broke", and so he'd had no choice but to comply with Manion's instructions.' Graham Shirley, 'The Coming of Sound: Standardtone versus Cinesound', *History: Magazine of the Royal Australian Historical Society*, September 2018, no. 137, p. 6.

184 'She works like a machine, cold and sure ...' *Labor Daily*, 23 August 1932, p. 4.

186 'It also featured an orchestra of twenty-four players ... and a permanent ballet of sixteen girls.' Ken G Hall, *Directed by Ken G Hall: Autobiography of an Australian Filmmaker*, Lansdowne Press, Melbourne, 1977, p. 48.

186 'On the one hand, he was an impatient, hard-driving dictator who believed that the way to get the best out of his staff ...' Hall 1977, p. 12.

186 'Only two years before, in 1931, film returns across Australia had been at their lowest for five years. In the second half of the same year, Hoyts Theatres lost 18 500 pounds. By the time Stuart Doyle refused to exhibit and distribute *Two Minutes Silence*, Union Theatres and Australasian Films together had lost an extraordinary 48 012 pounds in a single financial year.' Peter Fitzpatrick, *The Two Frank Things*, Monash University Press, Clayton, 2012, p. 127.

186 'To my thinking, with each film I made I got better and better ...' Joan Long, 'Australian Women Filmmakers, Part 1', *Cinema Papers*, June–July 1976, p. 89.

15   Cinderella's choice (1933–1934)

Paula Dornan interview with Graham Shirley [transcript], 1988, Title No. #1530844, National Film and Sound Archive.

Paulette McDonagh interview with Joan Long and Graham Shirley [transcript], c. 2010, Title No. #1062964, National Film and Sound Archive

Neville Macken interview with Graham Shirley [sound recording], 1971, Title No. #227531, National Film and Sound Archive.

Charles and Alan Stewart interview with Mandy Sayer, 2021, The Cinema Museum, 'Interview with Charles and Alan Stewart' [video], cinedumonde, YouTube, 31 July 2016.

187 'Directly after production on *Two Minutes Silence* was completed, Isabel and Charles Stewart announced their engagement ...' *Freeman's Journal*, 15 September 1932, p. 16.

187 '... Isabel and Charles Stewart announced their engagement in the press on 15 September 1932.' *Sydney Mail*, 21 September 1932, p. 24.

187 'Gregory moved the family to the small town of Molong, northwest of Orange, and with his brother opened a pharmacy there on 17 October 1933.' *Molong Express and Western District Advertiser*, 18 October 1933, p. 8.

189 'A desperate Blackall was forced to lobby the local medical association for equal referrals from the nearest hospital, but still the rivalry continued.' *Molong Express and Western District Advertiser*, 16 June 1934, p. 4.

191 'Each Poppy Day brings its share of romance. Cupid gets busy among the crowd of pretty girls who come forward each year ...' *Labor Daily*, 1 November 1933, p. 9.

191 'In January 1934, still under the banner of "the McDonagh sisters", ...' *The Canberra Times*, 24 October 1933, p. 2.

191 'Some of the best scenario writers in England and America are ... interpreted the script of some of the biggest stories ever filmed.' *Truth*, 18 February 1934, p. 27.

192 'Paulette's second inspiration, Dorothy Arzner, was a Hollywood film director ...' Damon Wise, 'Lumière Festival: Dorothy Arzner, a Hollywood Trailblazer', *Variety*, 10 October 2016.

193 'Furthermore, Arzner was the first woman to join the Directors Guild of America ...'
    Theresa Geller, 'Arzner, Dorothy', *Senses of Cinema*, May 2003.
194 'Through the memories of Armistice, it presents the problems of today and the ideals
    of tomorrow ...' *Stageland*, 1 November 1933.
196 'But to attract publicity for the release of their new film, cunning Phyllis had adapted
    and condensed the material ...' Alan and Charles Stewart interview with Mandy
    Sayer, 2021.
197 'Neville Macken remembered that the Council of Churches had invested some money
    into the film ...' Neville Macken interview with Graham Shirley [sound recording],
    1971, Title No. #227531, National Film and Sound Archive.
197 'One even complained about the lack of Australian subject matter in the film,
    unfairly comparing the sisters' expertise as filmmakers to those of "the big men in the
    business", Frank Thring and Ken Hall. But the journalist musters some patronising
    faint praise by calling "the girls" and their team 'sensible'. *The Sun*, 22 January 1933,
    p. 20.
197–98 'There are no changes in angle, and very few changes in distance, to give variety.
    In these ...' *Sydney Morning Herald*, 5 February 1934, p. 6.
198 'Mr Campbell Copelin and Miss Marie Lorraine both show the same weakness ...'
    Sydney Morning Herald, 5 February 1934, p. 6.
198 'A powerful and convincing story, intelligently directed and capable of challenging
    comparison with world standards.' Kenneth Slessor, *Smith's Weekly*, 10 February 1934,
    p. 7.

16   Inside the outback (1934–1936)
Paula Dornan interview with Graham Shirley [transcript], 1988, Title No. #1530844,
    National Film and Sound Archive.
Paulette McDonagh interview with Joan Long and Graham Shirley [transcript], c. 2010,
    Title No. #1062964, National Film and Sound Archive.
Sheila Collingridge interview with Graham Shirley [sound recording], 1977, Title
    No. #376624, National Film and Sound Archive.
Charles and Alan Stewart interview with Mandy Sayer, 2021.

202 'Local publishers in the past either published very few books or very dull ones ...'
    Labor Daily, 18 May 1935, p. 11.
203 'To refer to one of the most enterprising [publishers], Jackson and O'Sullivan Ltd
    have published over 30 books in the last two years ...' *Labor Daily*, 18 May 1935, p. 11.
203 '... a work of a most powerful nature, adding all the qualities of a first-class thriller to
    one of the strangest love stories ever told.' *Katoomba Daily*, 10 October 1935, p. 4.
203 'Unfortunately the author has been more ambitious than successful.' *Examiner*,
    Launceston, 24 August 1935.
203 'A book of no particular merit.' *Chronicle*, Adelaide, 5 September 1935.
203 'This master crook has, beside the unpleasant habit of disembowelling failures in his
    gang, the boring habit ...' *Labor Daily*, 18 May 1935.
204 The Bulli Lookout sketch appeared in the *Sydney Morning Herald*, 28 September 1935,
    p. 13.
204 'The sky has changed its azure robe for misty dark draperies and stoops low to
    catch its leaden reflection in the turbulent water below.' Phyllis McDonagh, 'The
    Parramatta, Varying Moods of the River', *Sydney Morning Herald*, 4 April 1936, p. 18.
204 'A grey submarine lies rammed against a modern liner ...' *Sydney Morning Herald*,
    8 November 1936, p. 6.
205 'He was glad they had sent him to the Military Hospital. In some curious fashion ...'
    'A Voice in the Darkness', *Smith's Weekly*, 27 February 1937, p. 16.

205   'A picture suddenly flashed into his brain ...' 'A Voice in the Darkness', *Smith's Weekly*, 27 February 1937, p. 16.

205   'That was, of course, before the fierce light of publicity had singled out No. 14 for its special beneficence ...' *The Daily Mail*, 18 November 1936, p. 12.

208   'These will show the tribal life of the aborigines, work on a big cattle station, and the highlights of the fauna, flora and scenery of the centre.' *The Sun*, 5 July 1934, p. 21.

209   'A fully-equipped expedition will leave Sydney about the end of August ...' *Sydney Morning Herald*, 6 July 1934, p. 8.

209   'A week later *The Sun* reported that Mrs Charles Stewart (Isabel) was expected to return ...' *The Sun*, 15 July 1934, p. 25.

210   'But Isabel replied, "No, I've got a son. I want to be a married woman and not work anymore".' The Cinema Museum, 'Interview with Charles and Alan Stewart' [video], cinedumonde, YouTube, 31 July 2016.

211   'The quota system that the McDonaghs had been fighting to establish for years was finally approved in September 1935, which recommended a five-year quota for Australian pictures in all programs ...' Peter Fitzpatrick, *The Two Frank Thrings*, Monash University Publishing, Clayton, 2012, p. 216.

211   'The Gaumont company, based in England, had for a long time wanted to shoot a film in Australia, and so it provided technical and financial assistance to National Productions.' 'Making films in Australia', *The Mail*, 7 September 1935, p. 3.

211   'The British Unit arrived in November 1935 and production began at the Pagewood studios in 1936.' 'Film experts', *The Sydney Morning Herald*, 13 November 1935, p. 9.

211   'In January [1936], Kenneth Slessor reported on the films that were currently in production in New South Wales ...' *Smith's Weekly*, 4 Jan 1936, p. 22.

212   '... the story is weak in the extreme. Instead of selecting and developing some definite dramatic subject ...' *Sydney Morning Herald*, 21 September 1936.

212   'The direction of "The Flying Doctor" is, to put it bluntly, a bit muddled ...' *Sydney Mail*, 23 December 1936, p. 24.

17   Desperately seeking sisters (1936–1946)

Paulette McDonagh interview with Joan Long and Graham Shirley [transcript], c. 2010, Title No. #1062964, National Film and Sound Archive.

Paula Dornan interview with Graham Shirley [transcript], 1988, Title No. #1530844, National Film and Sound Archive.

Alan and Charles Stewart interviews with Mandy Sayer, 2021–22.

Moya Joyes interview with Mandy Sayer, 2021.

Sheila Collingridge interview with Graham Shirley [sound recording], 1977, Title No. #376624, National Film and Sound Archive.

Susan Fryer interviews with Mandy Sayer, 2021–22.

Details about John Verner Cunningham-Browne: Chris Hutton (descendant) interview with Mandy Sayer, 2022.

215   'It had a sweeping driveway, a fountain ...' Gaby Naher, *The Truth About My Fathers*, Random House, Milsons Point, 2002.

216   'One day, after many attempts, Charles managed to catch a large swordfish ...' Zane Grey, *An American Angler in Australia*, Derrydale Press, New York, 2002, p. 48.

216   'Photographer Rennie Ellis remembered the atmosphere of the Belvedere as "New Orleans *belle epoque*"' Rennie Ellis and Wesley Stacey, *Kings Cross Sydney*, Thomas Nelson, Melbourne, 1971, p. 82.

219–20   'I was called on immediately to organise a Women's War Page – and was fortunate in having success on my hands ...' Phyllis McDonagh brief autobiography [manuscript], 26 May 1975, Title No. 790864, National Film and Sound Archive.

220 '... but also, in press interviews after her crowning, take the opportunity to promote the sisters' upcoming film, *Two Minutes Silence.*' *Daily Telegraph*, 26 August 1932, p. 5.

225 'In 1919, at the age of twenty-six, Cunningham-Browne became a clerk of the Holy Orders ...' Electoral Rolls, Australia, 1903–1930.

225 'The Catholic priests of St Joseph's in Woollahra, were so chuffed about welcoming a former Anglican clergyman ...' *Southern Cross*, 11 January 1929, no. 24, 28 September 1923, p. 8

18 Spliced together again (1941–1956)
Alan and Charles Stewart interviews with Mandy Sayer, 2021–22.
The Cinema Museum, 'Interview with Charles and Alan Stewart' [video], cinedumonde, YouTube, 31 July 2016.
Paula Dornan interview with Graham Shirley [transcript], 1988, Title No. #1530844, National Film and Sound Archive.
Details about John Verner Cunningham-Browne: Charles Stewart interview with Mandy Sayer, 2022; and Chris Hutton (descendant) interview with Mandy Sayer, 2022.
Susan Fryer interview with Mandy Sayer, 2021.

233 'With typical McDonagh bravado, he boasted, "it's harder to make one omelette"' *The Sun*, 25 August 1950, p. 15.

233 'Still, according to his wishes, she organised a funeral for him ...' *Sydney Morning Herald*, 9 May 1950, p. 20.

236 'And directly above Nosov's flat ... Moscow.' Sandra Hogan, *With My Little Eye*, Allen & Unwin, Crows Nest, 2021, pp. 107–10.

238 'Grant begins his article thus: "Dear Phyllis, Welcome home! We're proud of your achievements as an editress and authoress"' *Truth*, 19 September 1954, p. 11.

239 'When the first issue came out on the streets I had a whole front-page story with pictures, two feature news articles and one page of women's news ...' Phyllis McDonagh brief autobiography [manuscript], 26 May 1975, Title No. 790864, National Film and Sound Archive.

19 Isabel rising (1957–1965)
Hayes Gordon interview with Graham Shirley [sound recording], 8 November 1990, Title No. 799488, National Film and Sound Archive.
Moya Joyes interview with Mandy Sayer, 2021.
Alan and Charles Stewart interview with Mandy Sayer, 2021.
Graham Shirley interview with Mandy Sayer, 2021.
The Cinema Museum, 'Interview with Charles and Alan Stewart' [video], cinedumonde, YouTube, 31 July 2016.
Paula Dornan interview with Graham Shirley [transcript], 1988, Title No. #1530844, National Film and Sound Archive.
Paulette McDonagh interview with Joan Long and Graham Shirley [transcript], c. 2010, Title No. #1062964, National Film and Sound Archive.
Susan Fryer interview with Mandy Sayer, 2022.

245–46 'For defending his principles, Hayes was virtually blacklisted from the American stage, triggering his subsequent exile in Australia.' Katrina Strickland, 'An Ideal Life', *The Weekend Australian*, 23–24 August 1997, p. 11.

248 'One night during a play, some hooligans scaled the walls of the theatre and began throwing stones onto the roof ...' Unpublished interview of Alan and Charles Stewart with Graham Shirley, London, 20 April 2015.

250 'His timing is a joy to observe and every nuance of his facial expressions is a lesson in the art of comedy.' *The Australian Jewish News*, 11 May 1962, p. 20.

252 'In the late 1950s, a rare copy of *The Cheaters* surfaced in the library of an avid Australian film collector ... ' Graham Shirley, 'McDonaghs of Australian cinema', *Filmnews*, 1 December 1978.

253 'This is a private event. We don't need publicity. We've already made history.' Private correspondence between Charles Stewart and Mandy Sayer, 2022.

255 'He adds breezily, "You can idle along at three miles an hour, cruise in comfort at four or five miles an hour, accelerate at six miles an hour and, if you're really in a hurry, reach a top speed of eight miles an hour – and keep it going".' *Brandon Sun*, Manitoba, 11 October 1962.

20   Second coming (1966–1975)
Ken Hall interview with Graham Shirley [sound recording], 1976. Title No. # 326468, National Film and Sound Archive.
Charles Stewart interview with Mandy Sayer, 2022.
Paula Dornan interview with Graham Shirley [transcript], 1988, Title No. #1530844, National Film and Sound Archive.
John and Catherine Dornan interview with Mandy Sayer, 2021.
Paula Dornan interview by Judith Kelly [sound recording], 1983, Title No. #330324, National Film and Sound Archive.
Paulette McDonagh interview with Joan Long and Graham Shirley [transcript], c. 2010, Title No. #1062964, National Film and Sound Archive.
Susan Fryer interview with Mandy Sayer, 2022.
David Stratton interview with Mandy Sayer, 29 March 2021.

258 '... the only vestiges of the grand colonial mansion are some ornamental sandstone steps and balustrading near the Parramatta River.' <sydneylivingmuseums.com.au/ stories/drummoyne-house-remembered>.

259 '"Probably the biggest revelation", she admitted, "was the work of the McDonagh sisters"' Joan Long and Martin Long, *The Pictures that Moved*, Hutchinson of Australia, Richmond, 1982, p. 94.

263 'I hate women. Most of them have nothing on top ...' *Sun Herald*, 24 April 1977.

265 'Up until 1951, film stock was composed of cellulose nitrate ... which then dehydrates into a coarse brown dust.' Ray Edmonson and Andrew Pike, *Australia's Lost Films*, National Library of Australia, Canberra, 1982, p. 22.

266 'In the 1990s, yet another copy would be created from all available prints and sequences, with a music track by Ron West added to the film ...' Ina Bertrand, *The Cheaters*, Metro Magazine #206, 2020, p. 114.

267 'Australian critics Andrew Pike and Ross Cooper, for example, praised the sisters for their "unusual sensitivity to the expressive range of the camera and their awareness of careful scenario construction as a key to emotionally powerful cinema"' Andrew Pike and Ross Cooper, *Australian Film, 1900–1977*, Oxford University Press, Melbourne, 1998, p. 152.

267 'Film historian Graham Shirley admired "the care and dramatic unity" of the silent version ...' Graham Shirley, 'McDonaghs of Australian cinema', *Filmnews*, 1 December 1978.

267 'Film historian Hartney Arthur judged the surviving McDonagh production as among the best silent movies ever made.' Ina Bertrand, *The Cheaters*, Metro Magazine #206, 2020.

270 '... once you had entered her world, had been summed up and invited again ...' Graham Shirley, 'McDonaghs of Australian cinema', *Filmnews*, 1 December 1978.

270 'Paulette's friend Brian Seamark remembers her as one of the "characters who made the Cross so colourful", calling her "highly intelligent and a fun person from the day I met her"' Bertrand, Ina, *The Cheaters, Metro Magazine #206*, 2020, p. 114.

270 'After he knocked on her door mid-morning, he was bemused to find seventy-three-year-old Paulette ...' Private conversation between Andrew Pike and Mandy Sayer, 2022.

271–72 'In it, Phyllis compares new feature film release *Love Story*, starring Ryan O'Neal, with the first film by the McDonagh sisters ...' Lorraine Hickman, 'When Three Dashing Sisters Made a Movie', *Australian Women's Weekly*, 21 April 1971, p. 4.

21   Curtain call (1976–1982)
The Cinema Museum, 'Interview with Charles and Alan Stewart' [video], cinedumonde, YouTube, 31 July 2016.
Paula Dornan interview with Graham Shirley [transcript], 1988, Title No. #1530844, National Film and Sound Archive.
Suzanne Spunner interview with Mandy Sayer, 2021.
John and Catherine Dornan interview with Mandy Sayer, 2021.
Susan Fryer interview with Mandy Sayer, 2022.
Charles Stewart interview with Mandy Sayer, 2022.

277 'The following year, Phyllis contributed an article to her old high school's newsletter, again repeating the myth that "our father, who had complete faith in our capabilities, put up one Thousand Pounds"' Phyllis McDonagh newsletter article [manuscript], 26 May 1975, Title No. 790864, National Film and Sound Archive.

278 'I grew up in the lap of luxury and now I have nothing ...' Barbara Muhvich, 'She Helped to Put Us on the Film Map', *Sun Herald*, 24 April 1977.

279 '... the last of the few really great conductors of his generation.' Hans Keller, 'Otto Klemperer', *Musical Sketchbook*, Cassirer, Oxford, 1957.

283 'She lived the theatre. Phyllis was a great supporter of the arts. She was the Music Hall's mascot.' Sandy Savos, 'Tributes in Sad Farewell to Beloved Writer', *North Shore Times*, 25 October 1978.

286 'Why seek ye the living among the dead? He is not here, but is risen ...' (Luke, 24:5).

286 'Late in her life, perhaps anticipating her own death, Paulette decided to go to confession, most probably at St Canice's in Rushcutters Bay ...' Sheila Collingridge interview with Graham Shirley [sound recording], 1977, Title No. #376624, National Film and Sound Archive.

ACKNOWLEDGMENTS

This biography could not have been written without the generous support of the 2021 Hazel Rowley Literary Award. Many thanks to Della Rowley and the 2021 judging panel.

My deepest gratitude to Louis Nowra for introducing me to the McDonagh sisters, suggesting that they deserved a dedicated biography, and convincing me to write it.

Deepest gratitude also goes to Graham Shirley, whose early research on the sisters and their contemporaries, contained in numerous recorded oral histories with Paulette McDonagh, Paula McDonagh, Neville Macken, Bud and Estelle Macken, Ken Hall, Hayes Gordon, and Sheila Collingridge, as well as his numerous articles, proved to be a rich source of material and points of view. Shirley also graciously provided me with the contact details of the McDonagh descendants and shared further research from other sources. His critical responses to an early draft of the manuscript, coupled with his generosity, have strengthened this narrative in countless ways.

Many thanks to Simon Drake, Access Co-ordinator at the NFSA, for providing easy access to the McDonagh archival material, and for his enduring support of this project.

I'm also indebted to the descendants of the McDonaghs, who made themselves available to me for a number of interviews and allowed this virtual stranger to probe their personal and family history with good cheer and equanimity: Alan and Charles

Stewart, John and Catherine Dornan, Moya Joyes, and Susan Fryer. Thank you for sharing your memories with me.

My thanks to the fabulous team at NewSouth Publishing: publisher Elspeth Menzies, project manager Sophia Oravecz, and fearless leader, Kathy Bail. And I tip my hat with gratitude to editor Gabriella Sterio for her expert literary midwifery. Any errors in the book are undoubtedly my own.

Thank you also to designer Debra Billson for her brilliant art deco cover design. The McDonagh sisters would have adored it.

Thanks also to filmmaker Margot Nash for sharing her research material and images; John Johnson, Councils Local Studies Librarian for information on the sales history of Drummoyne House; Tracy Bradford, archivist at Kincoppal-Rose Bay, School of the Sacred Heart, for providing photos and information on the sisters' time at the school; film historian Andrew Pike for sharing his anecdotes about Paulette McDonagh in her later life; Frank Shields for putting me in touch with the Dornan brothers; writer Meg Stewart for sharing her great aunt's memories of Isabel McDonagh; Chris Hutton and Cheryl Shurin for sharing information on their ancestor, John Verner Cunningham-Browne; film critic David Stratton for sharing his memories of Paulette McDonagh and the 1975 screening of *The Cheaters*; Susan Spunner for loaning me her copy of *Lip,* and for granting me an interview; and writers Suzanne Falkiner and Ken Hurry for providing a translation of Bruno Valletty's poetic tribute to Paulette contained in her autograph book. Many thanks also to my witty and wonderful literary agent, Jeanne Ryckmans, of Cameron's Agency.

Ingram Content Group UK Ltd.
Milton Keynes UK
UKHW010624150523
421501UK00029B/343